To Dottie & Ray -
Hope you Enjoy!

W. Bragg Brown

Through the Ocean Window

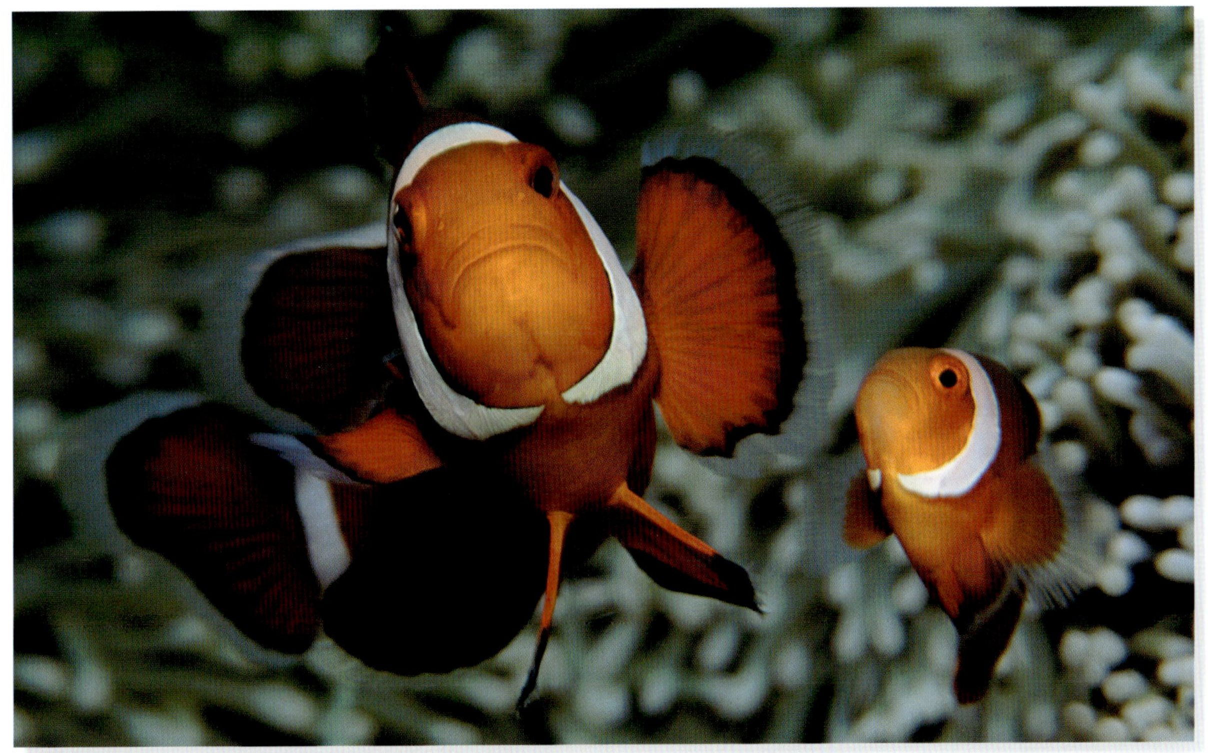

W. Gregory Brown

OWP

For Ariel - You are a treasured gift. You are my miracle.

Acknowledgements

My beautiful wife, Bonnie, who for the past 25 years congratulated me when I succeeded and lifted my spirits when I failed. You have enriched my life in so many ways. I love you more with each passing moment. Indeed, you are heaven sent.

Margaret Brown, my Mom, is a strong and remarkable woman. Throughout my life, she has chosen to put my dreams ahead of her own. Thank you, Mom, for your continued love and support. At every turn, I know you are with me.

For the past two decades, Steve and Deb Freligh have given scientists, naturalists, and photographers a platform to celebrate the beauty of nature and to share with others the environmental challenges facing our planet. Steve and Deb, I owe you a debt of gratitude. www.naturesbestmagazine.com

Captain Greg Lawlor: Since 1985, Greg and his amazing crew (Sam & Moses) have stocked my cerebral shelves with a lifetime of wonderful memories. They are, quite simply, the best.

Extreme Graphixs: Mark McCall performed all prepress functions for this book. He is extremely kind, extremely generous, and most importantly, he is extremely talented. www.extg.com

Cover Design: Neal Jones is a creative, young man destined for great things.

Printed in China on acid-free paper by Everbest Printing

Library of Congress Control Number: 2005902302

ISBN-13: 978-0-9766749-0-0
ISBN-10: 0-9766749-0-4

Ocean World Photography **OWP**
6461 Running Brook Rd.
Manassas, VA 20112

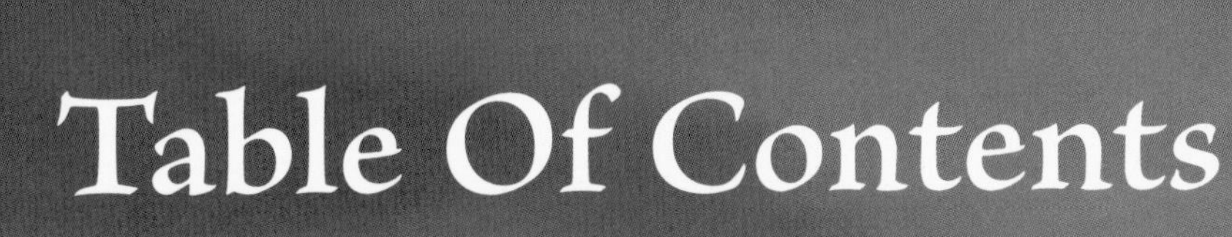

Table Of Contents

Introduction

For the past quarter century, I have had the rare privilege of photographing marine life on coral reefs around the world. It has been a rewarding and humbling enterprise. Beyond that, words alone fall considerably short of conveying the pure joy I have experienced from my time in the sea. Fortunately, I carried a camera to support my inadequate vocabulary. So join me now as we, for a time, shed our terrestrial bonds and journey through the ocean window.

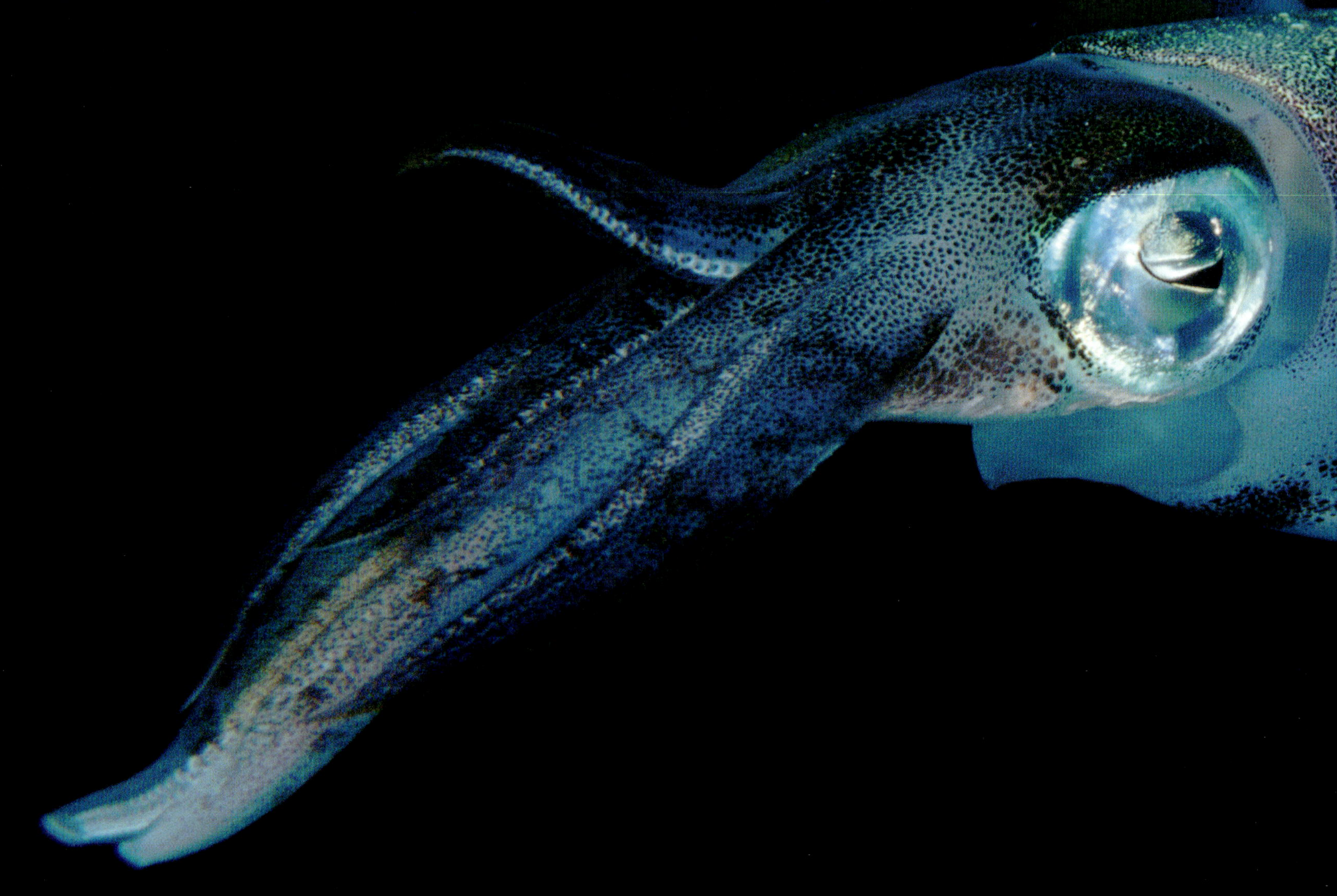

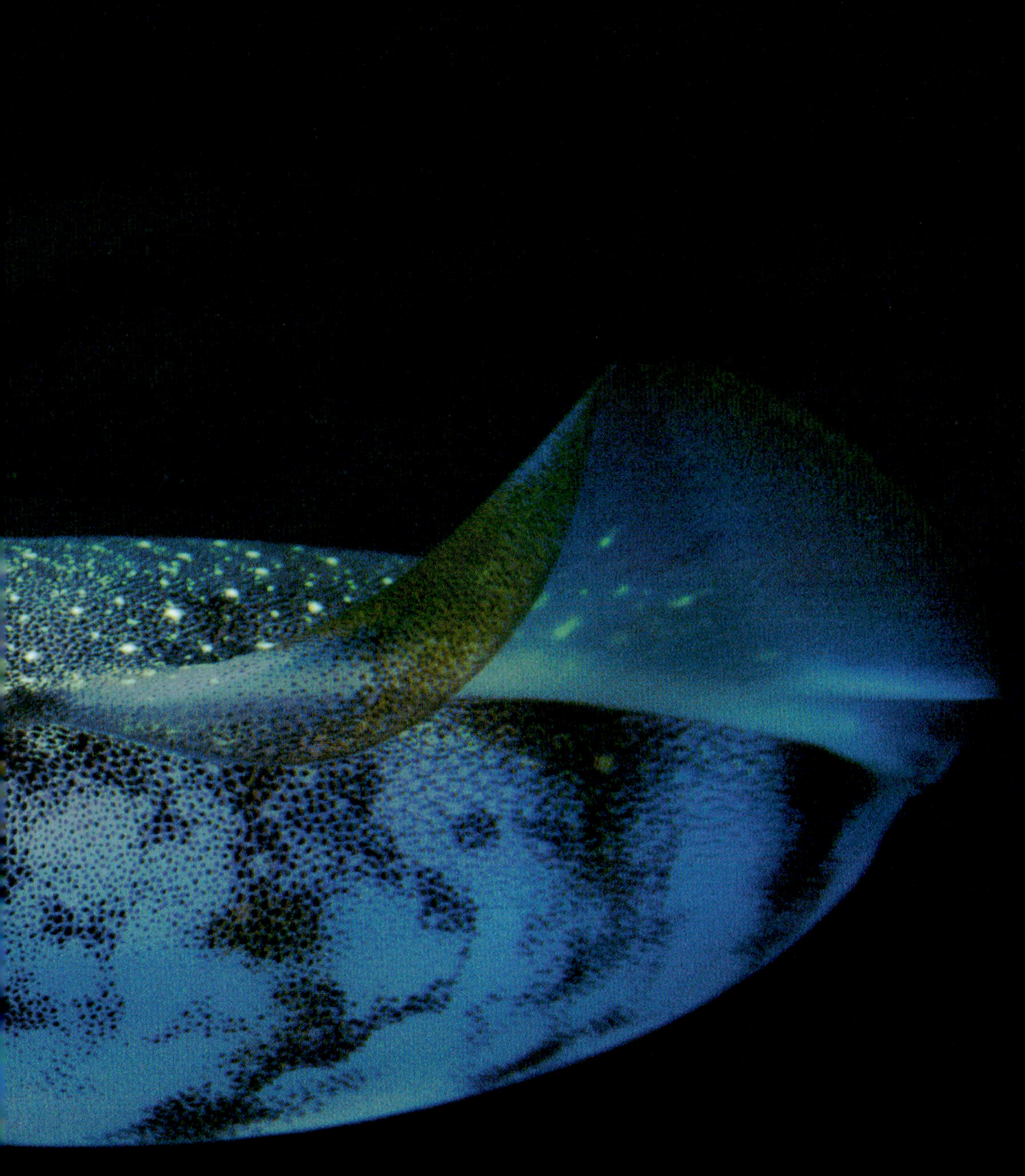

" They that go down to the sea in ships, that do business in great waters; these see the works of the Lord, and His wonders in the deep."

Psalm 107: 23-24

Life On The Reef

Life On The Reef

When I peer into the depths of the living reef, I am awed by its presence.It is both overwhelming and consuming: an ecological production that is, perhaps, unequalled in the universe. In relative terms, the ocean is a desert. It is a nutrient-poor ecosystem. How can the reef, one of nature's most diverse, abundant collections of animals, thrive in a nutrient-deficient environment? The answer is quite amazing. The Scleractinian corals (hard corals) are farmers! In addition to capturing food with their nematocyst-lined tentacles, they, as well as other invertebrates such as Tridacna Clams, share a unique symbiotic relationship with a microscopic algae. This algae, called zooxanthellae, lives within the coral polyp tissues and helps provide the coral with its nutrition requirements through photosynthesis. Every coral head has its own internal garden. The beautiful colors of hard corals are also provided courtesy of the zooxanthellae. This profound relationship is but one of the many symbiotic associations found within the coral kingdom. In fact, the reef environment abounds with beneficial groupings that enhance the ability of organisms to feed and reproduce. Life is stacked upon life on the coral reef, permitting resources to be tightly coupled and recycled. It's a system of interdependency designed for one thing: survival.

In this section of the book, the portraits and behaviors photographed are but a miniscule testament to the enchanting world of the coral reef. The collection of images represent approximately one tenth of a second. I have found a lifetime of memories in that fraction of time.

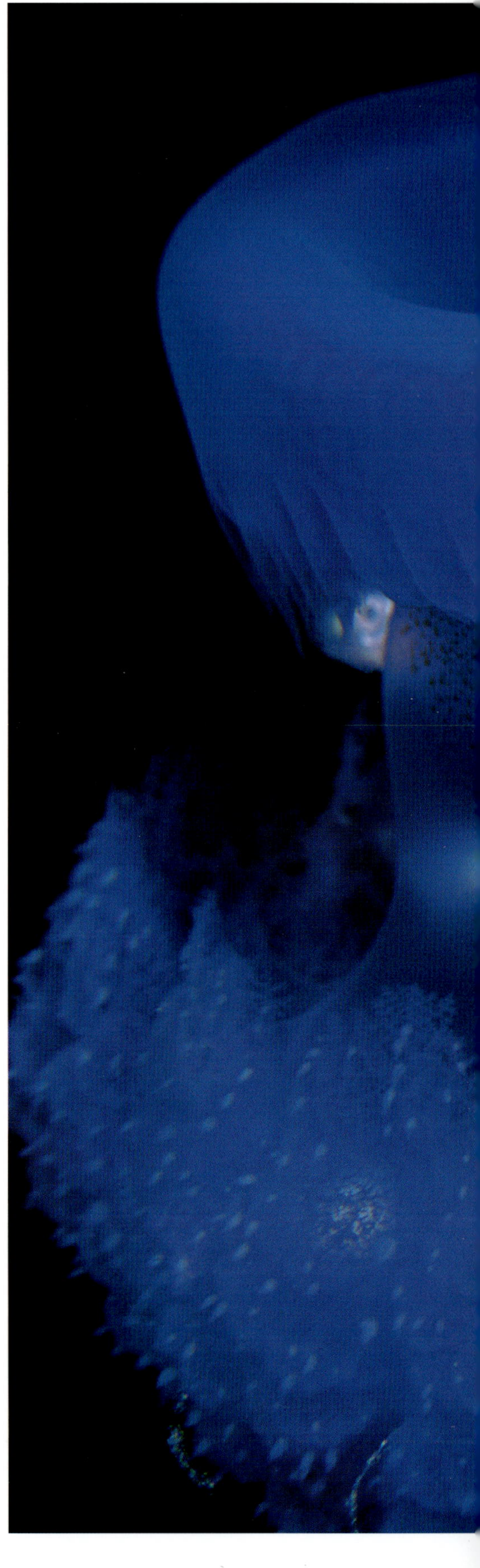

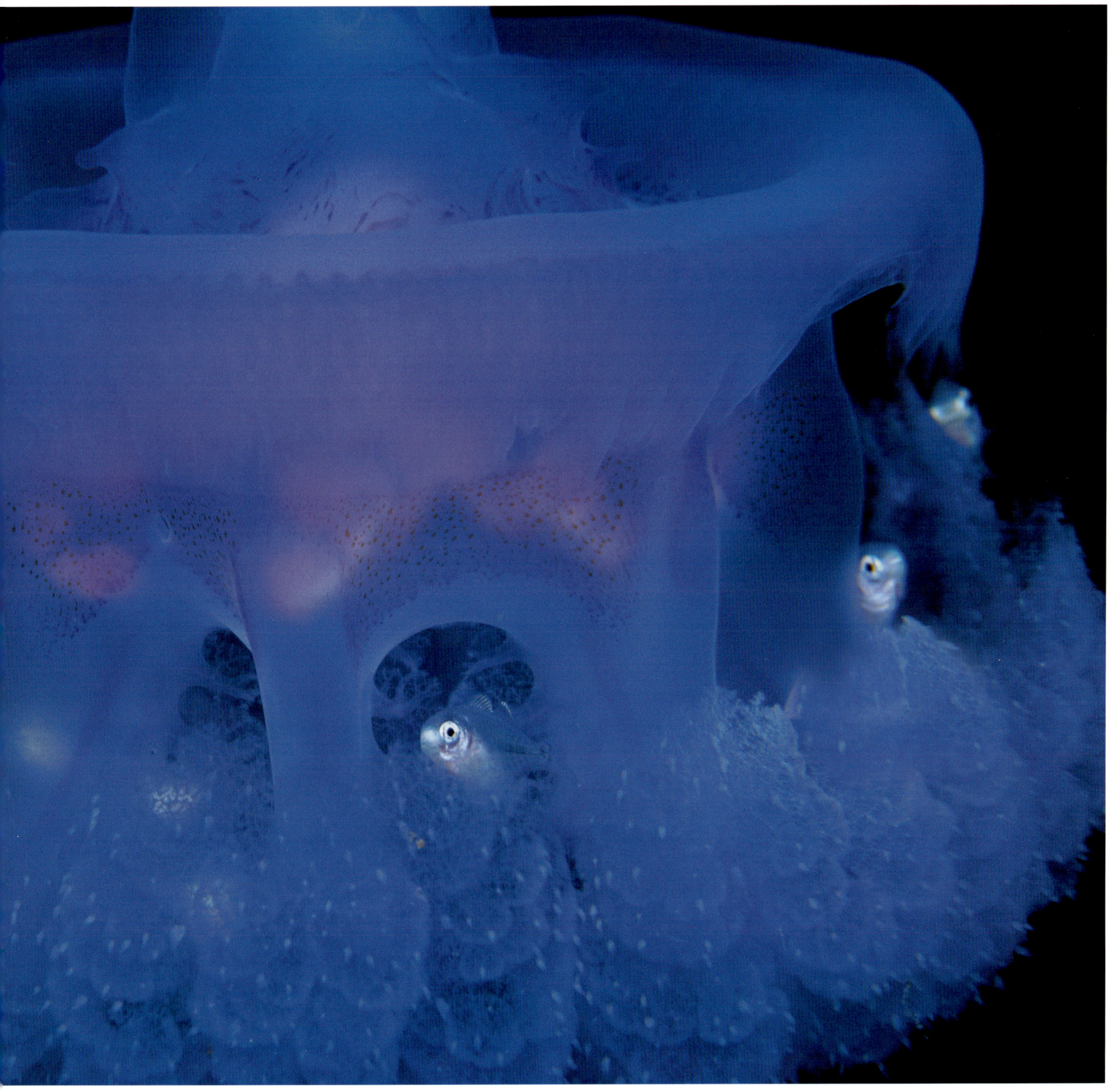

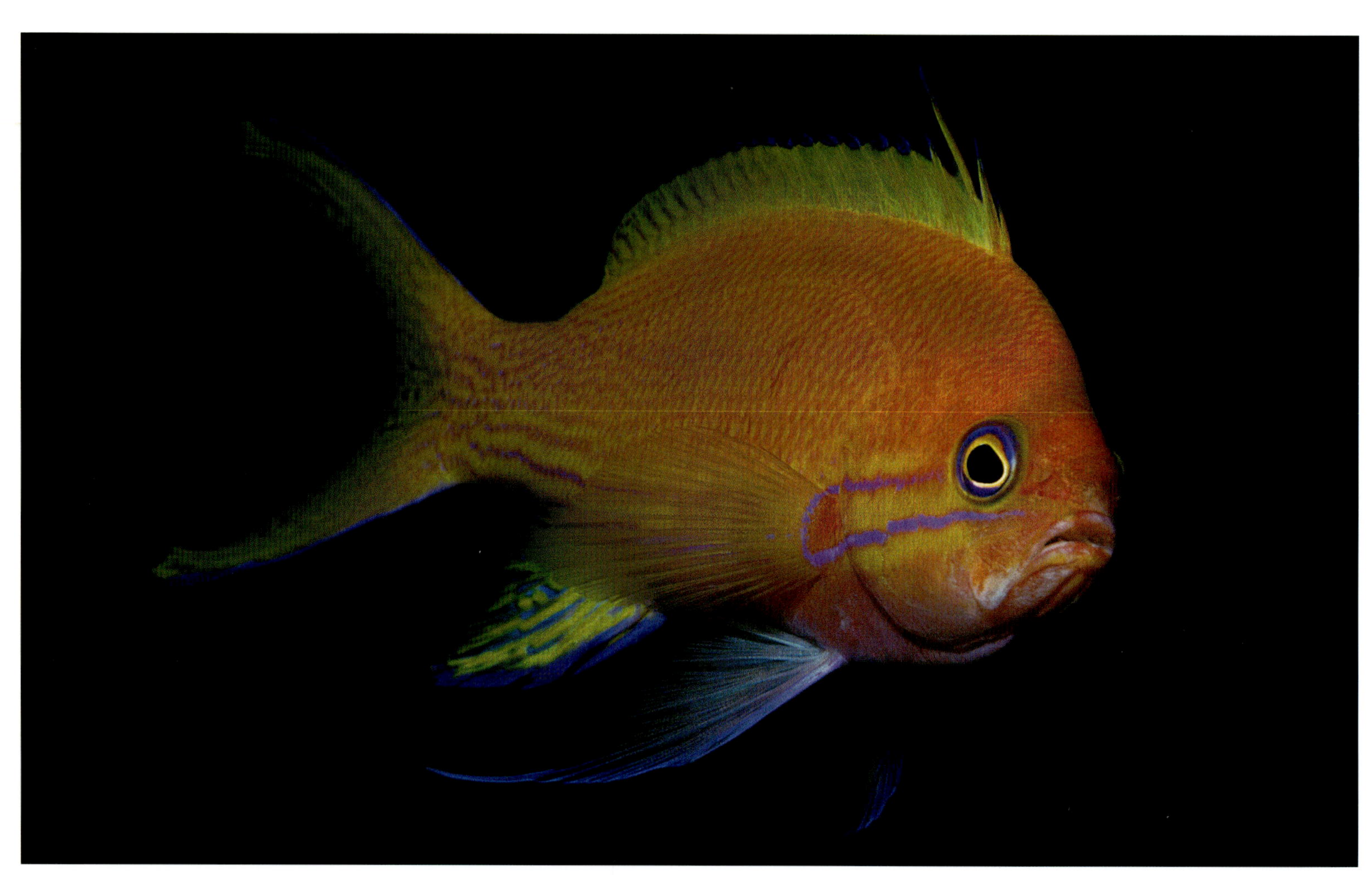

BLOTCHED BASSLET, FEMALE

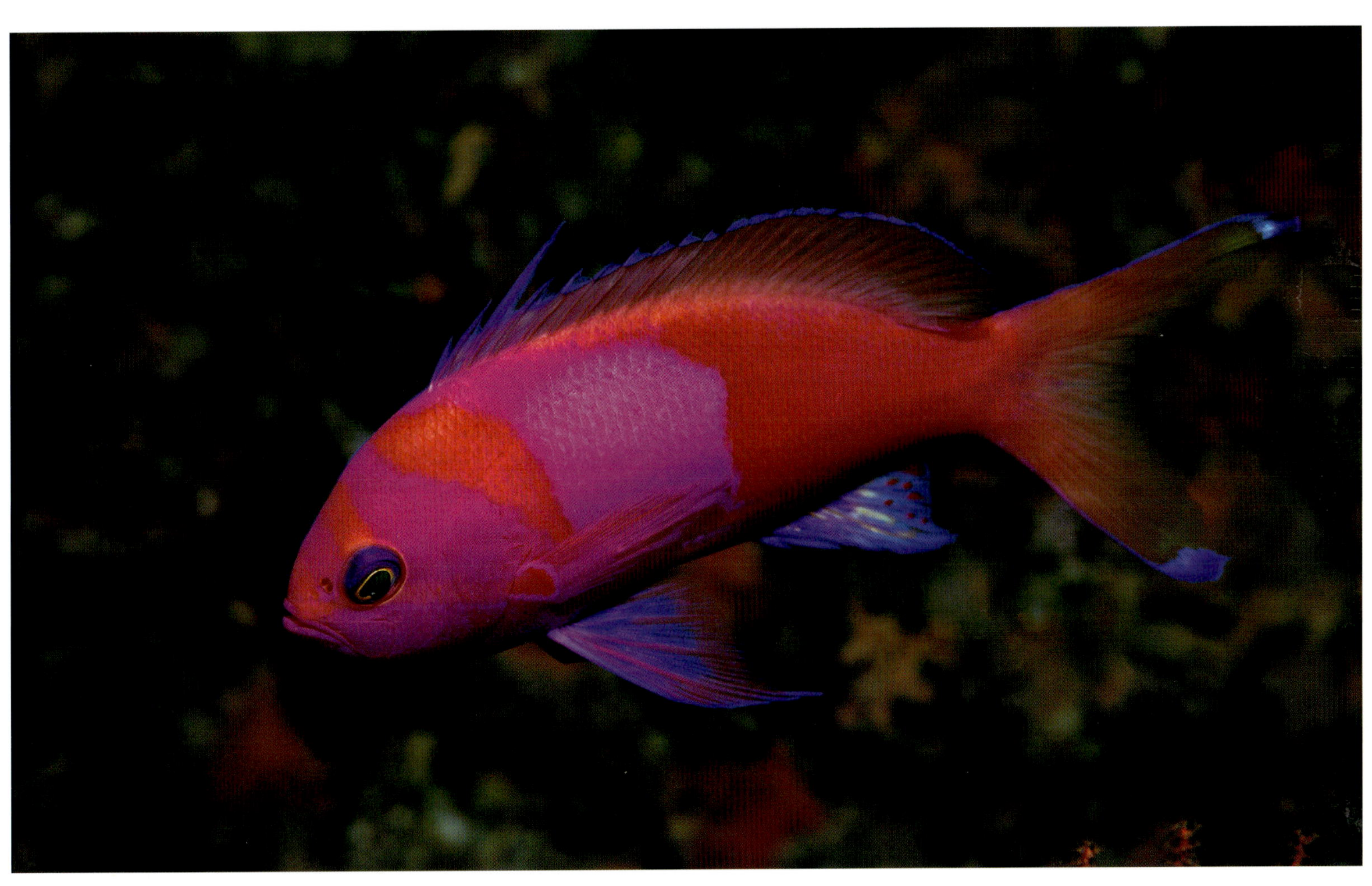

BLOTCHED BASSLET, MALE

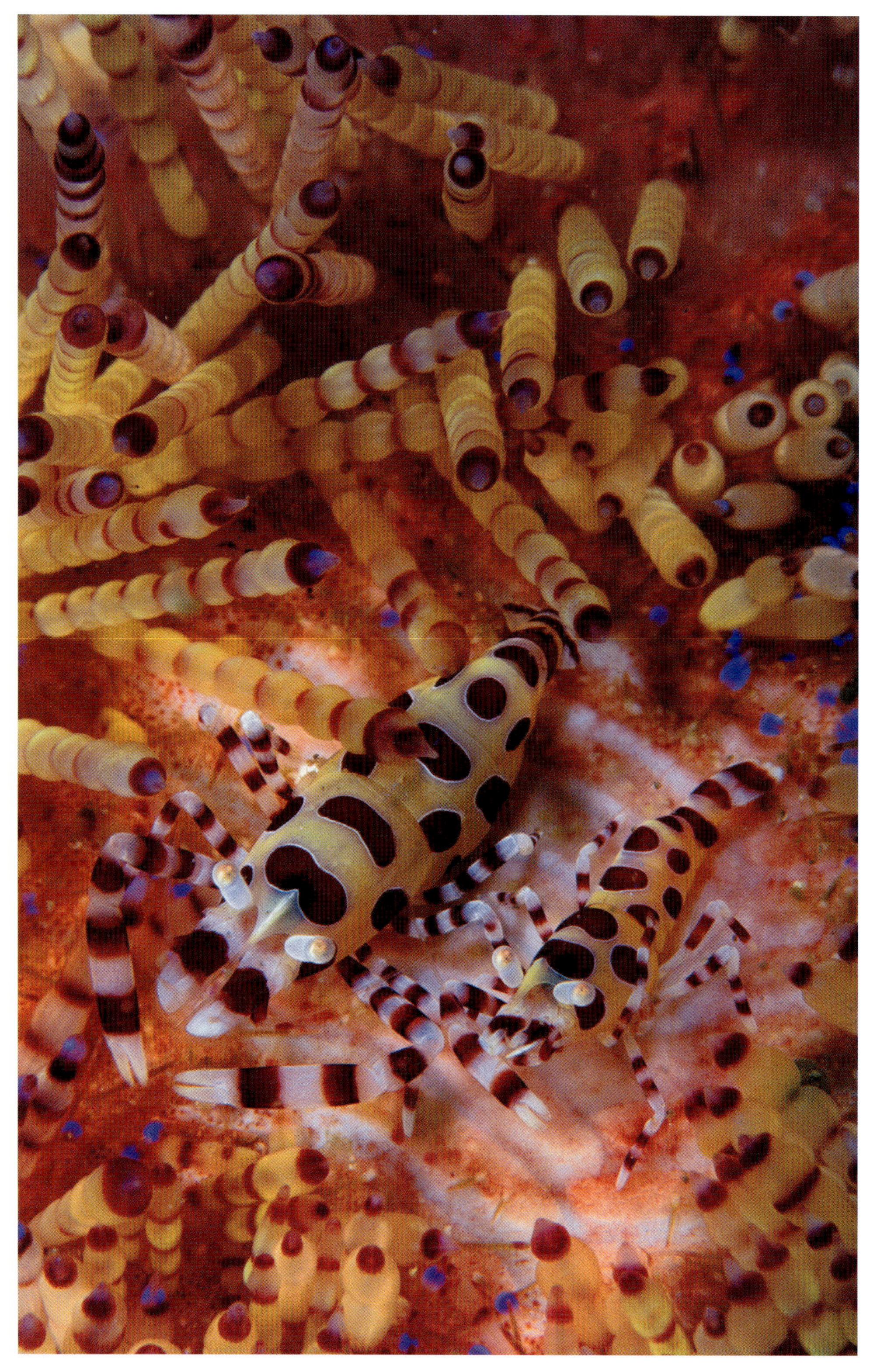

COLEMANS SHRIMP ON FIRE URCHIN

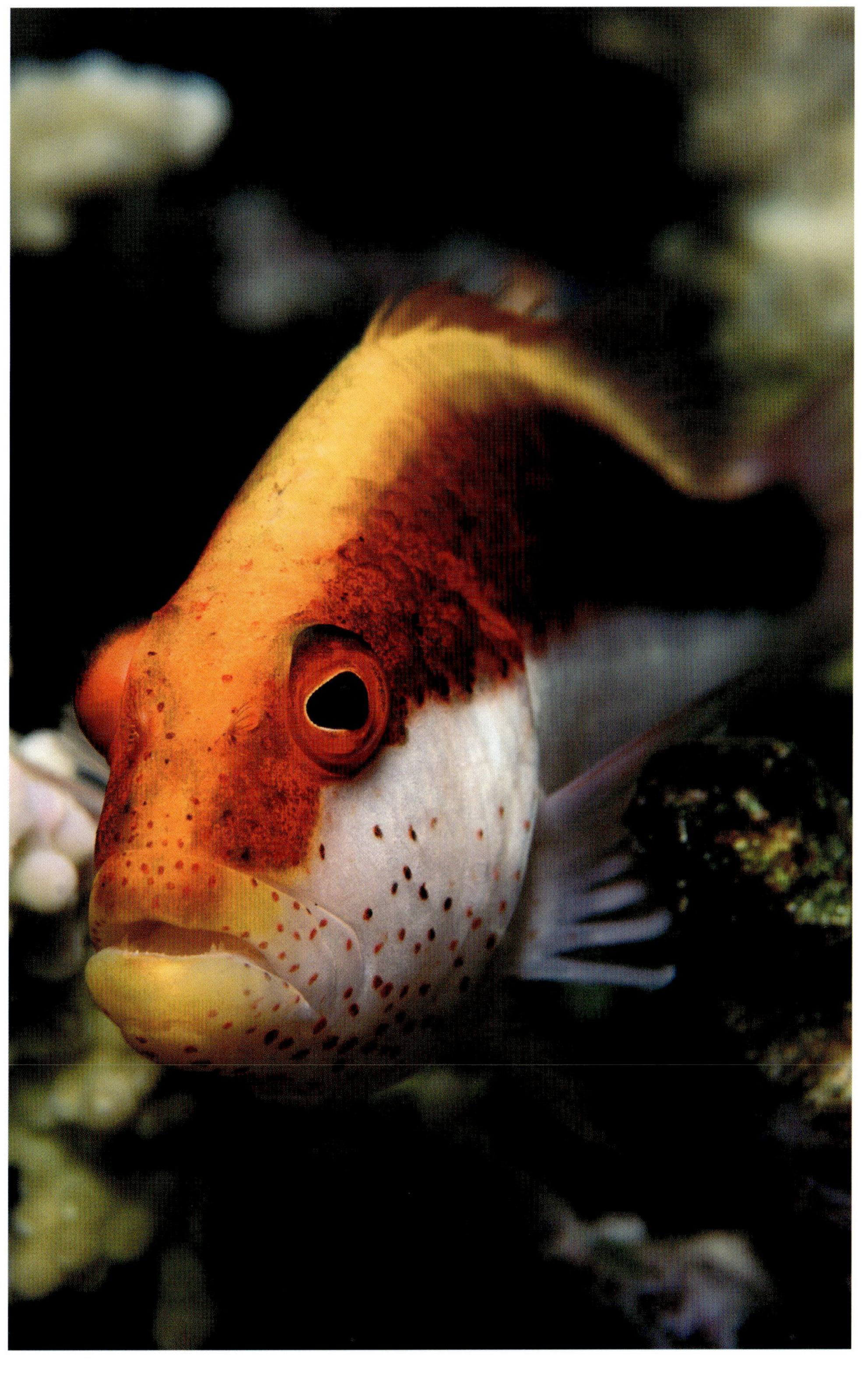

FORSTER'S HAWKFISH

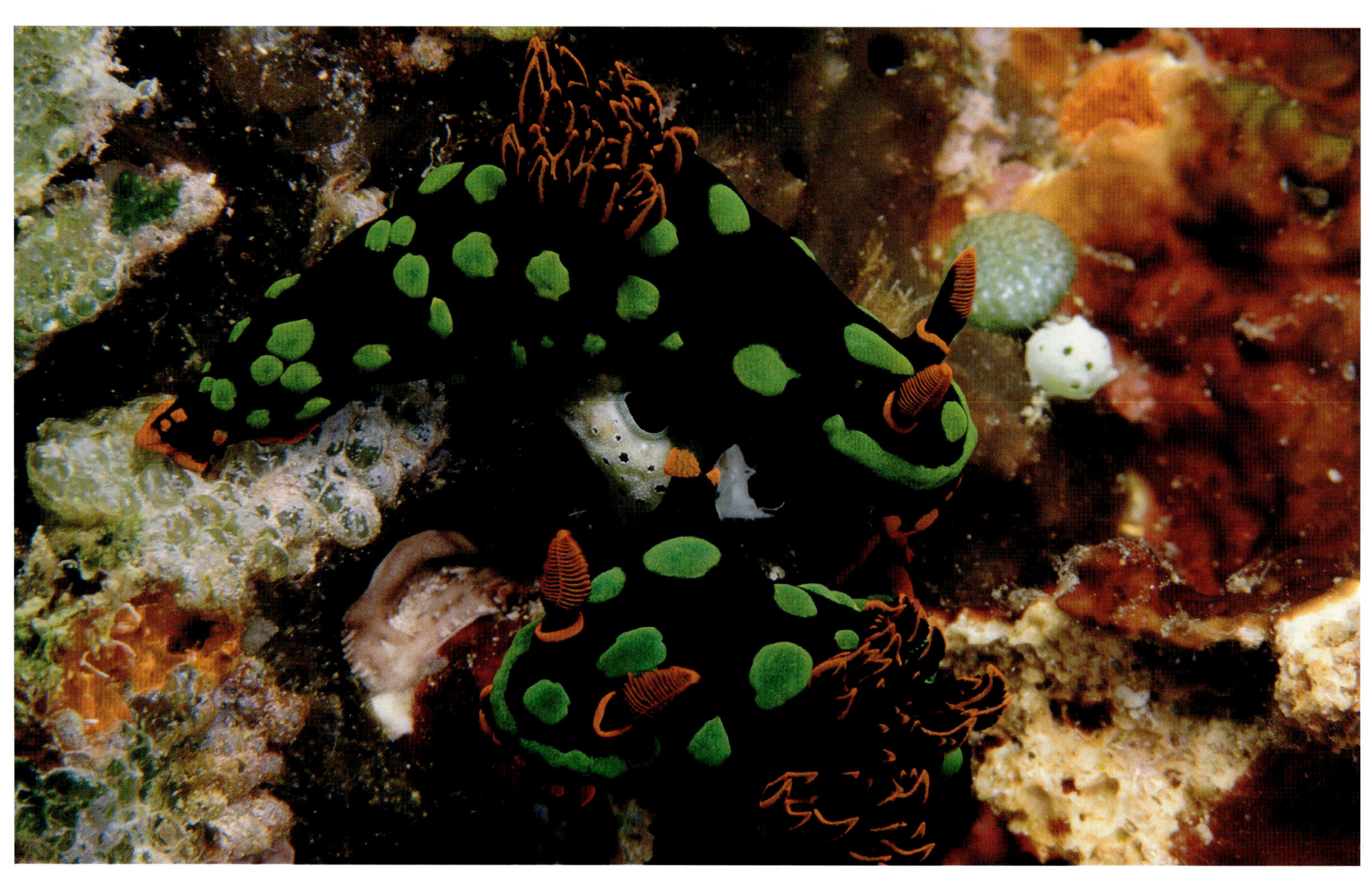

MATING POLYCERID NUDIBRANCHES

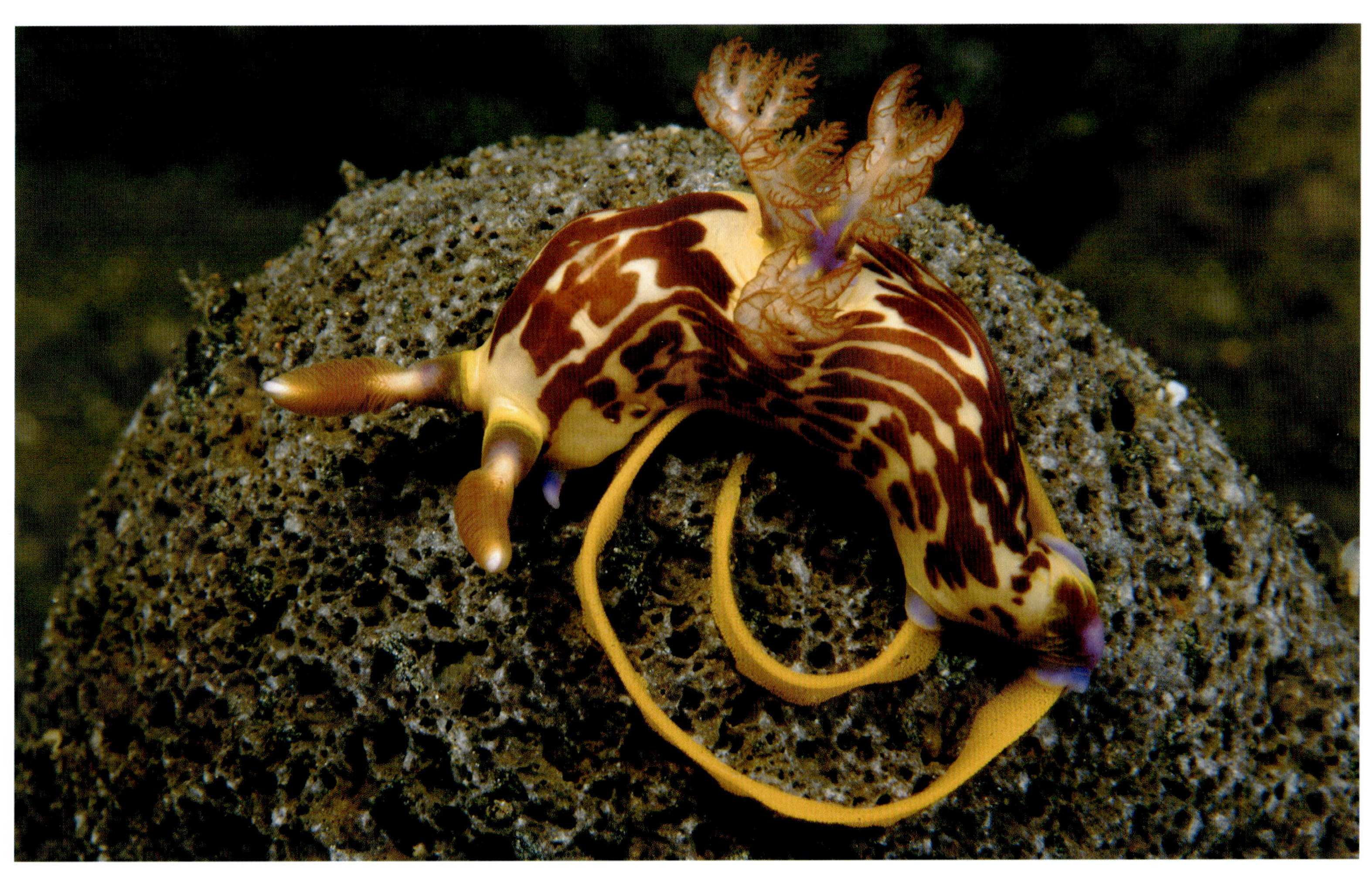

LINED NUDIBRANCH LAYING EGGS

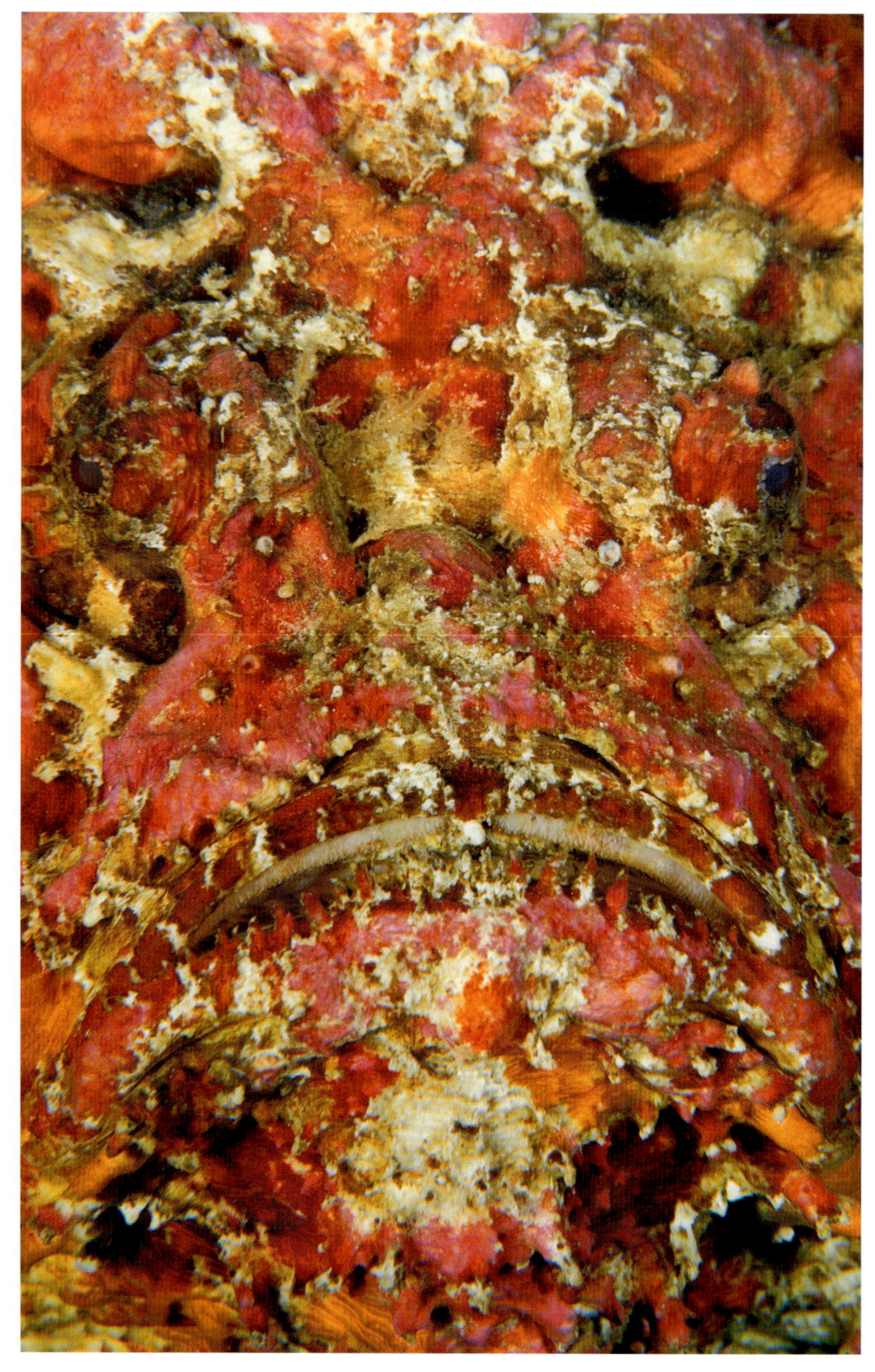

STONEFISH FACE

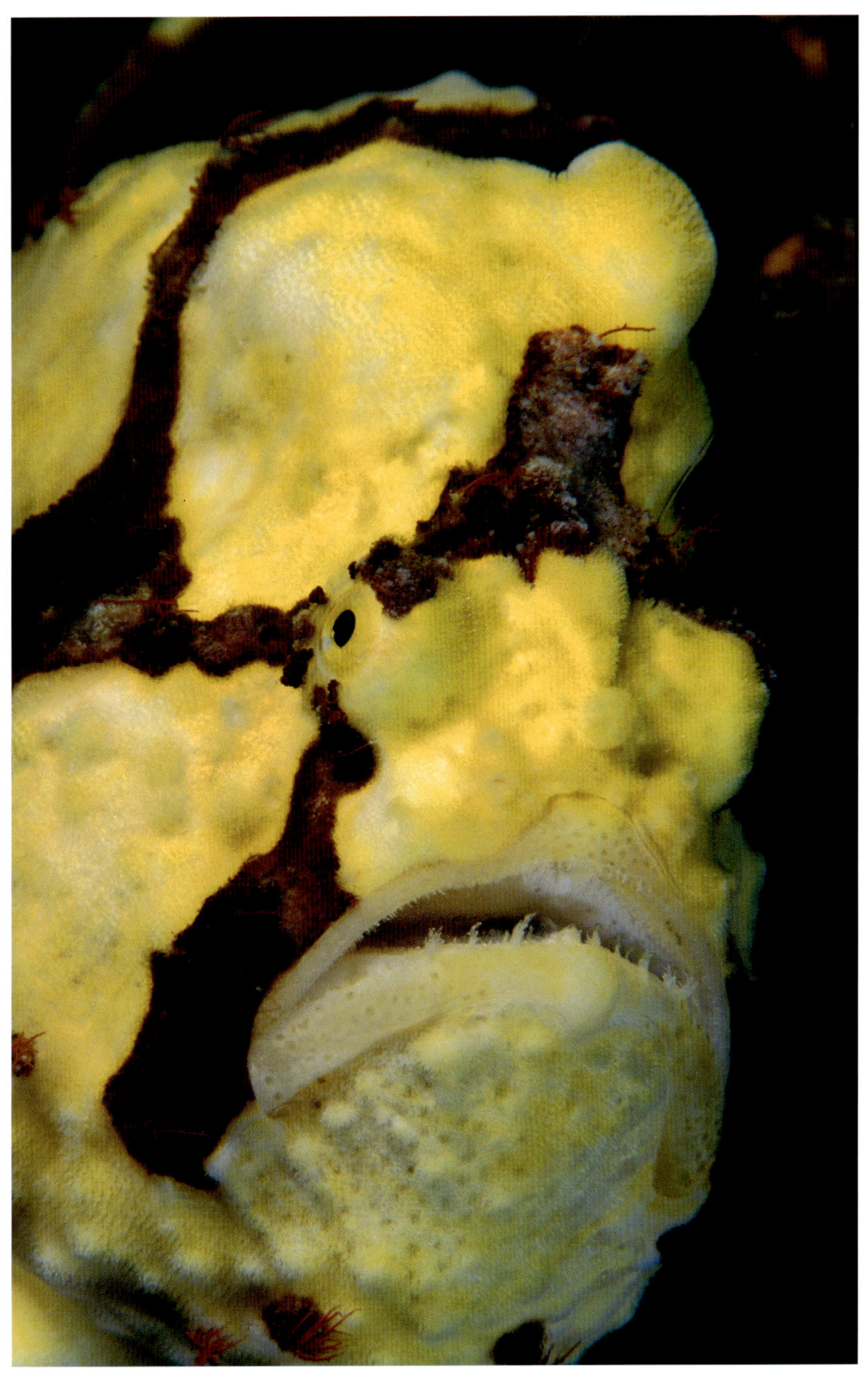

LONGLURE FROGFISH

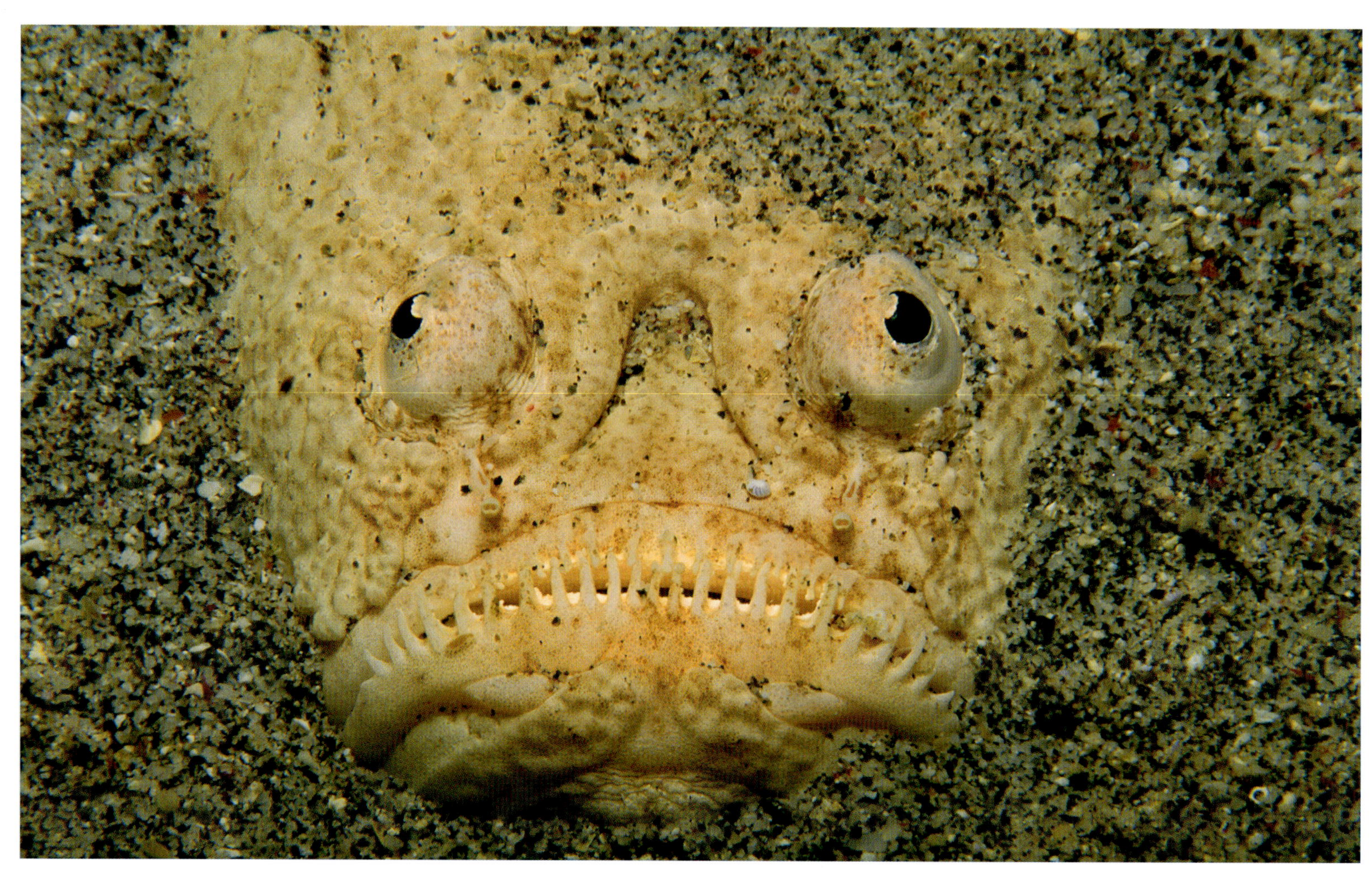

STARGAZER

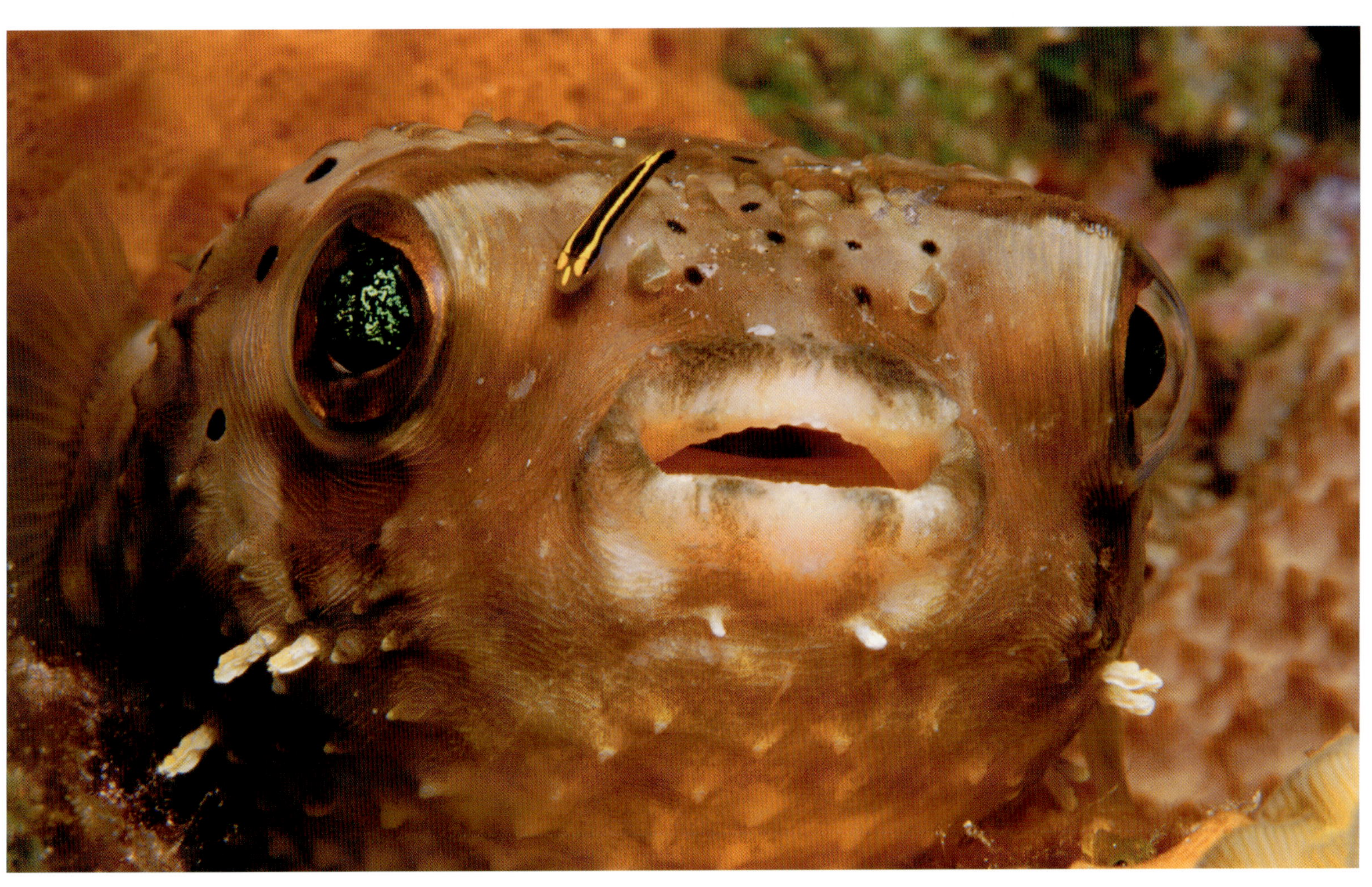

BALLOONFISH WITH CLEANER GOBY

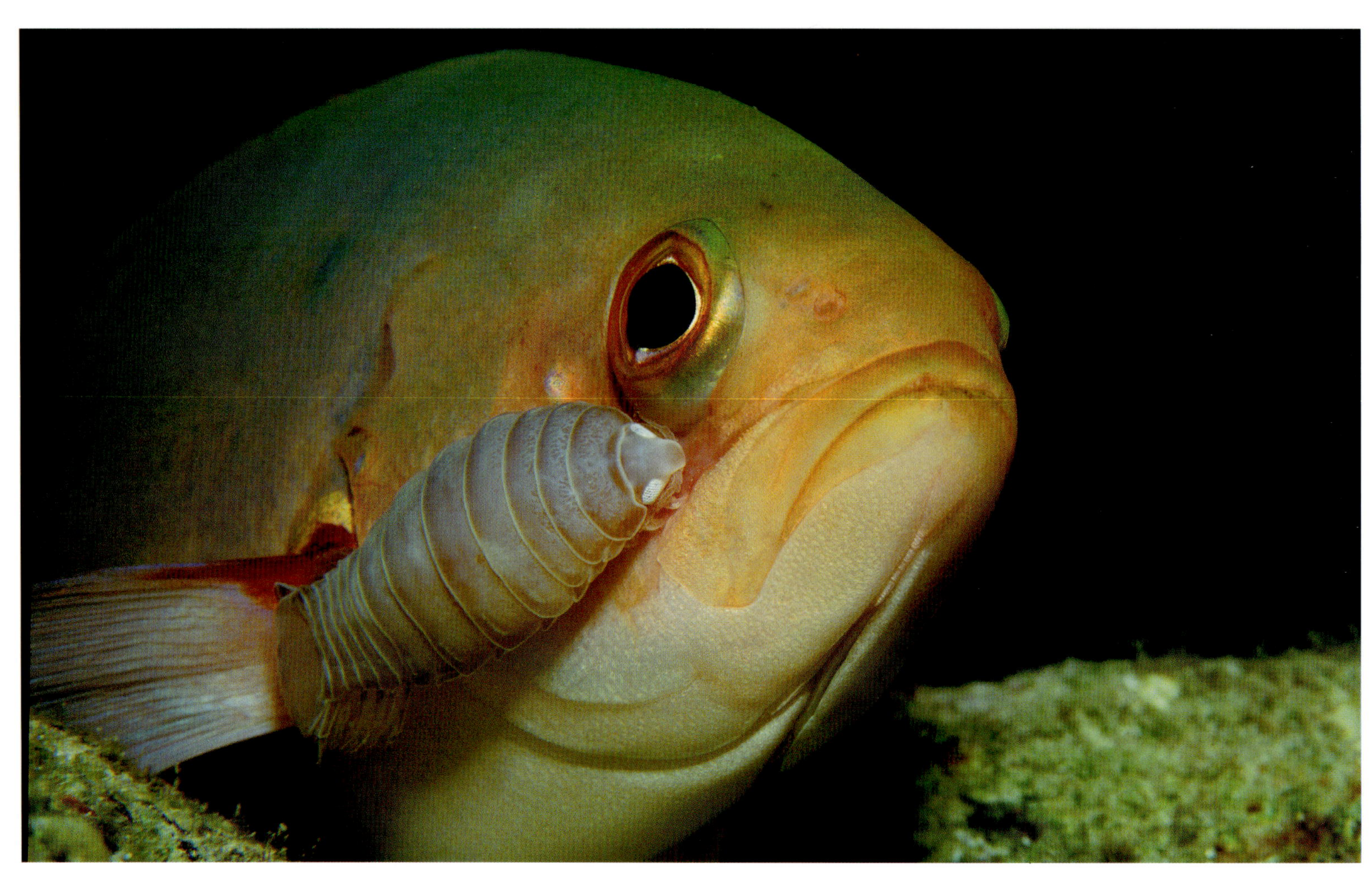

CREOLE FISH WITH PARASITIC ISOPOD

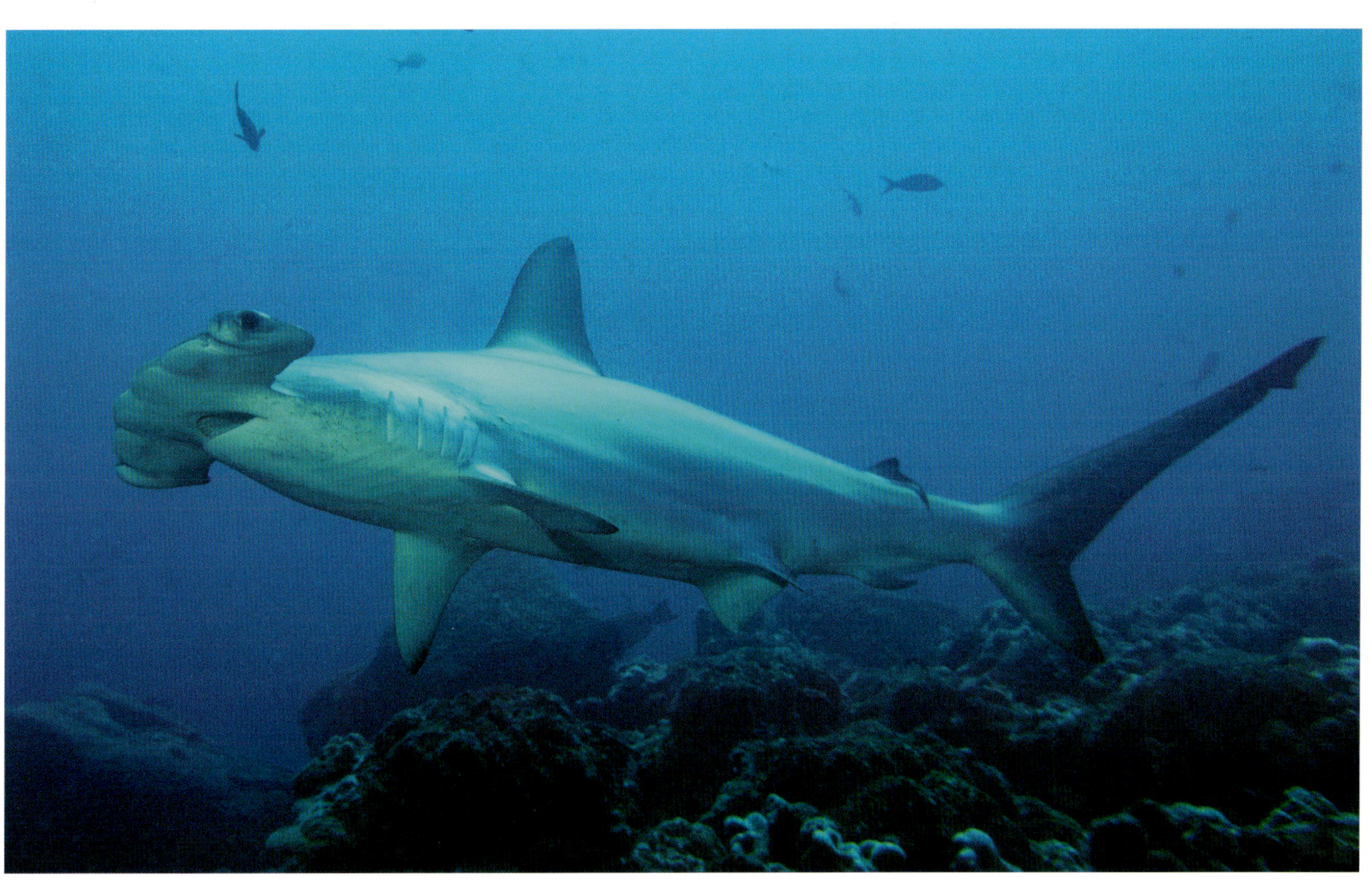

SCALLOPED HAMMERHEAD

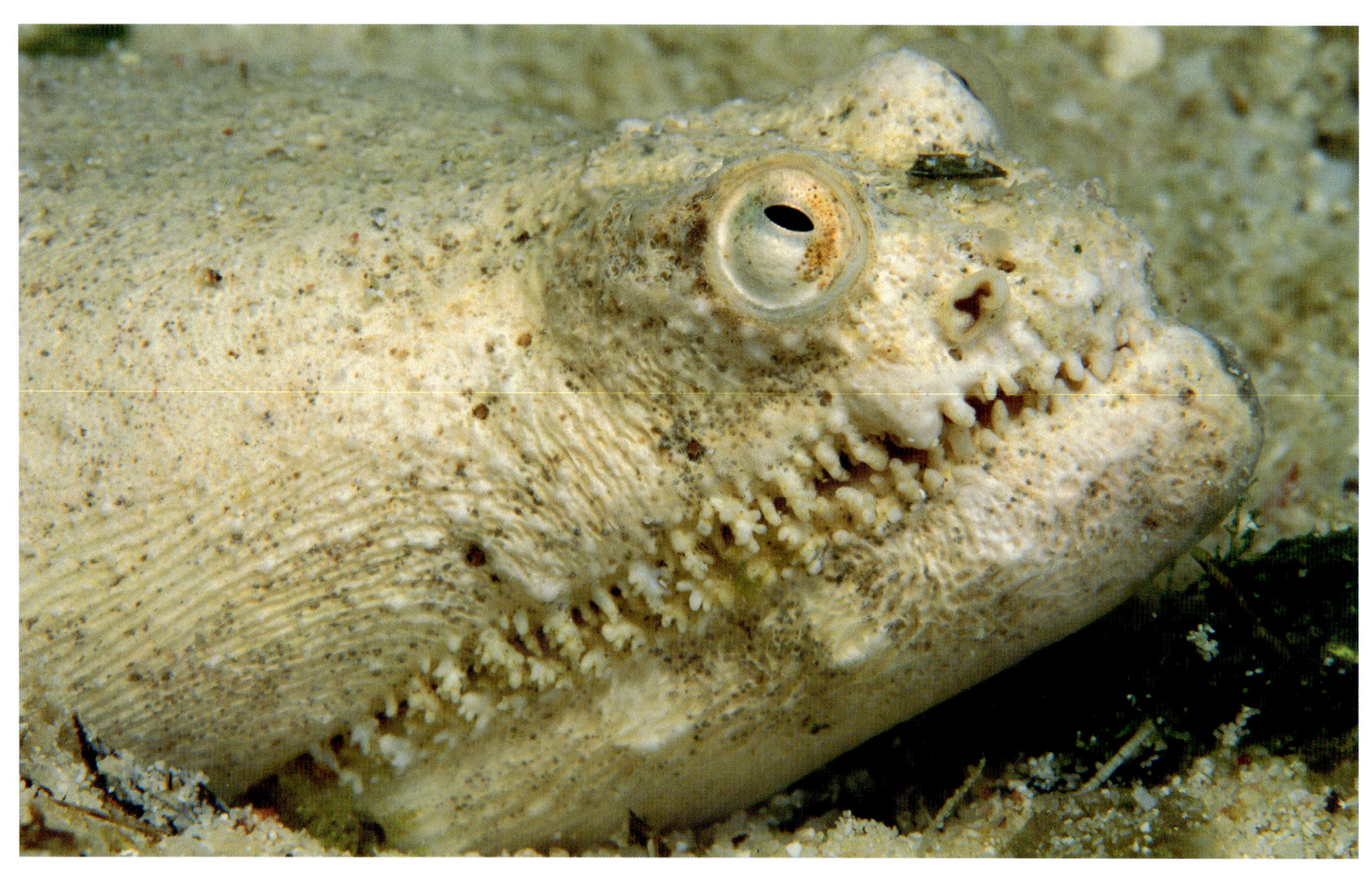

GHOST SNAKE EEL

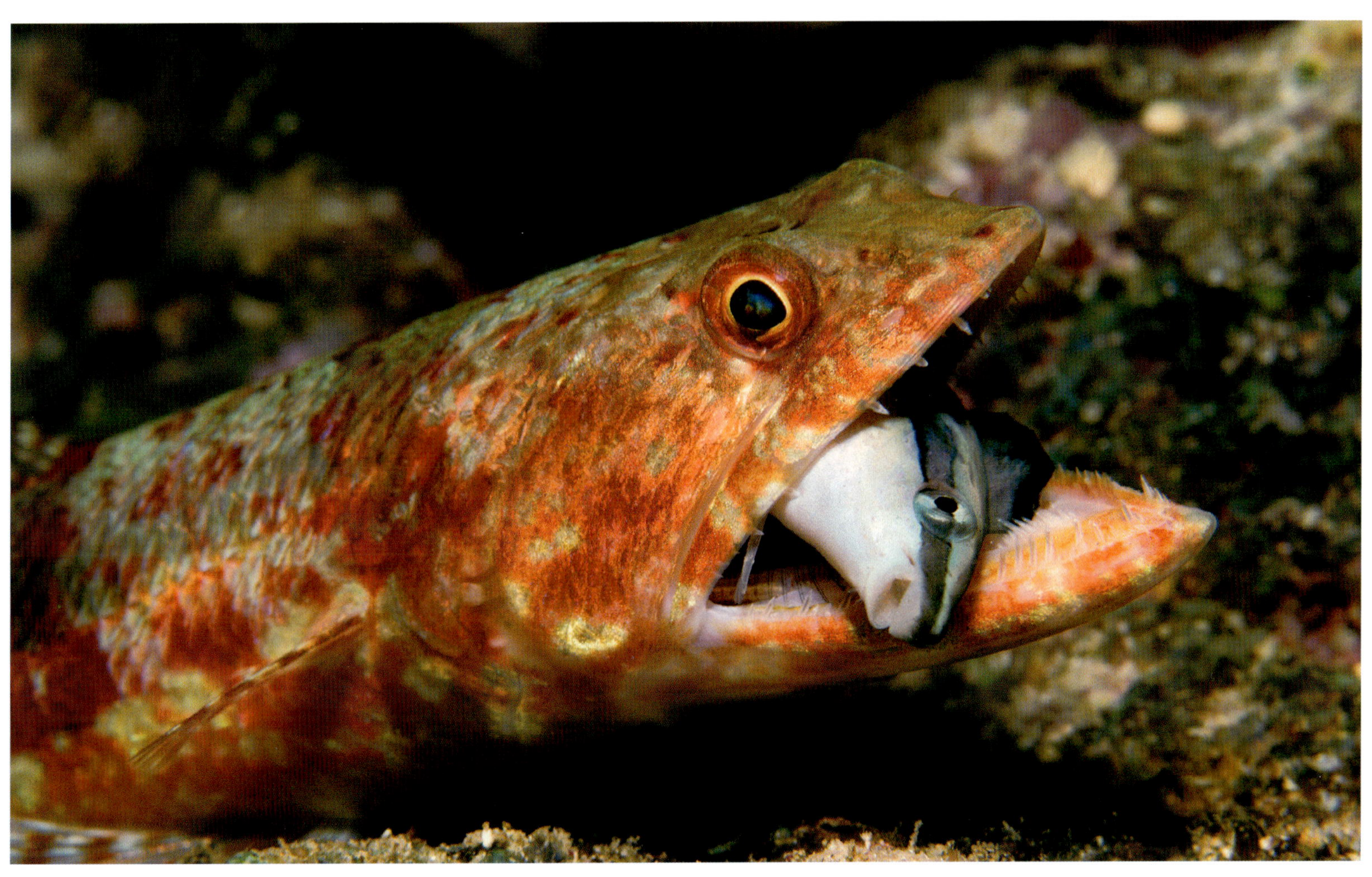

LIZARDFISH EATING FALSE CLEANER BLENNY

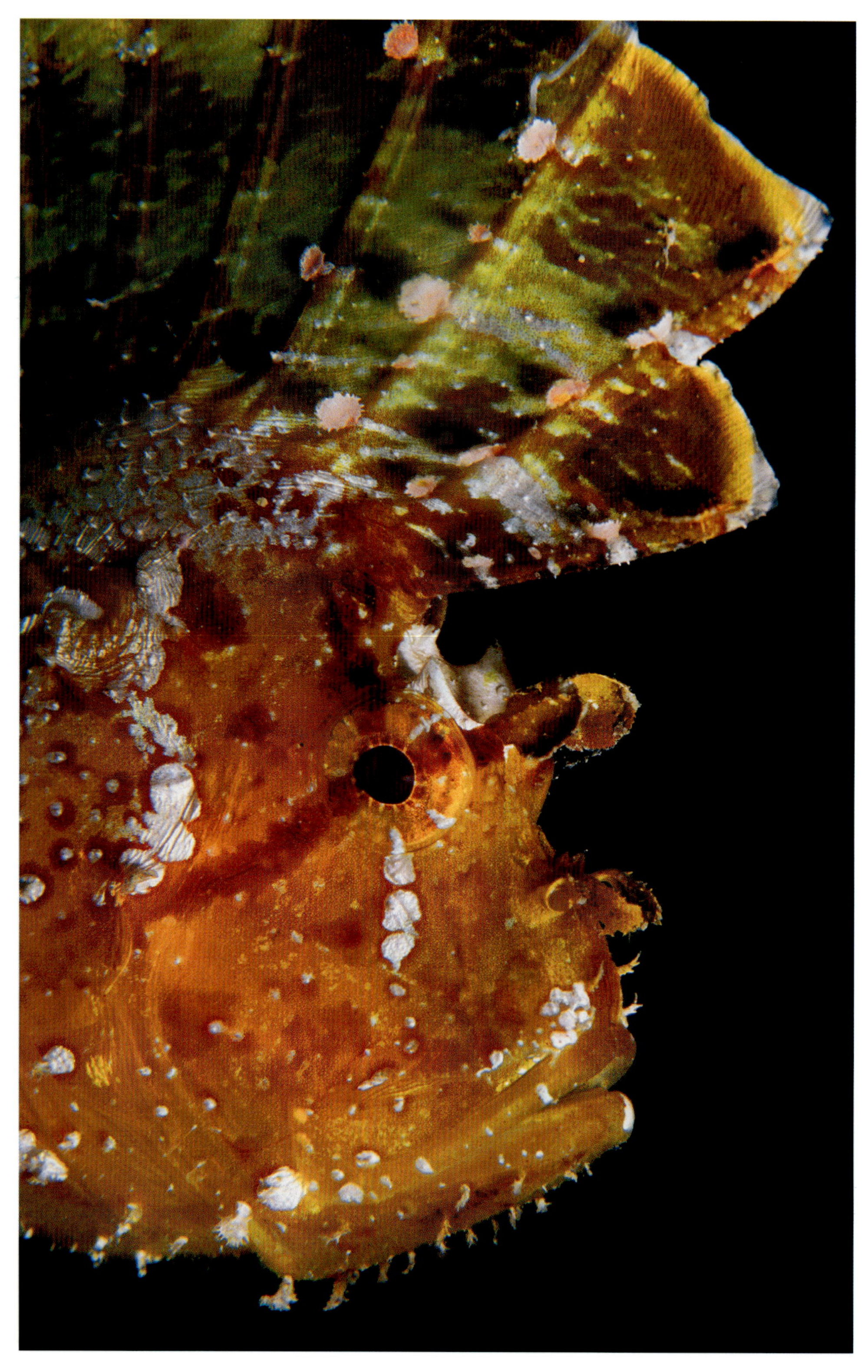

SAILFIN LEAF FISH

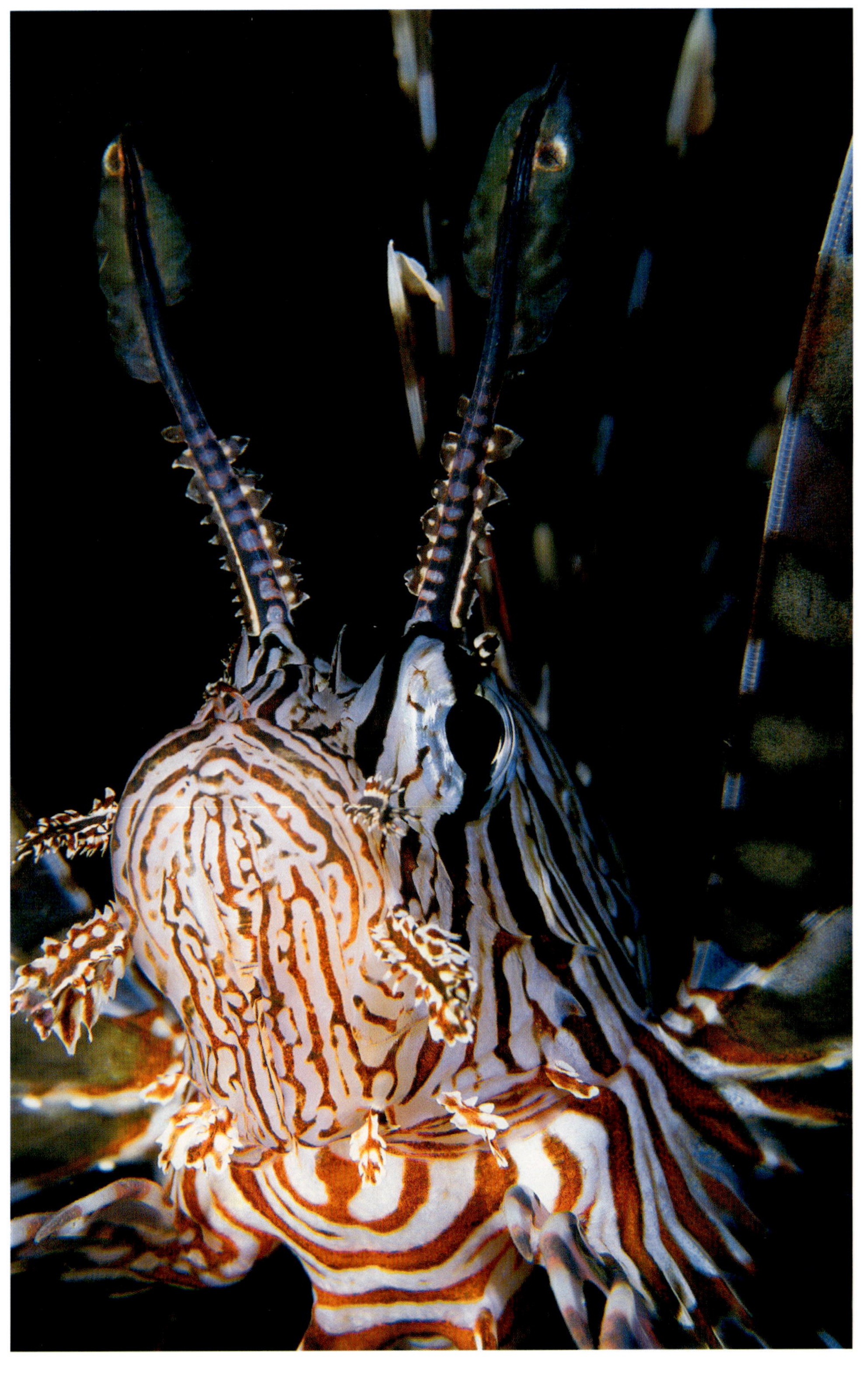

LIONFISH FACE

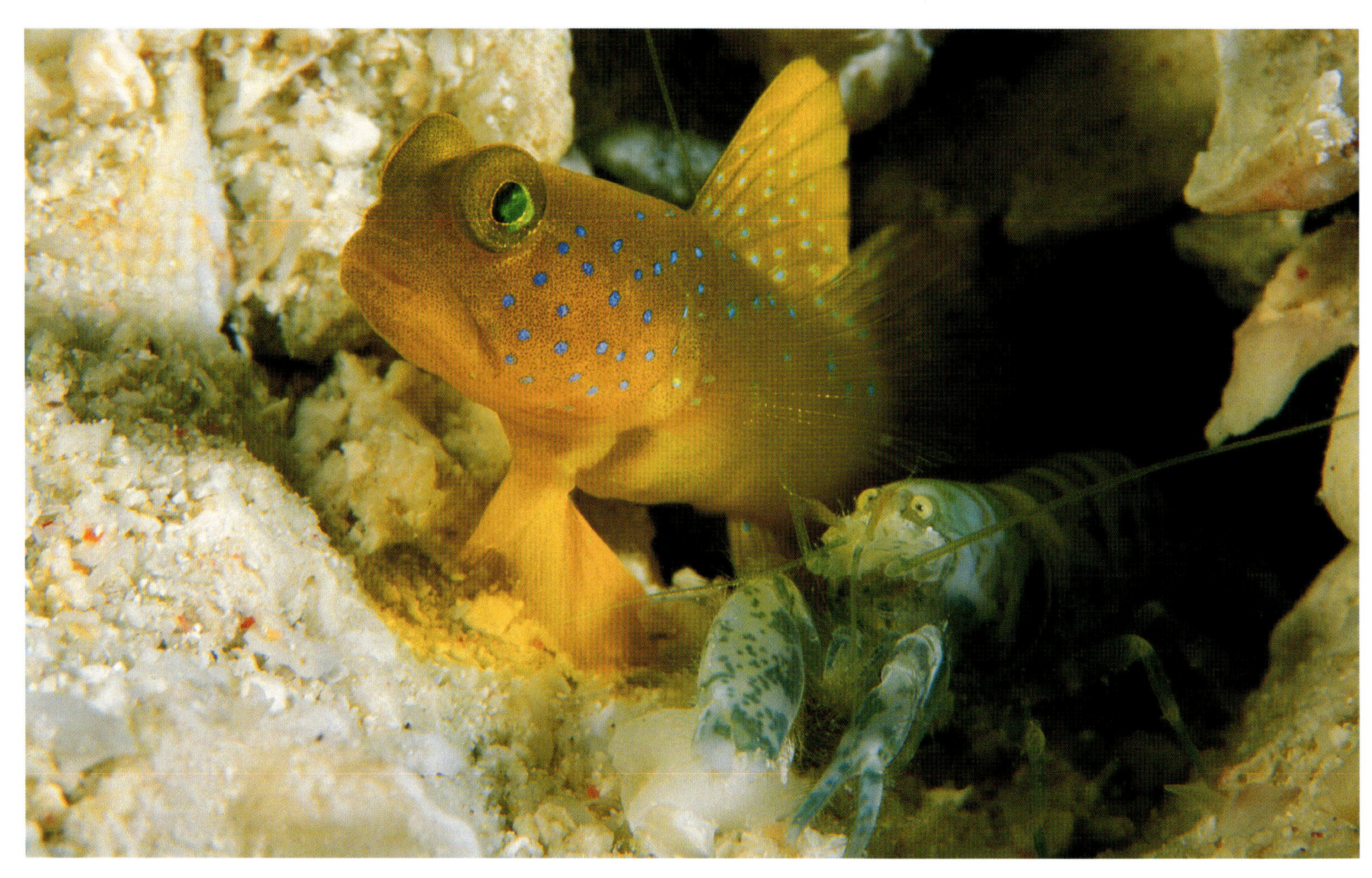

SENTINEL GOBY WITH ALPHEID SHRIMP

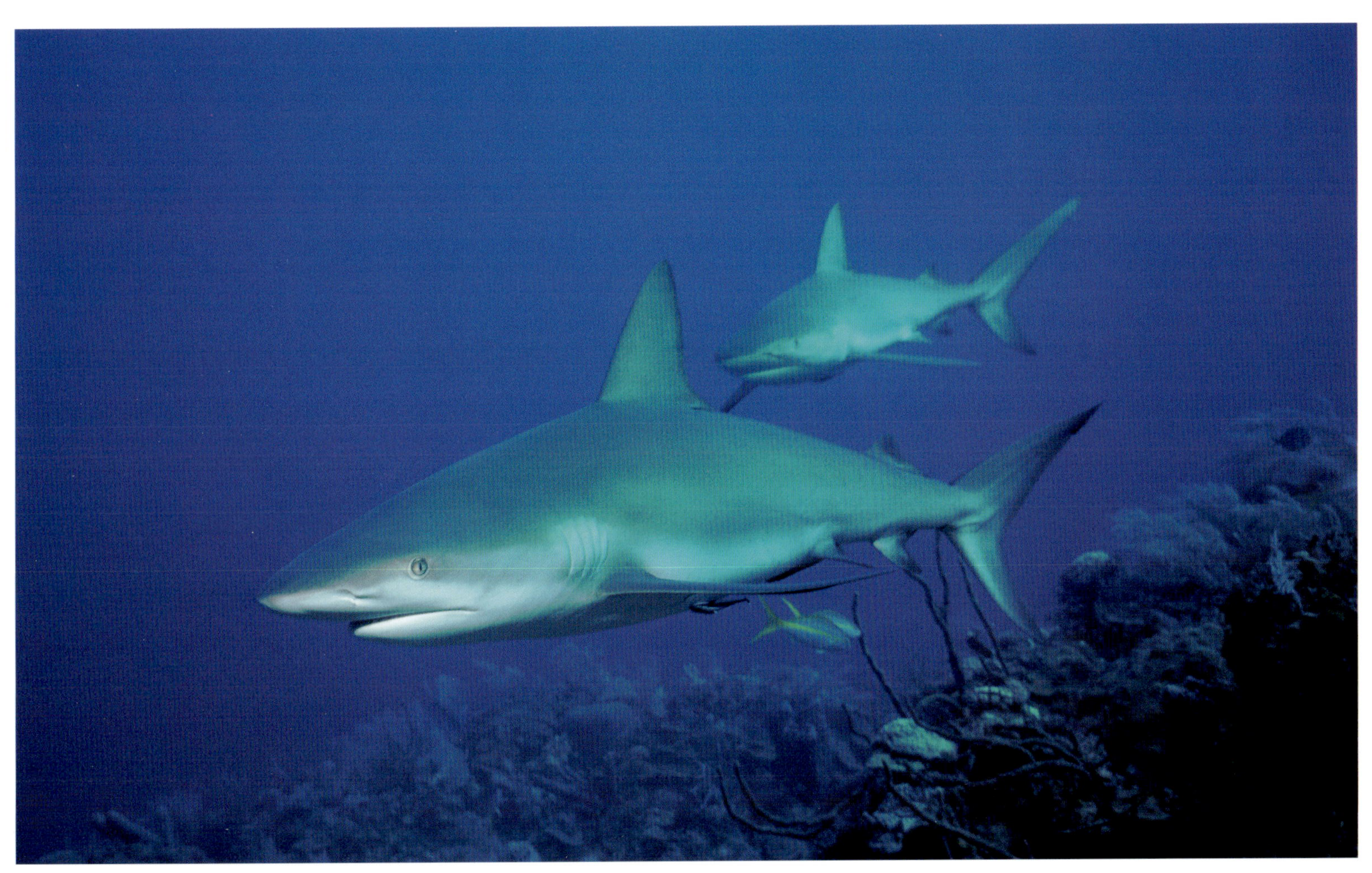

CARIBBEAN REEF SHARKS

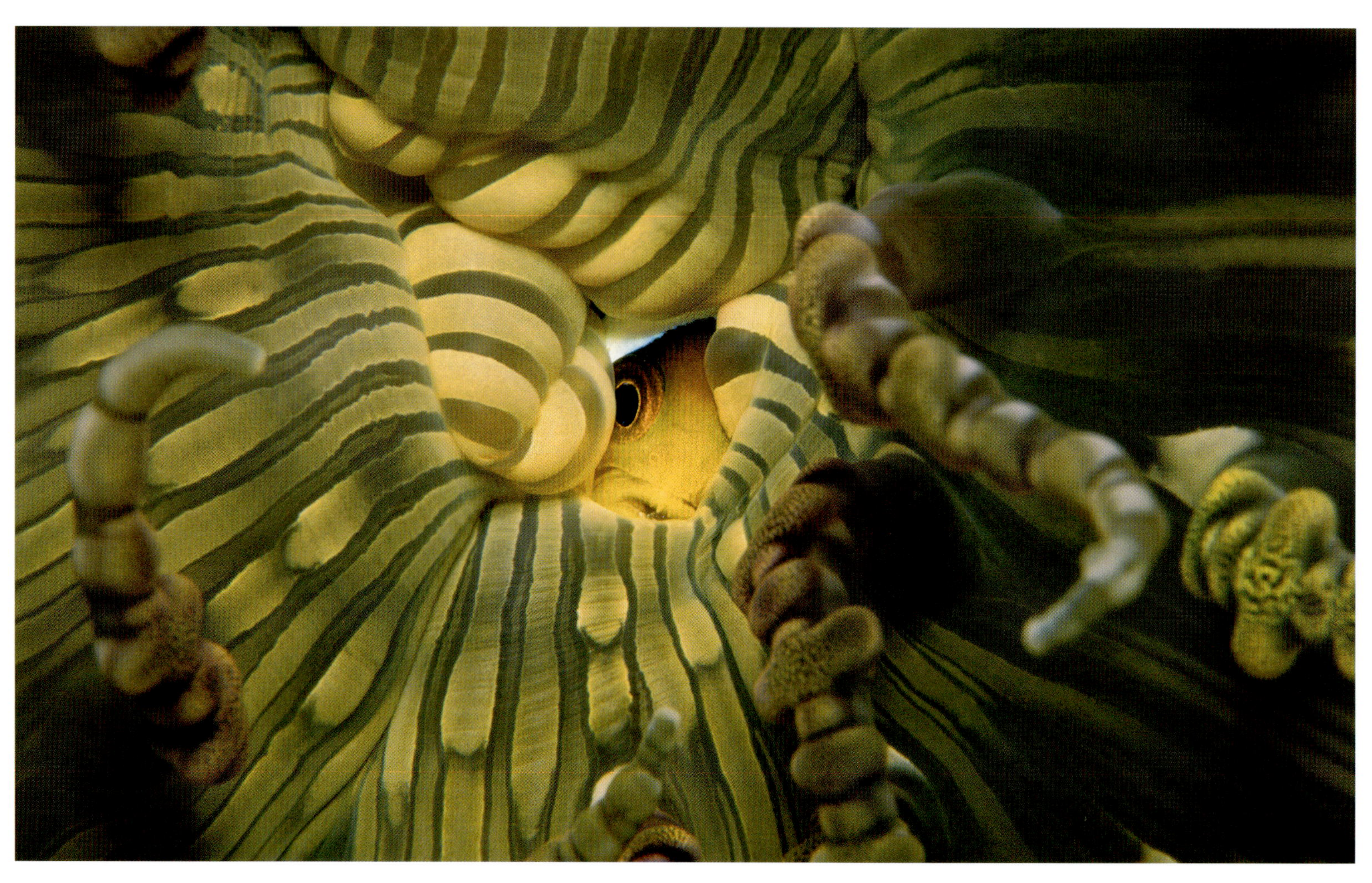

ORANGE - FIN ANEMONEFISH HIDING IN ANEMONE'S ORAL GROOVE

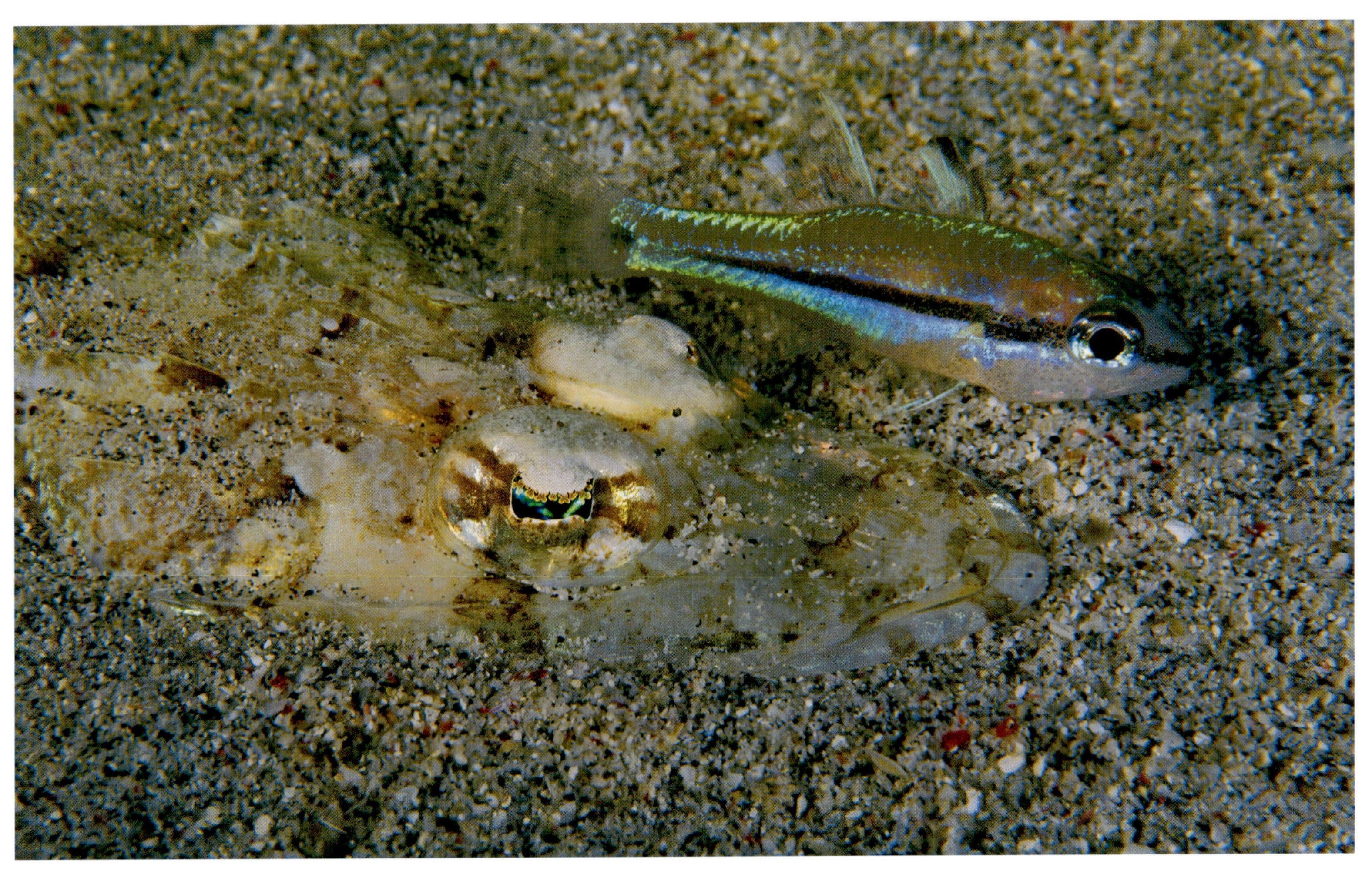

FLATHEAD ABOUT TO SWALLOW CARDINALFISH

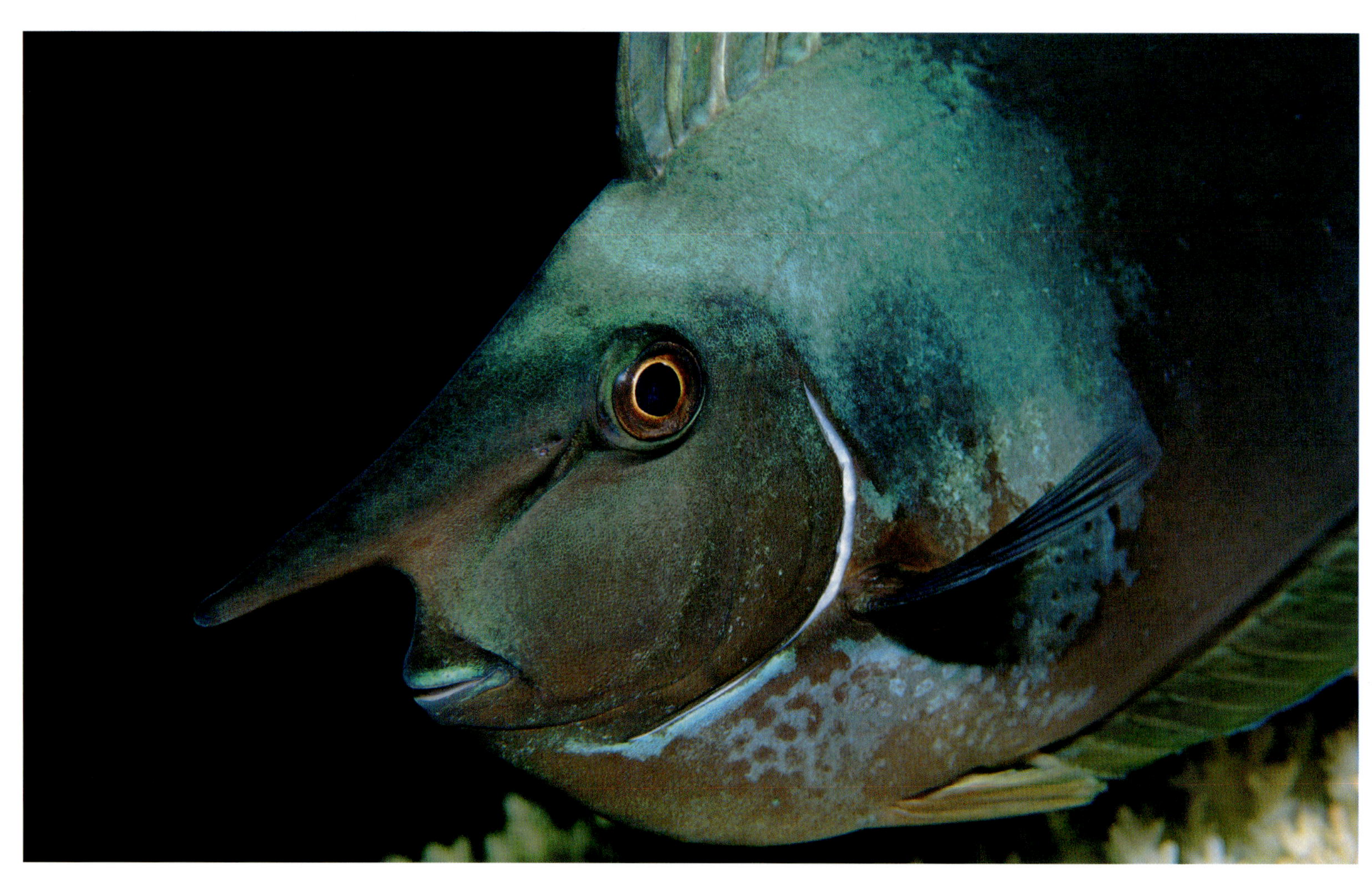

UNICORN SURGEONFISH

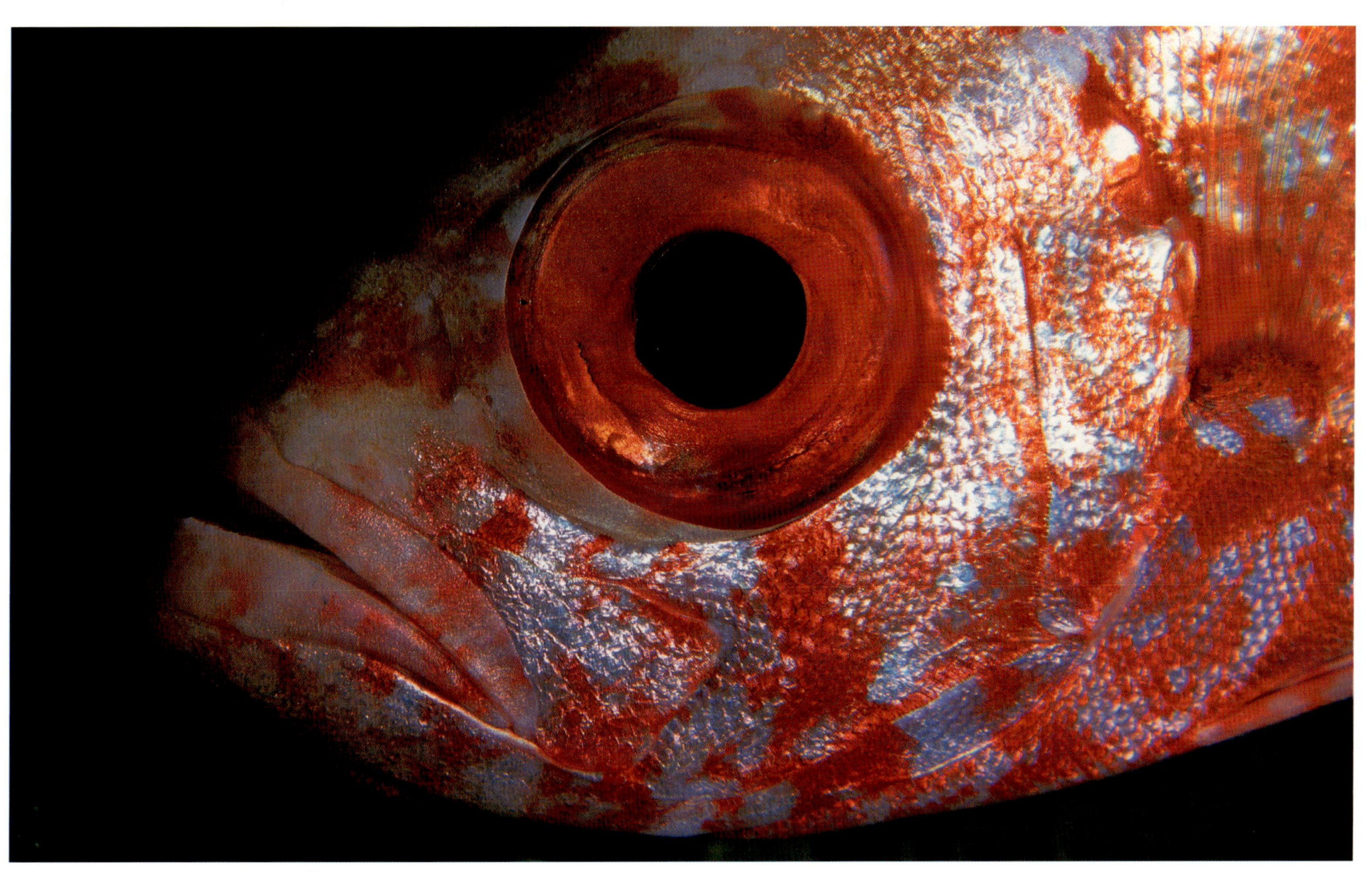

BLOTCHED BIGEYE

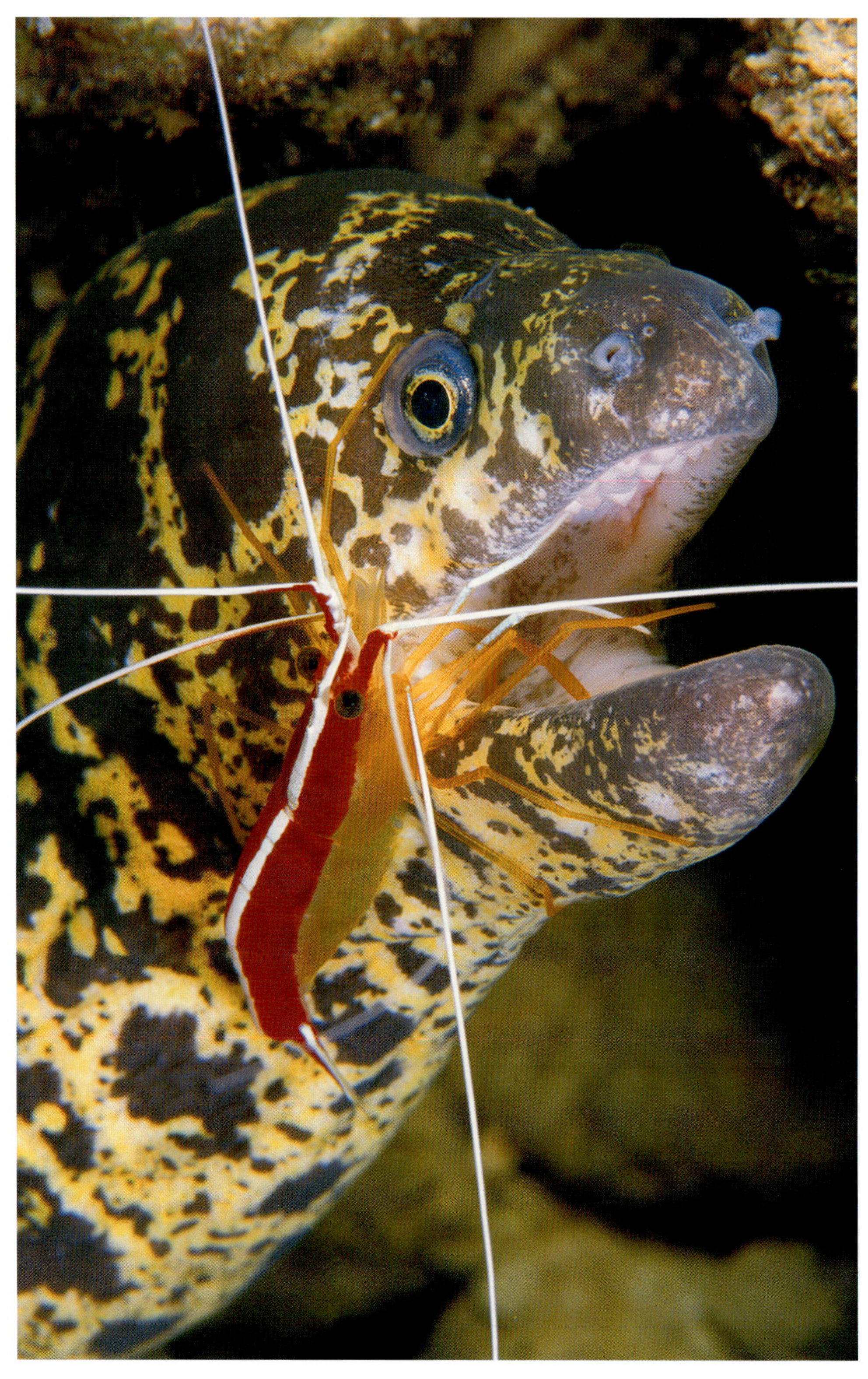

CHAIN MORAY CLEANED BY LYSMATA SHRIMP

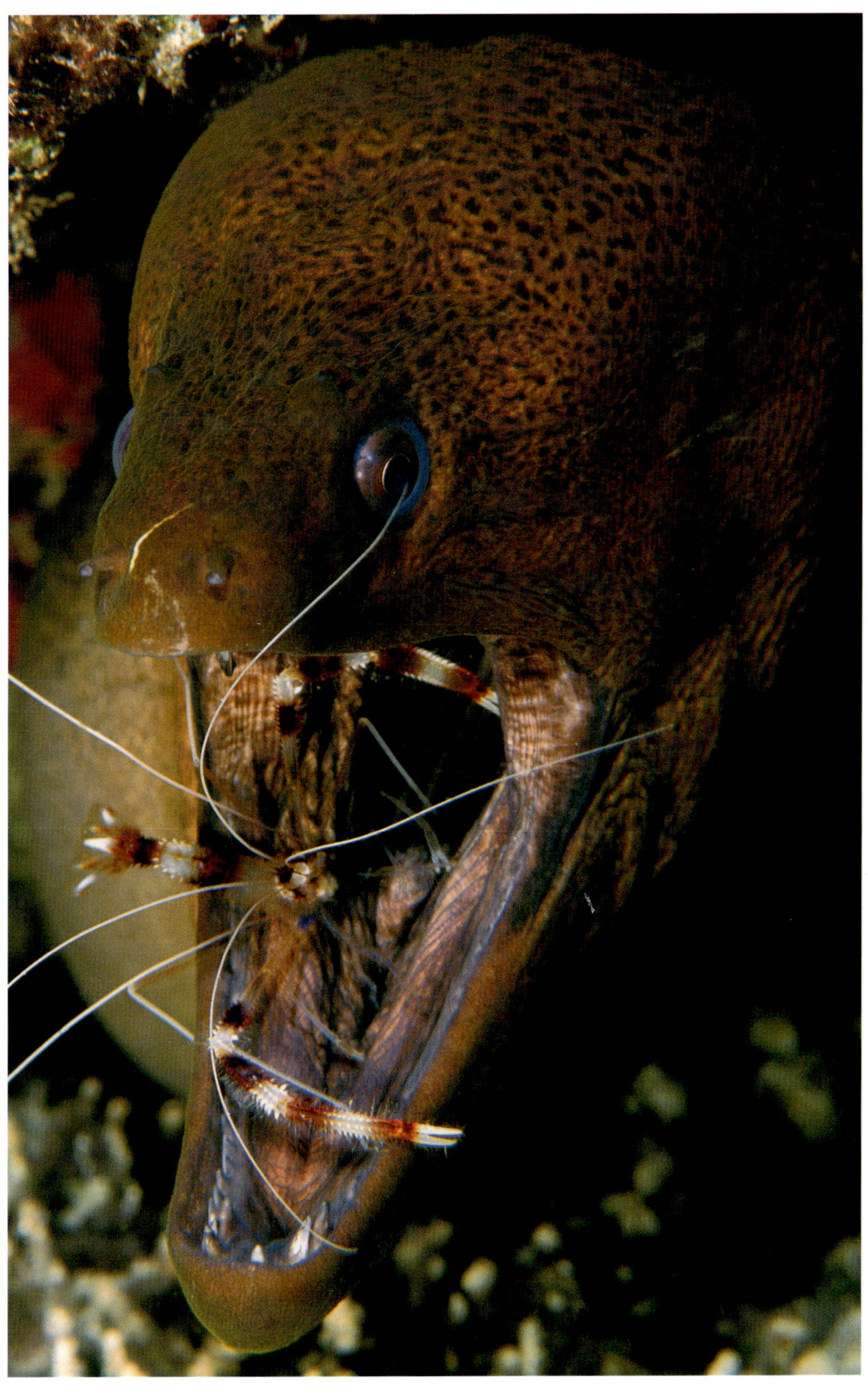

JAVAN MORAY CLEANED BY BANDED CORAL SHRIMP

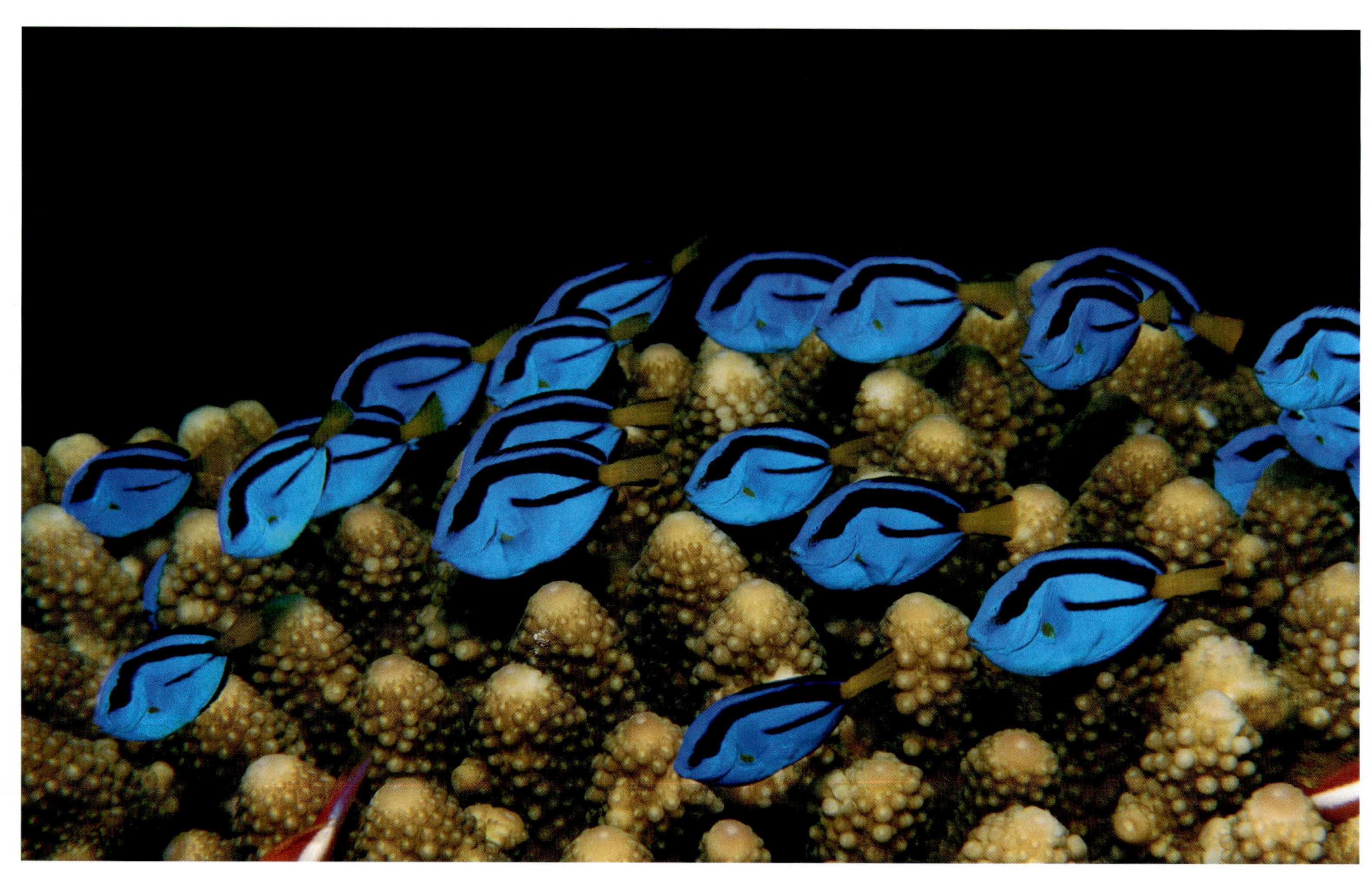

JUVENILE REGAL SURGEONFISH

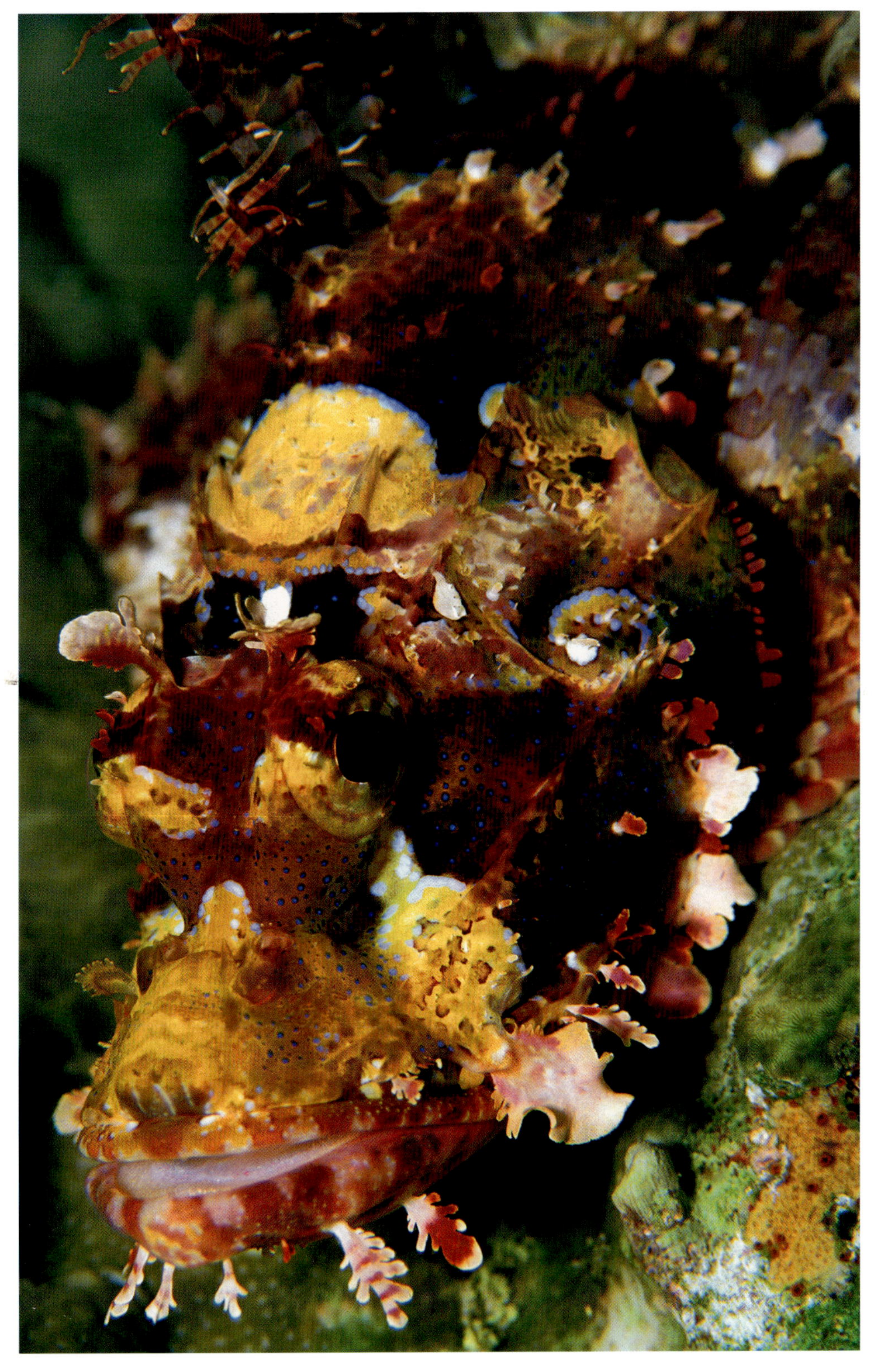

REFF SCORPIONFISH

Oceanic Design

Oceanic Design

The patterns and designs of the natural world are all around us. From the camouflaged coat of a white-tail fawn to the intricate design of a coral trout, nature is fine art brought to life. But it is not art for the sake of art. It is form for the sake of function...design with a purpose.

In the sea, nature completely abandons its leanings toward the understated. Complex patterns and outrageous color schemes are the norm on the coral reef. It is the ultimate art project.

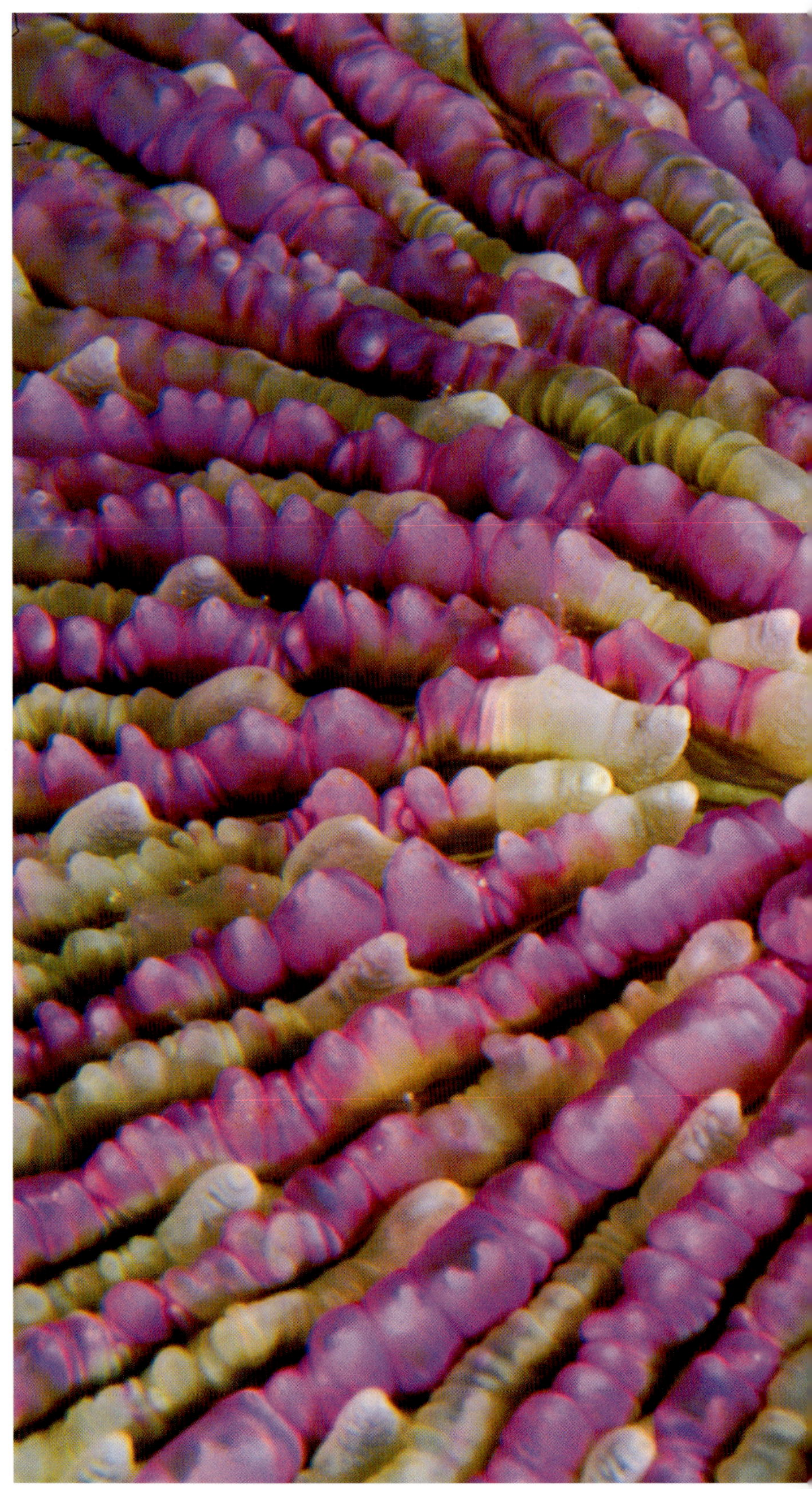

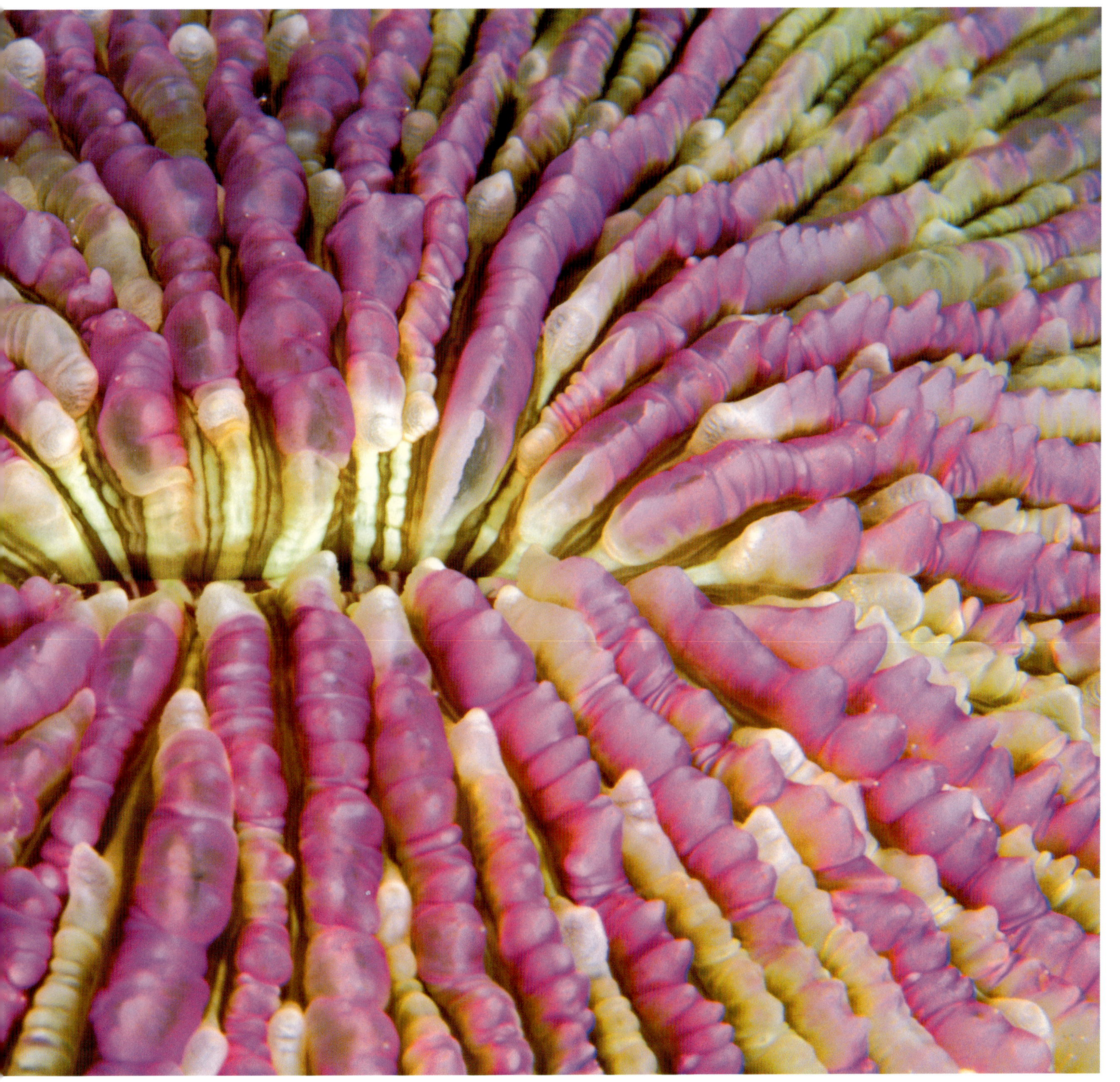

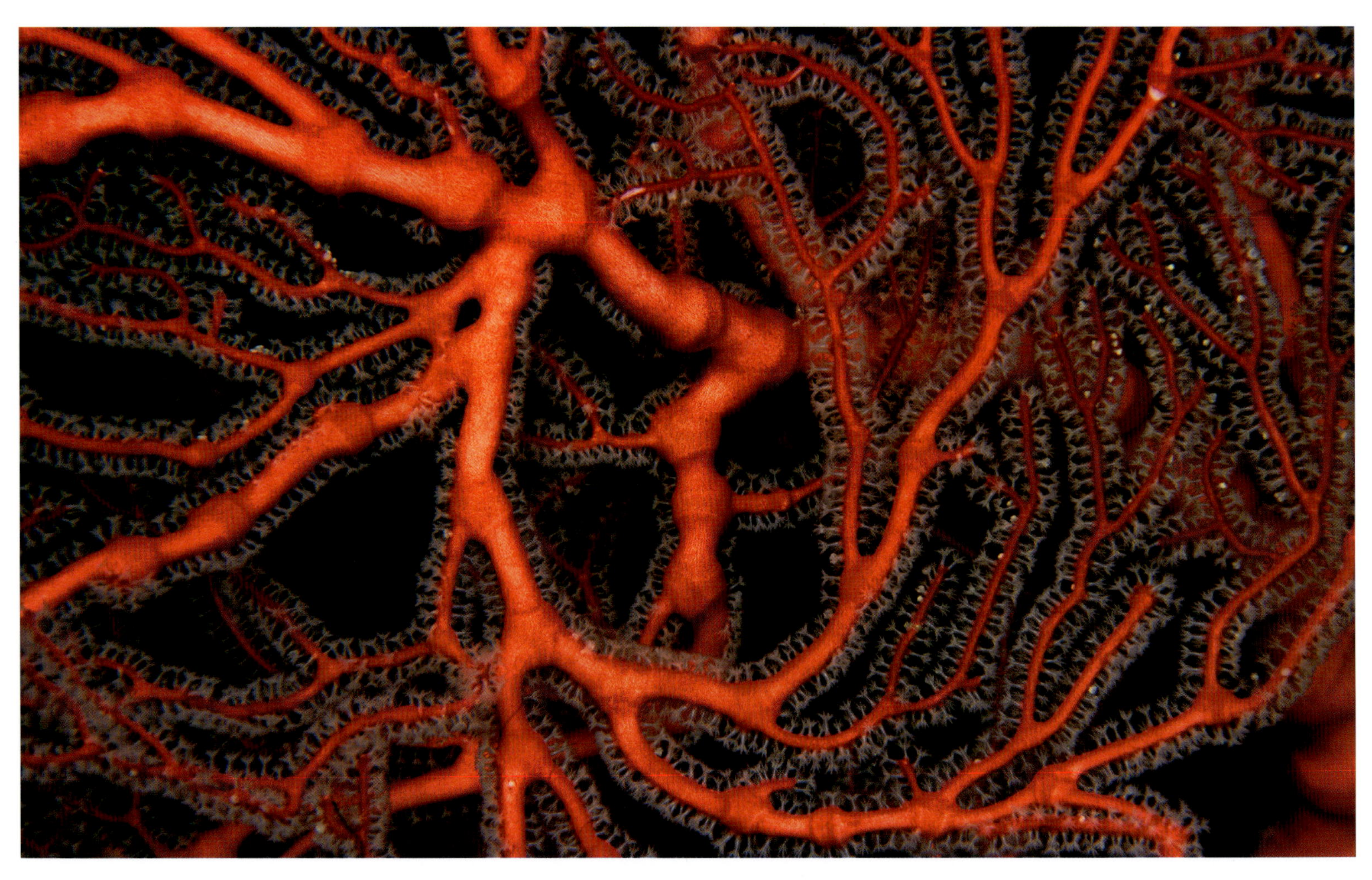

GORGONIAN FAN

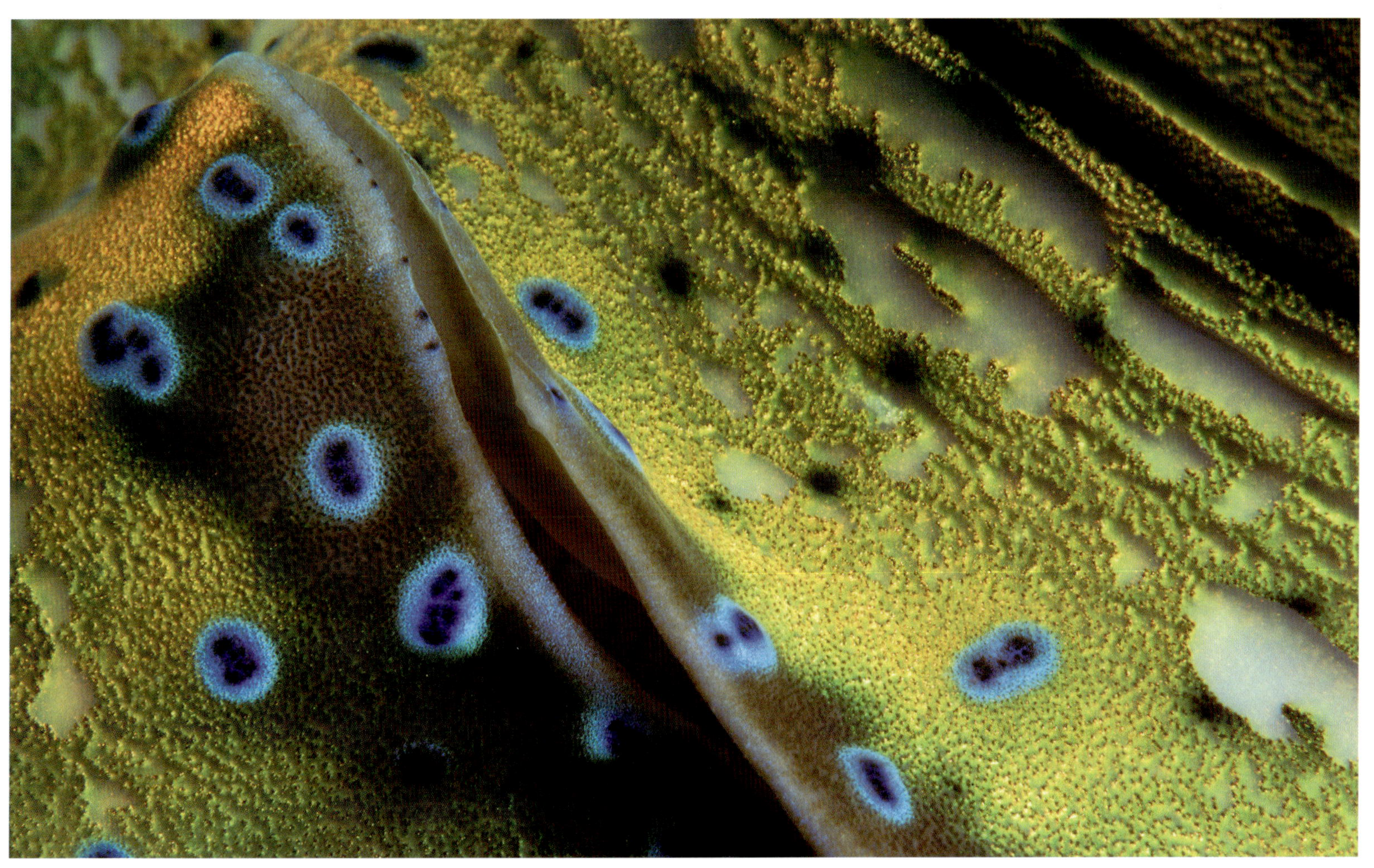

TRIDACNA CLAM SIPHON

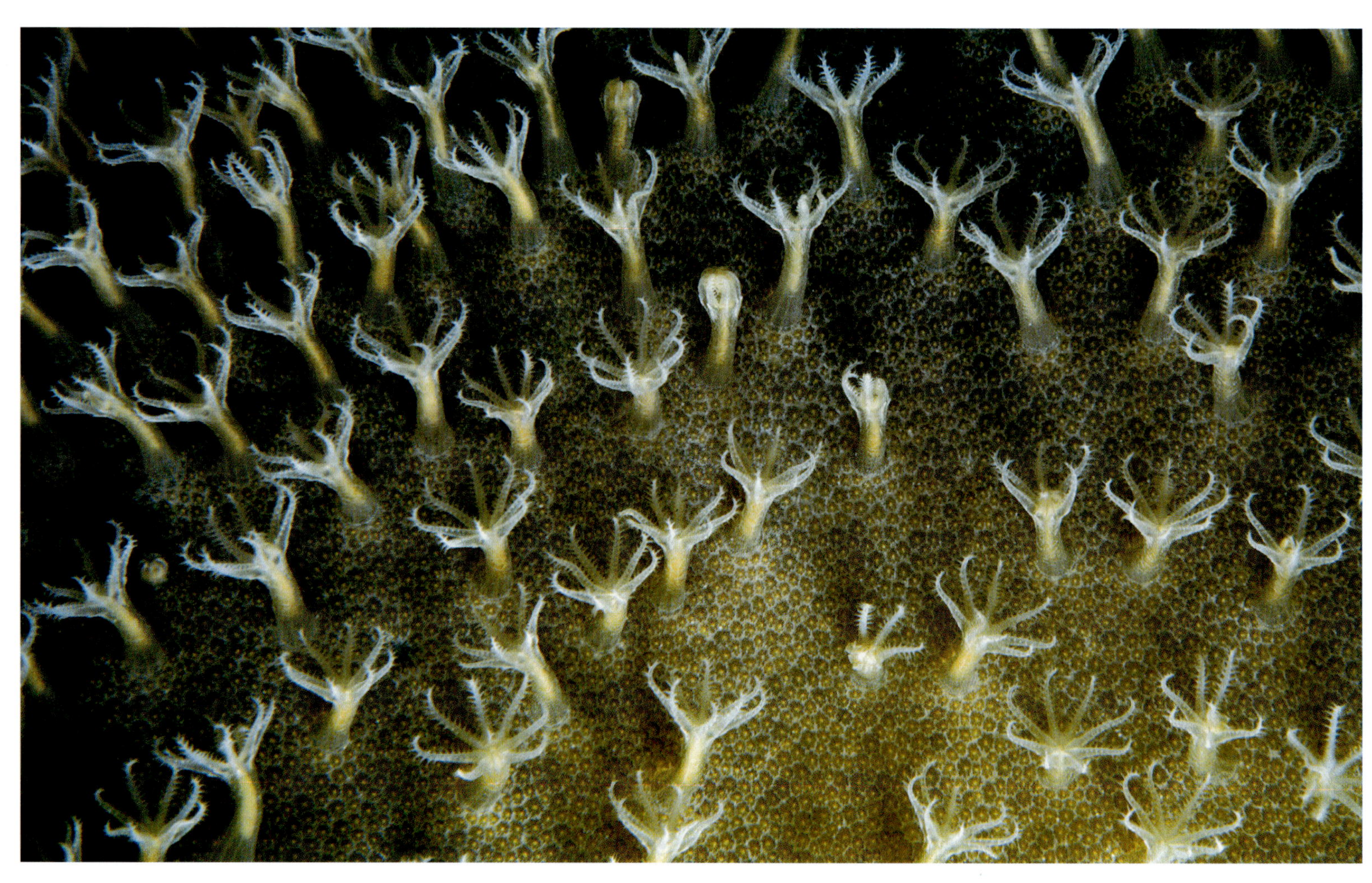

SOFT CORAL TENTACLES

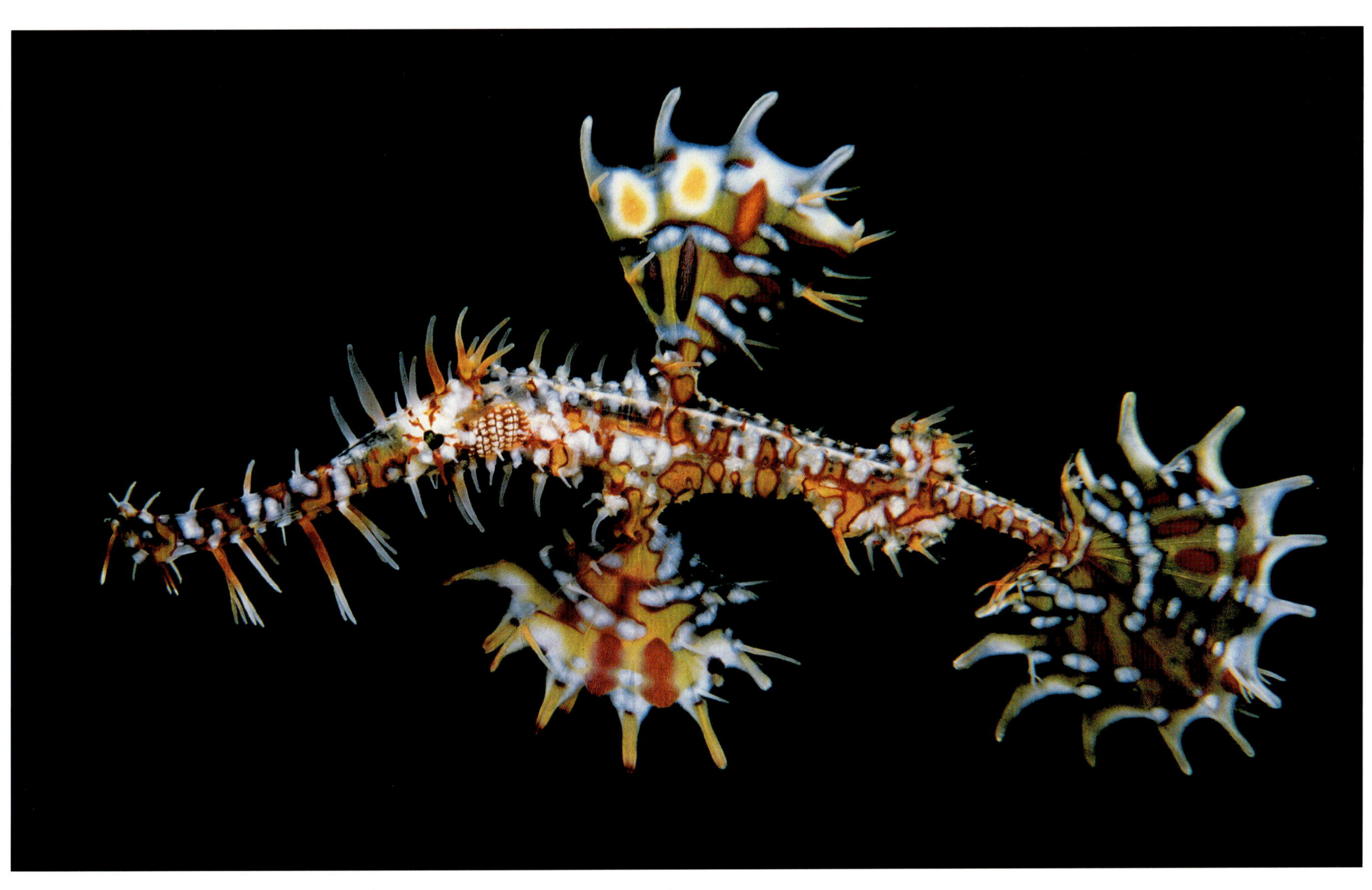

ORNATE GHOST PIPEFISH

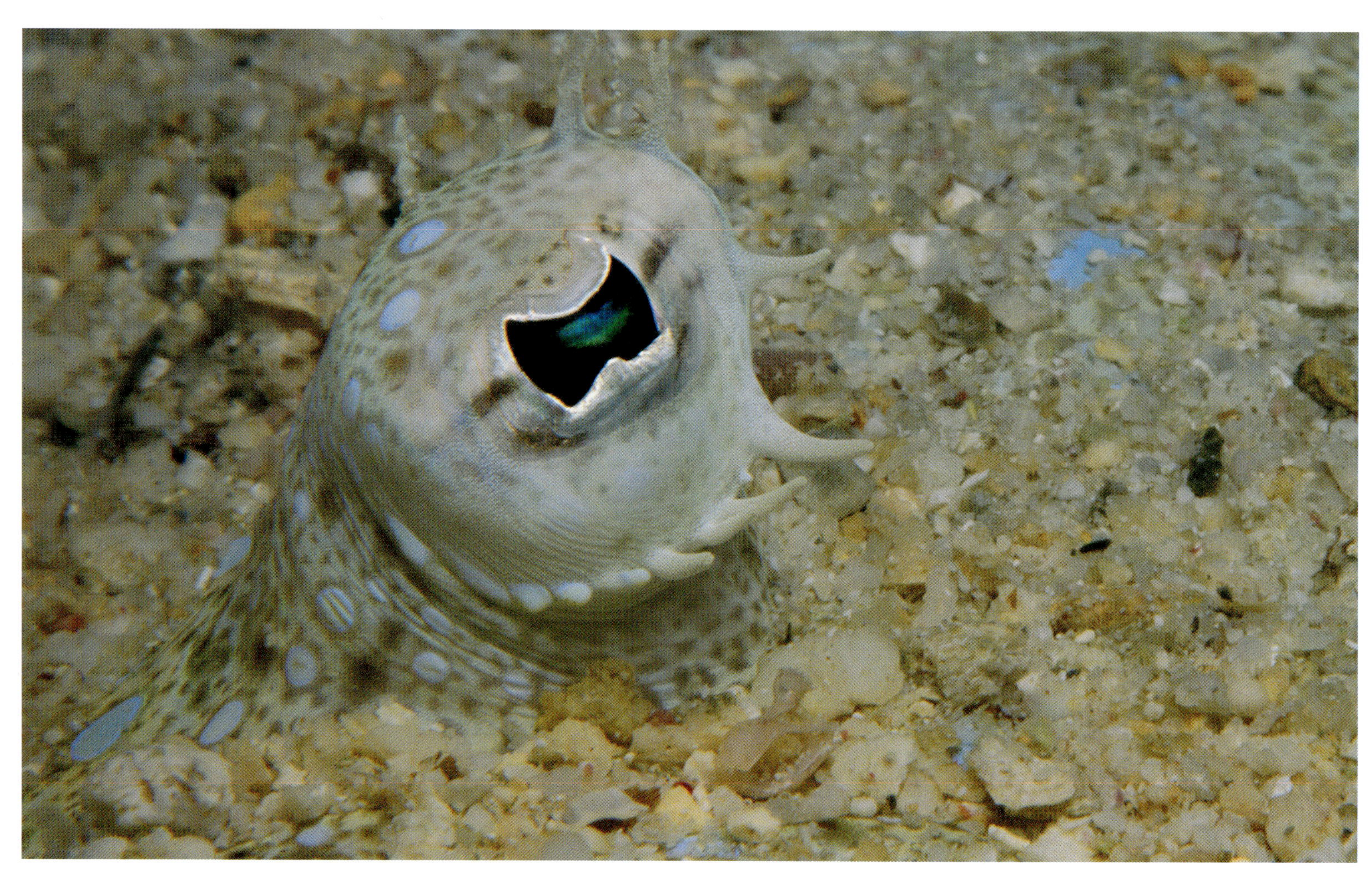

PEACOCK FLOUNDER EYE

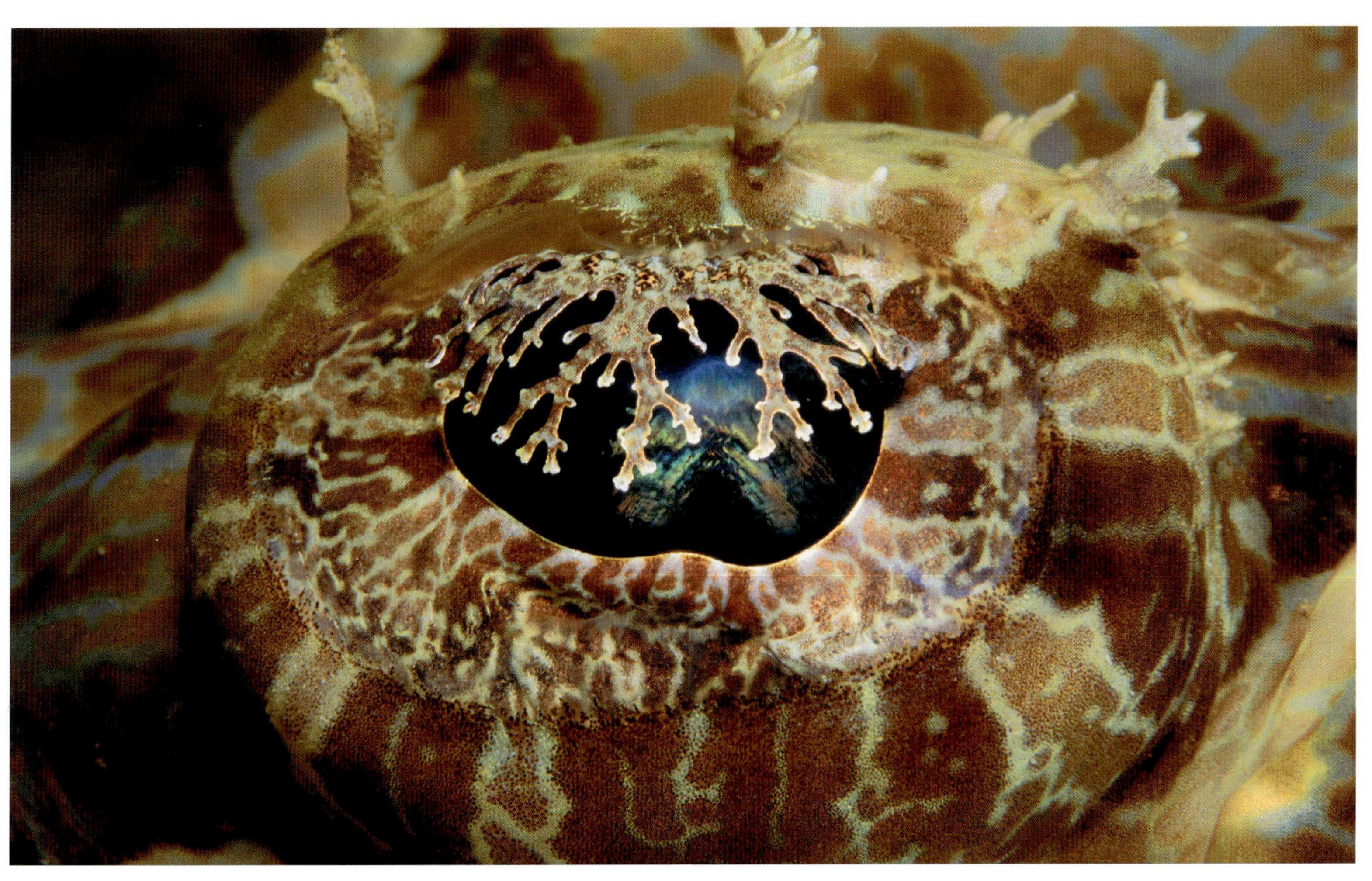

CROCODILE FISH EYE

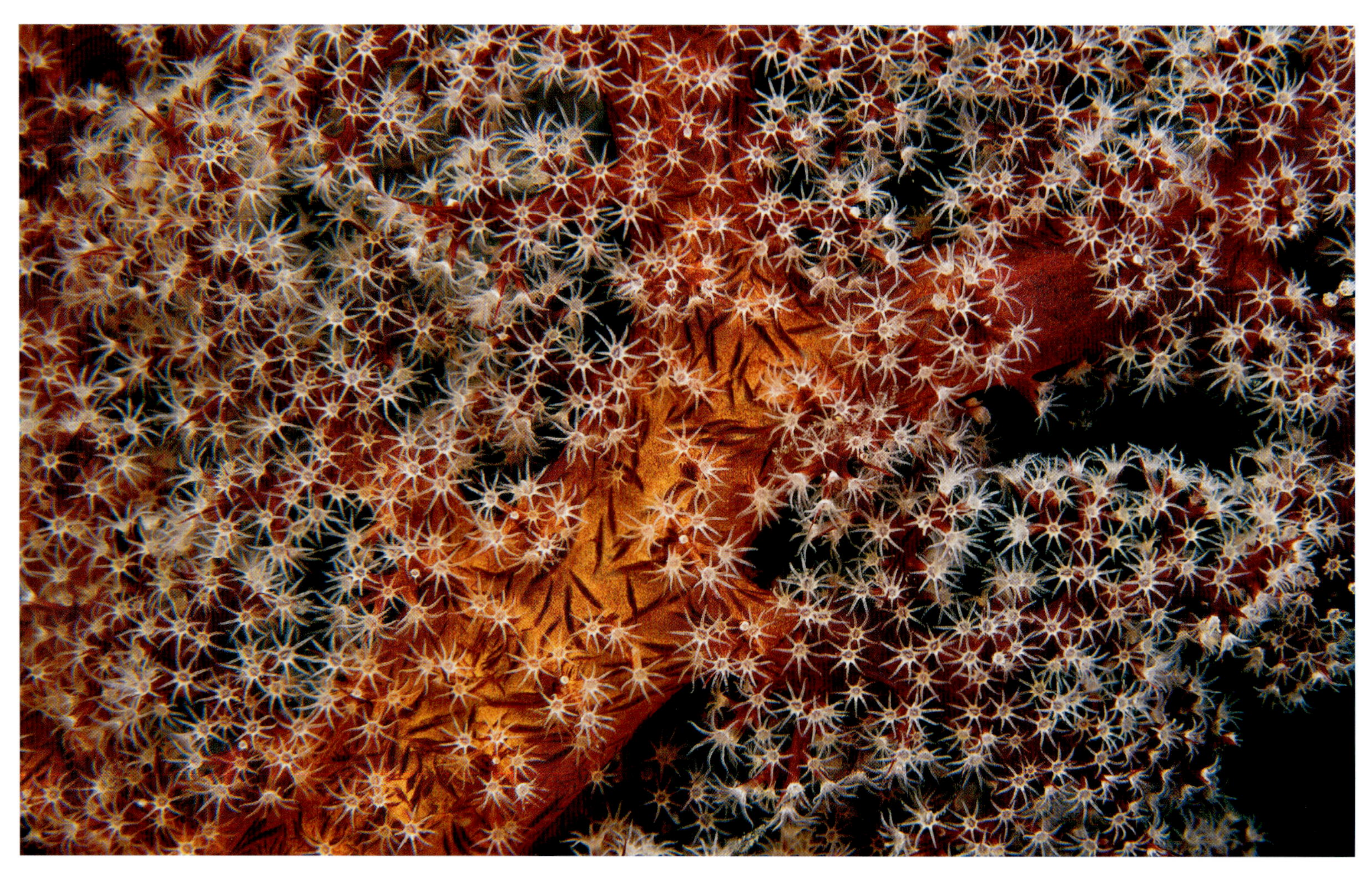

SOFT CORAL FEEDING

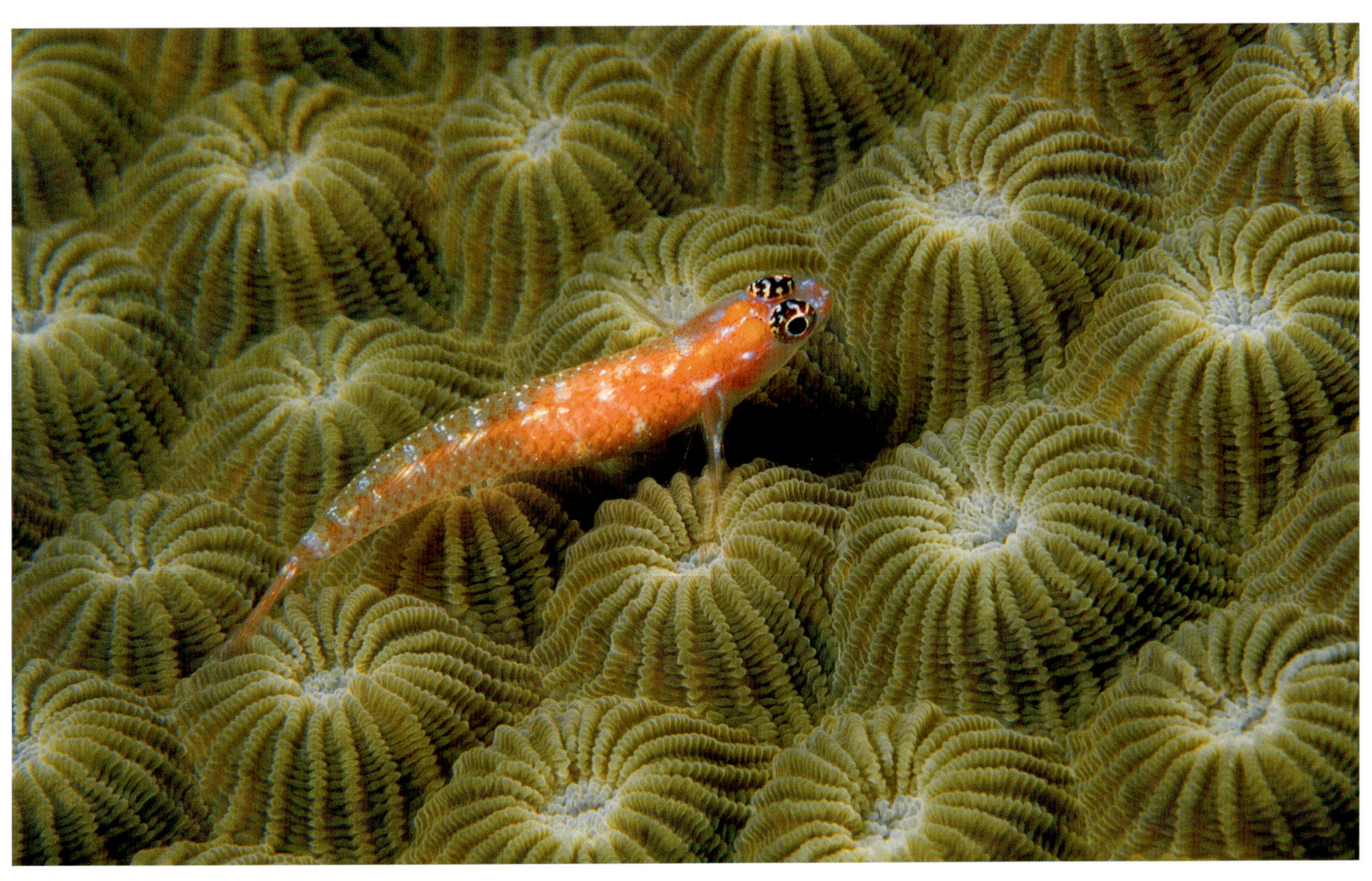

FRINGEFIN GOBY ON HARD CORAL

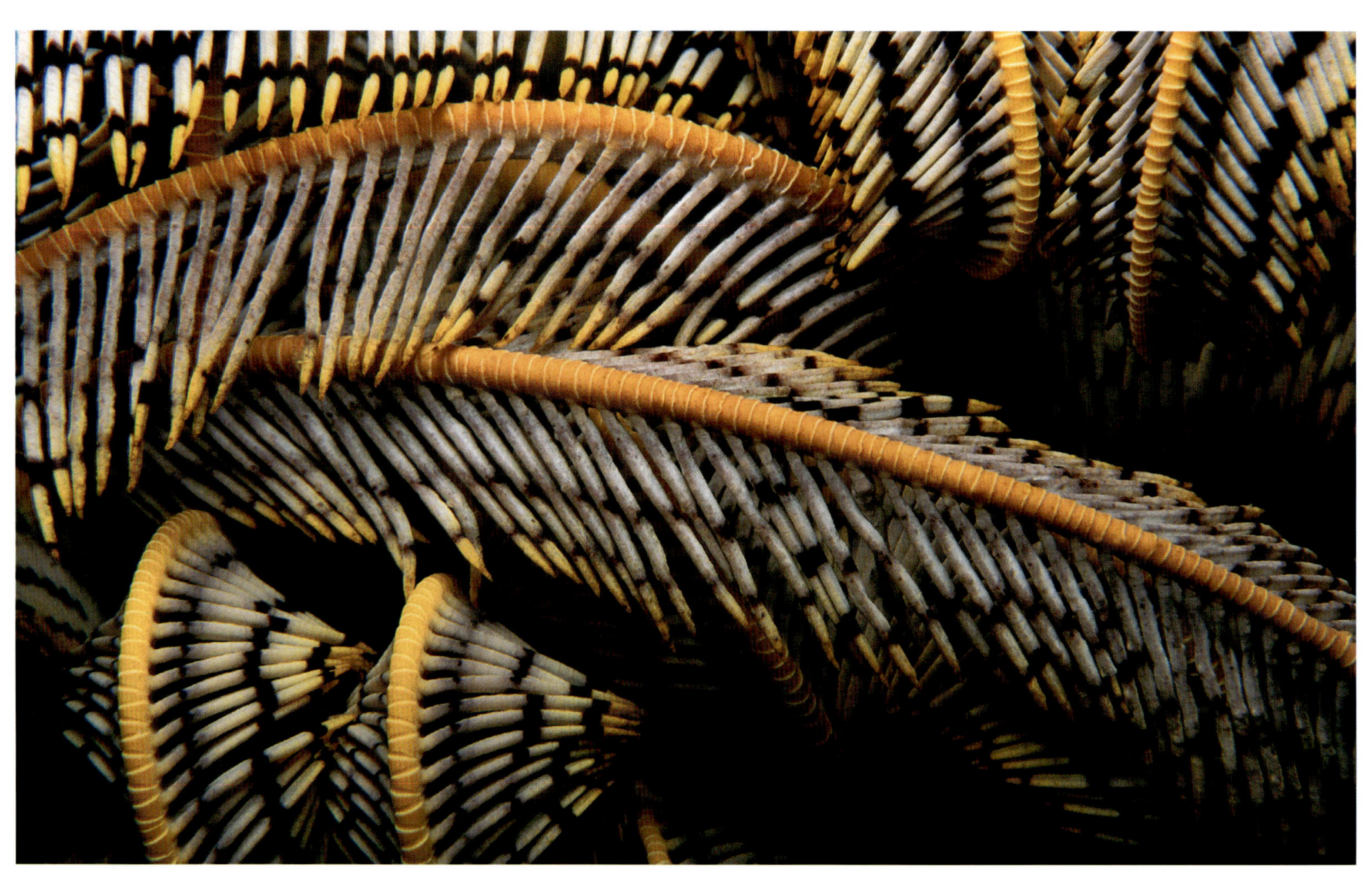

CRINOID ARMS

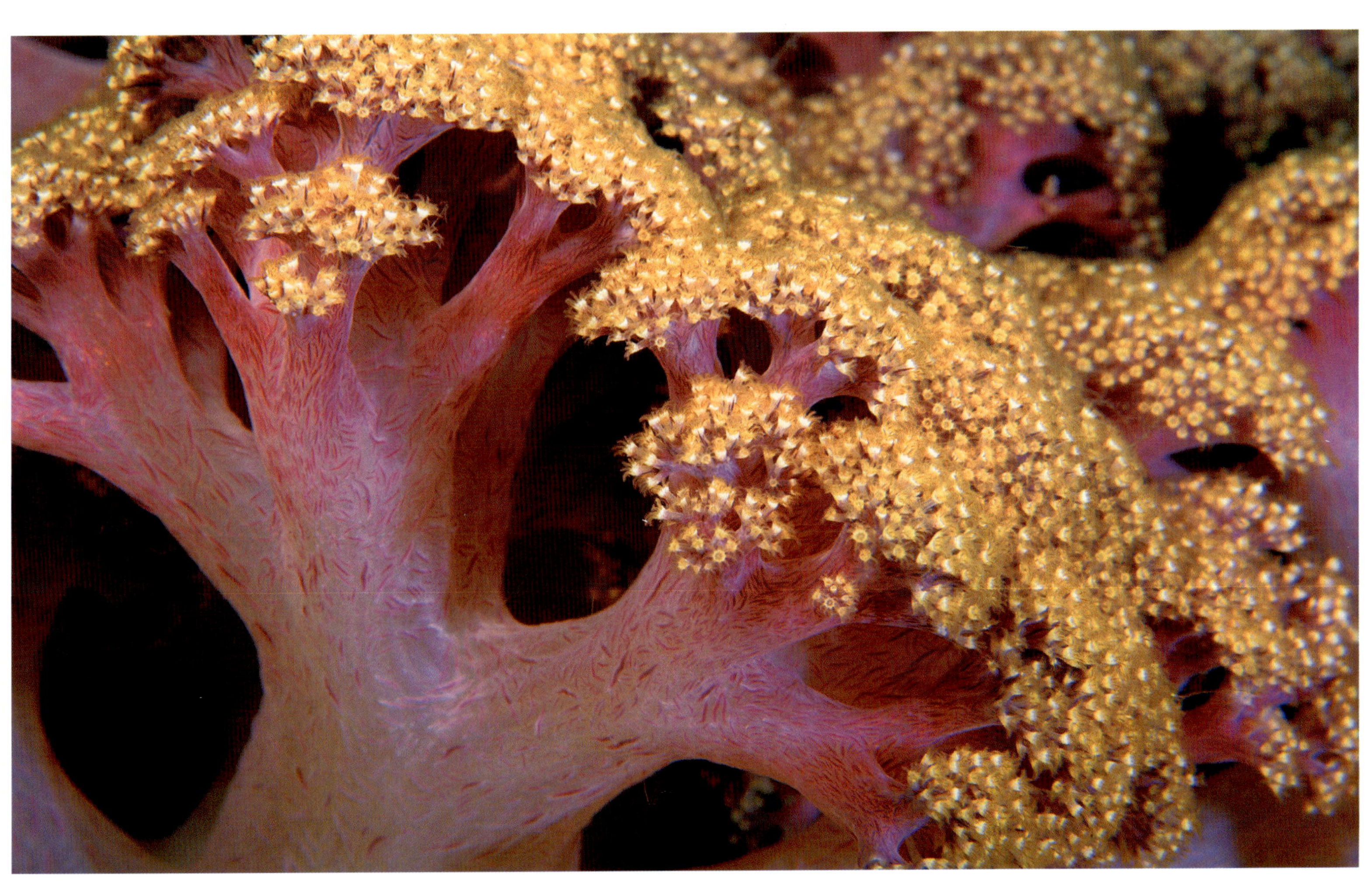

UMBELLATE TREE CORAL

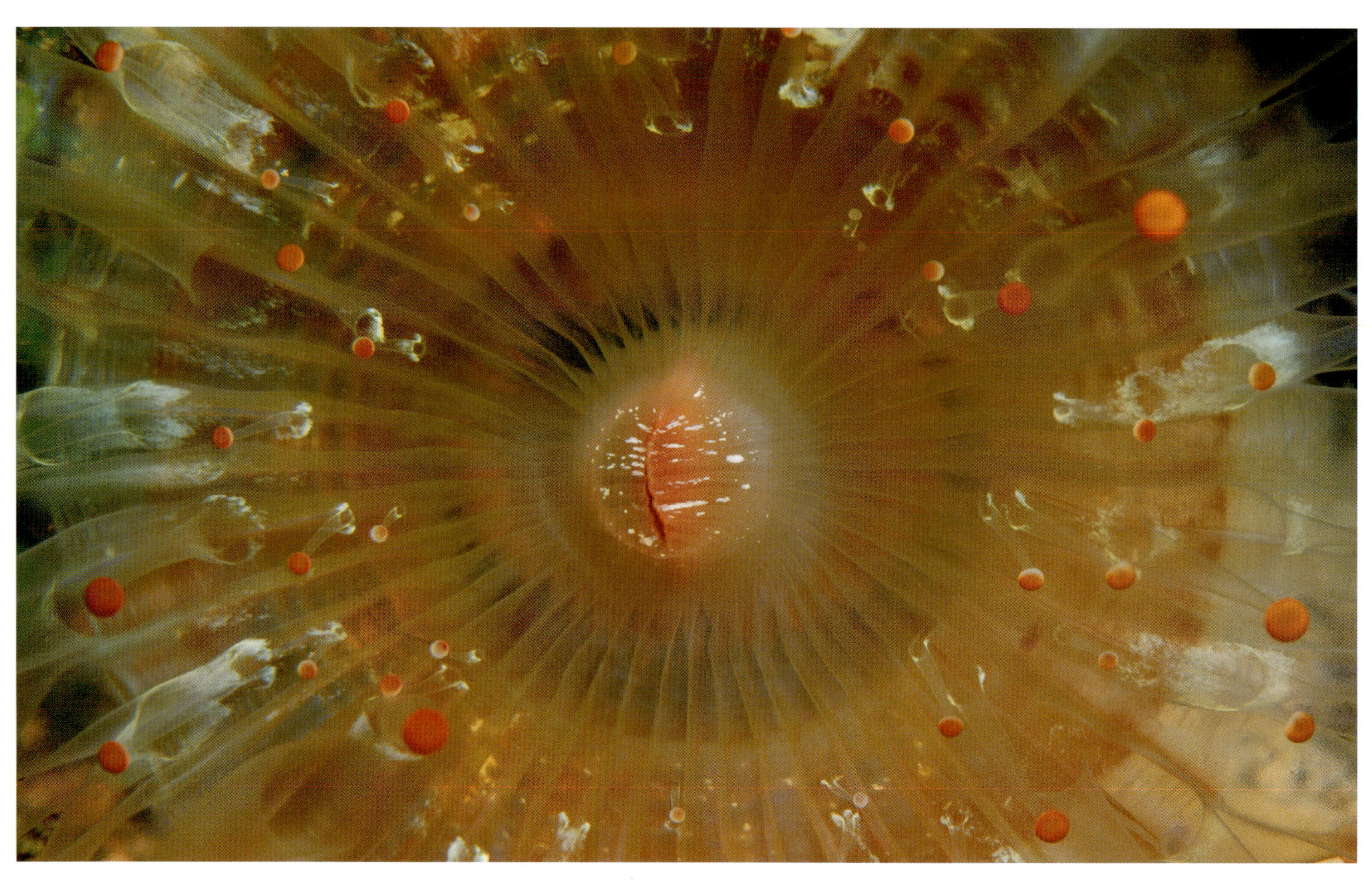

ORANGE BALL ANEMONE

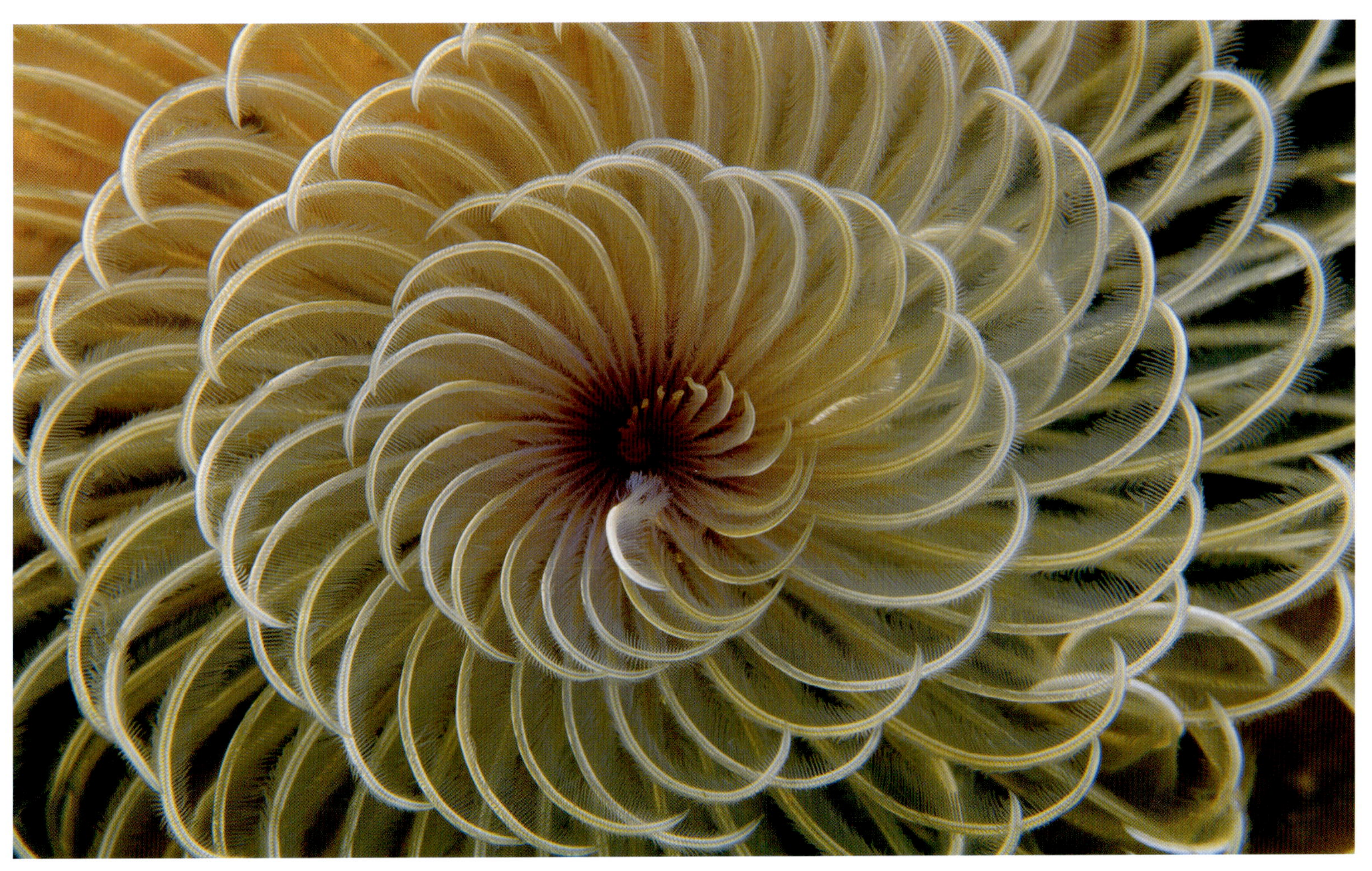

SABELLID TUBE WORM

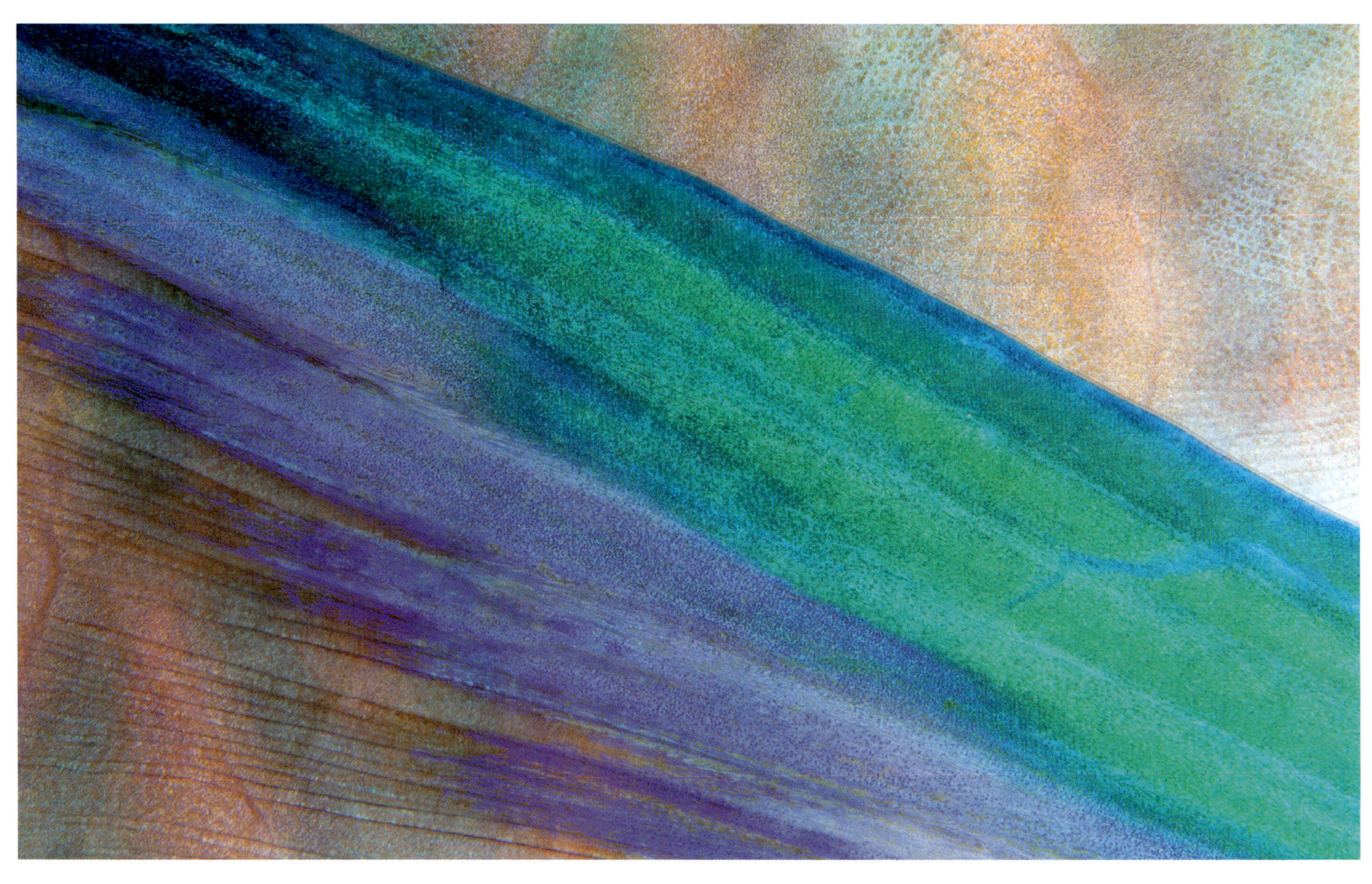

PARROTFISH FIN

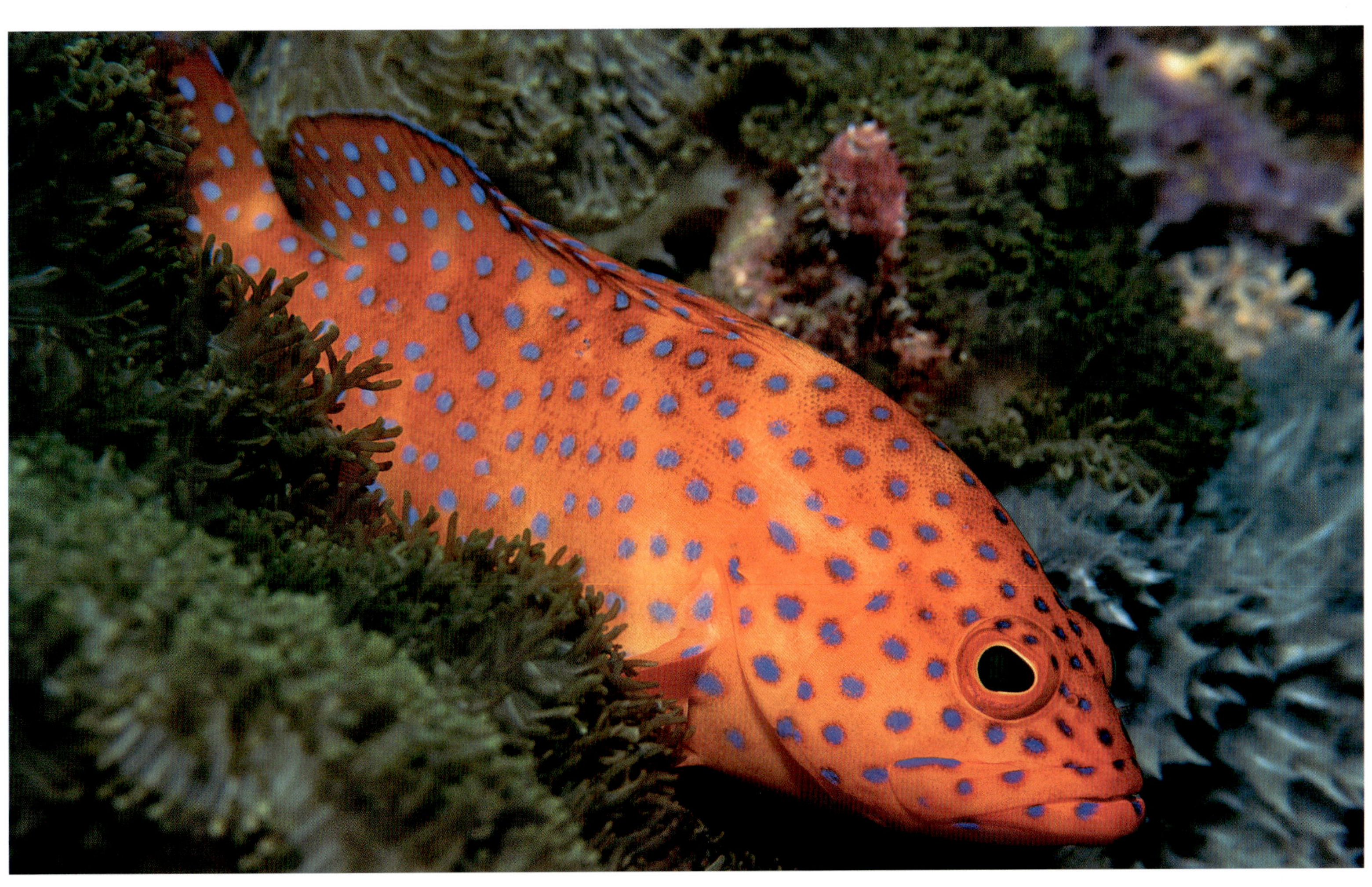

CORAL TROUT

Travelogue: Beneath Cerulean Seas

This part of the book features photography from some of the most exotic, remote coral kingdoms on the planet, as well as a couple of destinations that are more frequently visited. They are my top picks, chosen primarily from my perspective as a marine life photographer. I openly acknowledge my bias in the selection process. To be certain, there are numerous, incredible reef ecosystems that could - and should - have merited attention in these pages. Perhaps with your recommendations and several suitcases full of money, they can be included in the next edition. In the interim, I hope you will enjoy this visit to the wondrous reefs of cerulean seas.

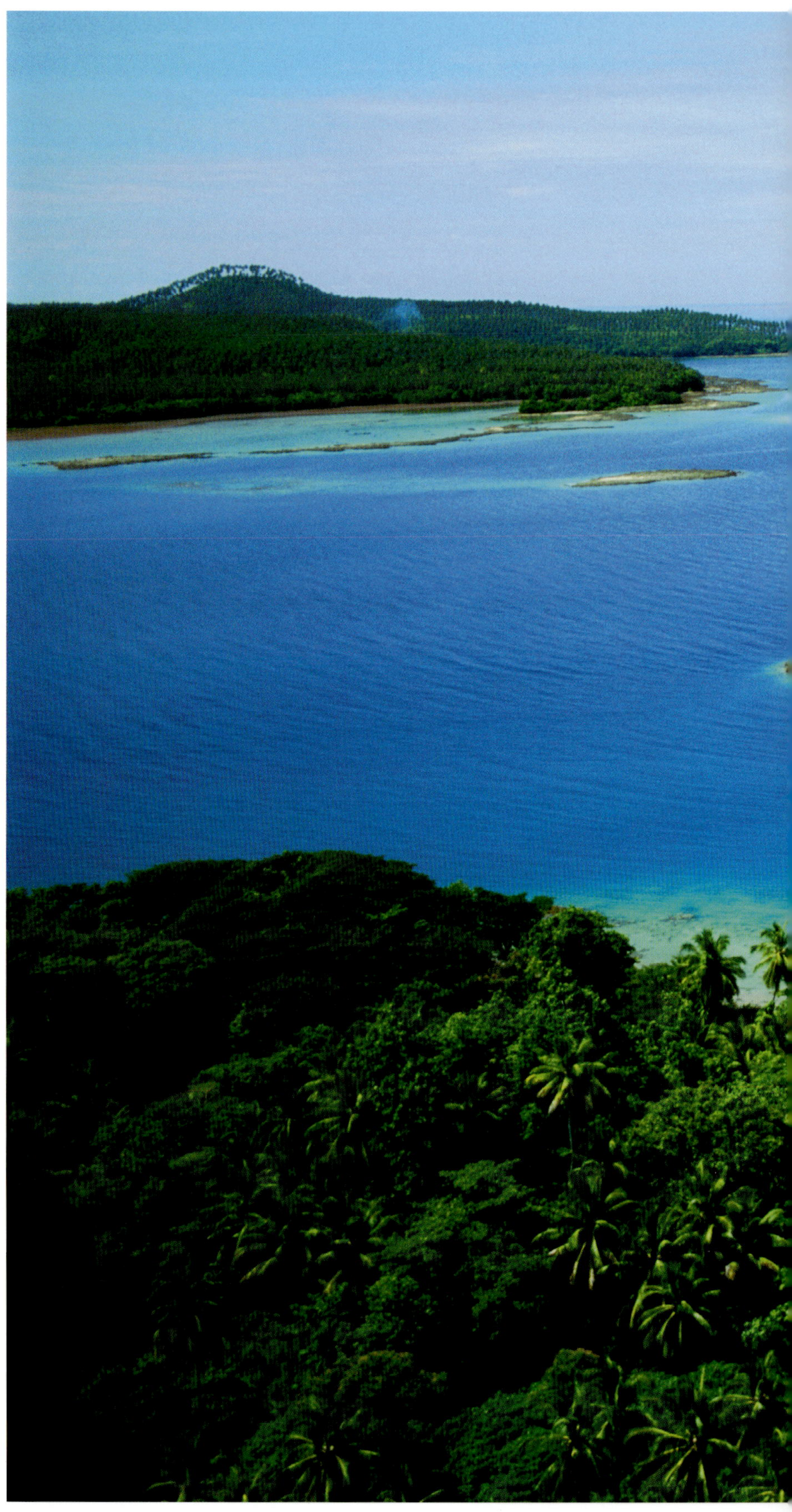

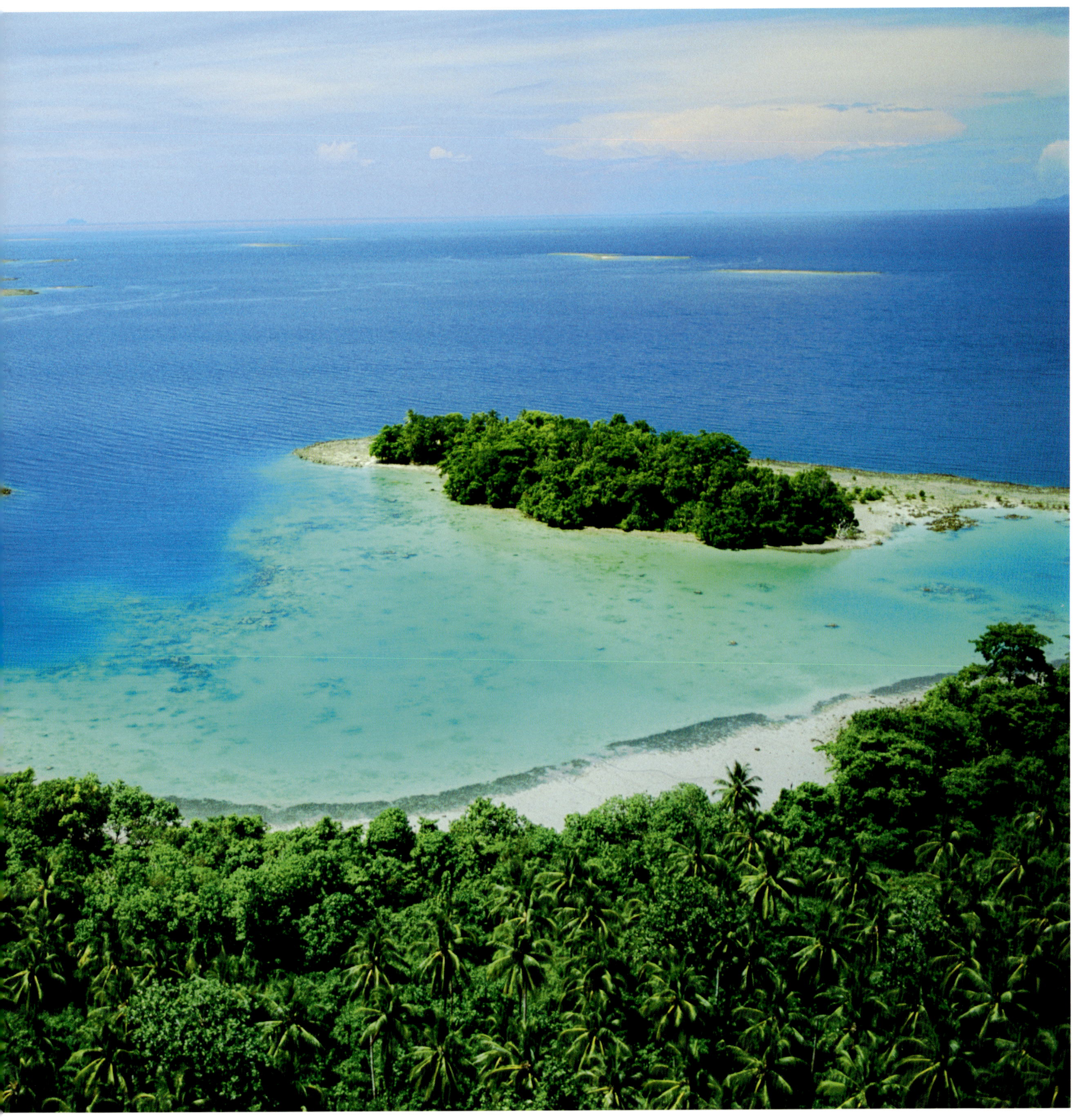

Bonaire

Bonaire

I took my first underwater photos in Bonaire. This sleepy, laid back, little island is my favorite place to dive in the Caribbean. Apparently, I'm not in the minority. These days, Bonaire hosts more divers each year than any other place on the planet. This desert-like island is nestled in the southern Caribbean, some 50 miles north of Caracas, Venezuela. It is part of the Dutch Antilles island group which includes its renowned sisters, Aruba and Curacao.

Bonaire is not considered a beautiful island. It is covered with infertile soil, cactus thickets, and an assortment of lizards. But step into the water and the transformation is amazing. Instant oasis! In the island's lee, the ocean resembles an enormous swimming pool teeming with a diverse assemblage of marine life. Along much of the coastline, the fringing coral reefs begin only a few feet offshore. In 1979, Bonaire's reefs were declared a marine park.. This protective status offers the hope that diving here will generate wonderful memories for generations to come.

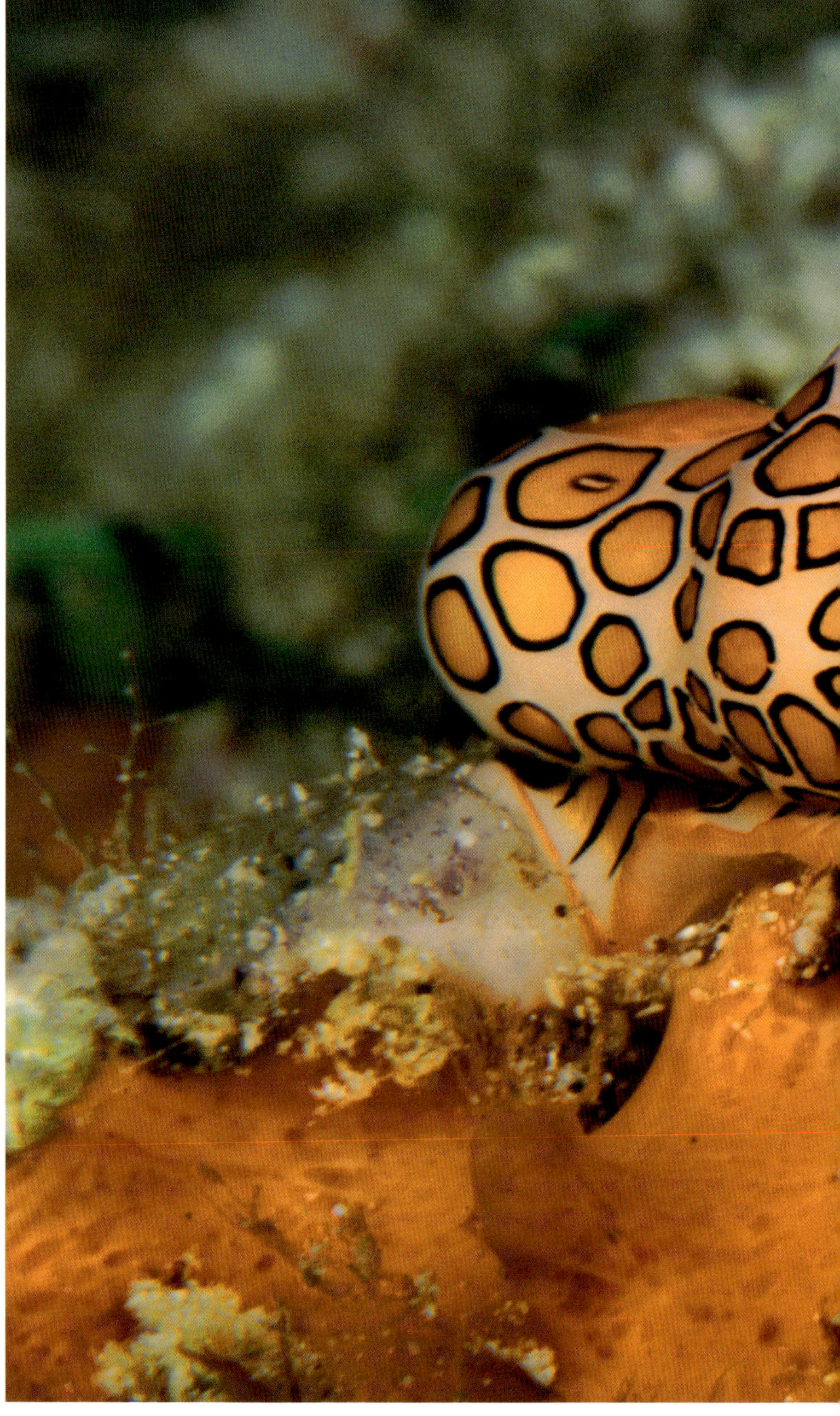

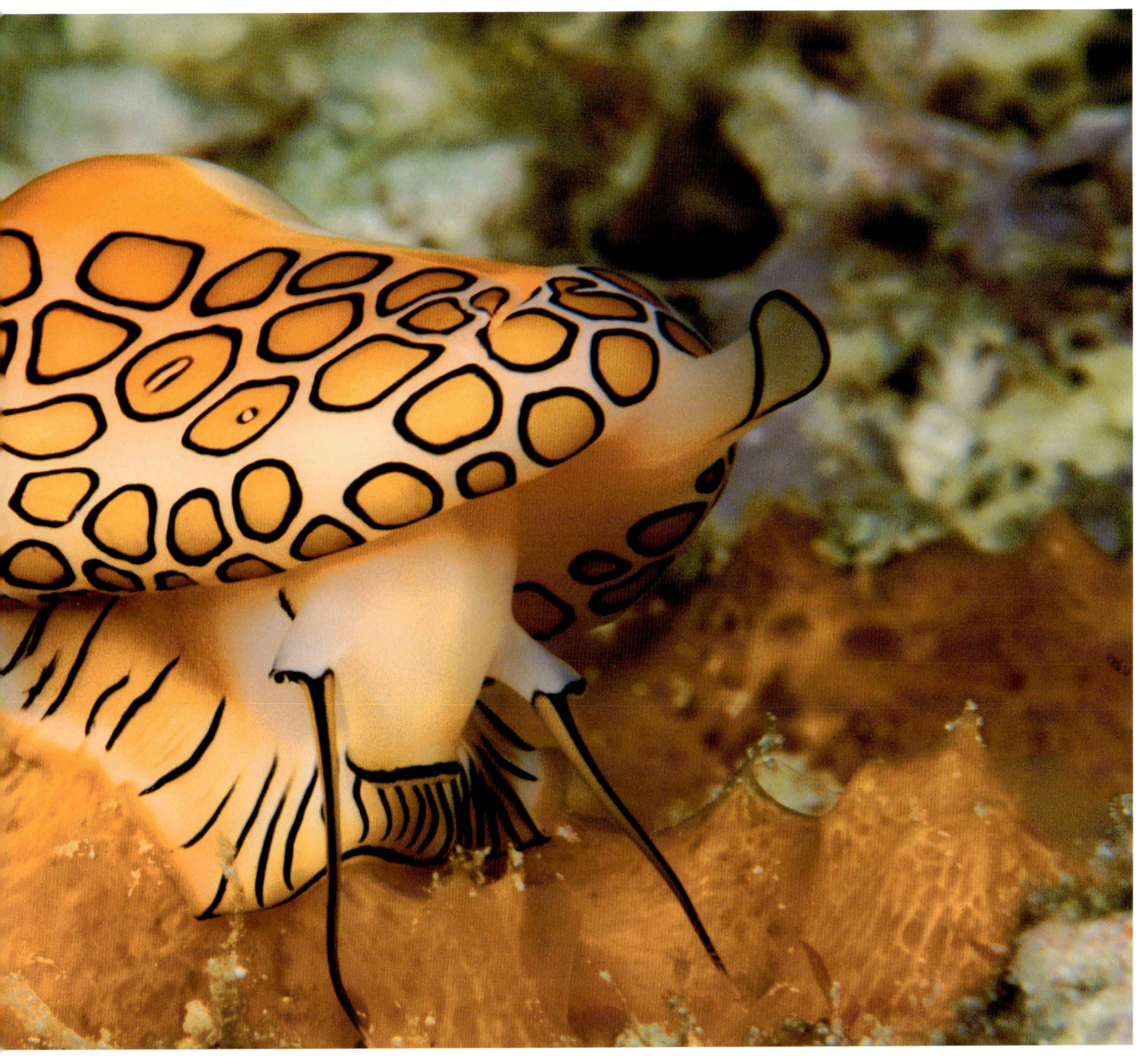

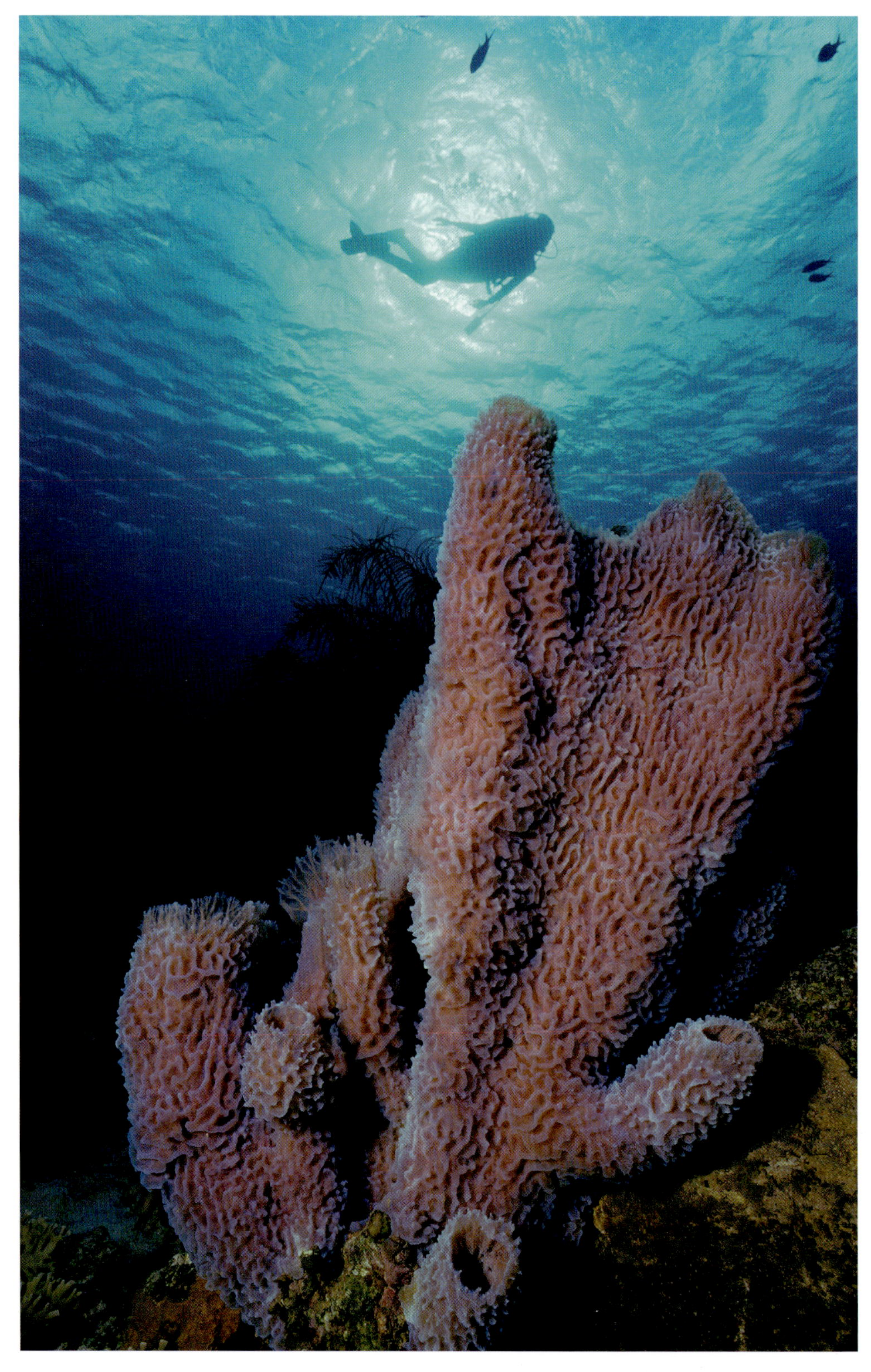

VASE SPONGE

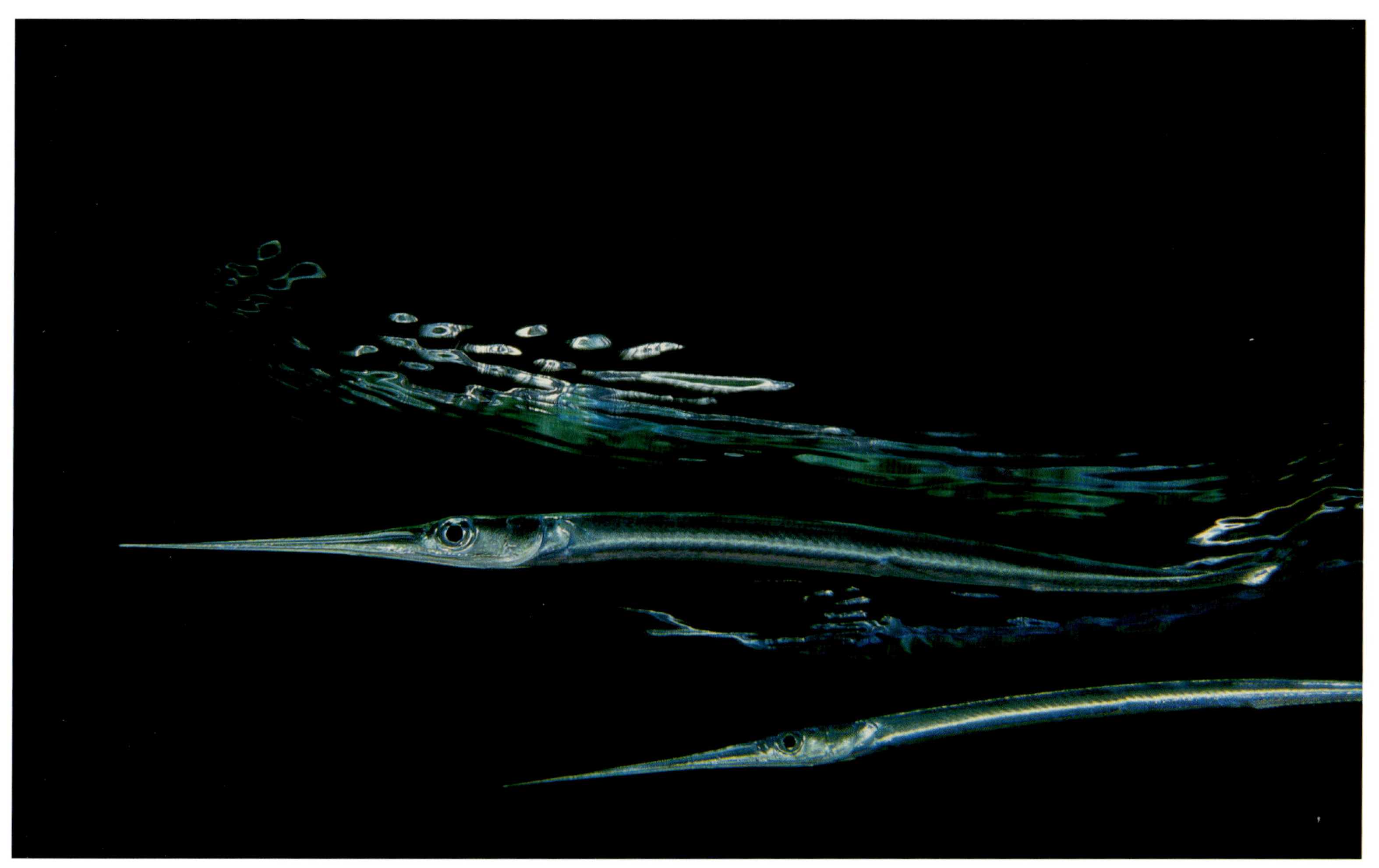

KEELTAIL NEEDLEFISH

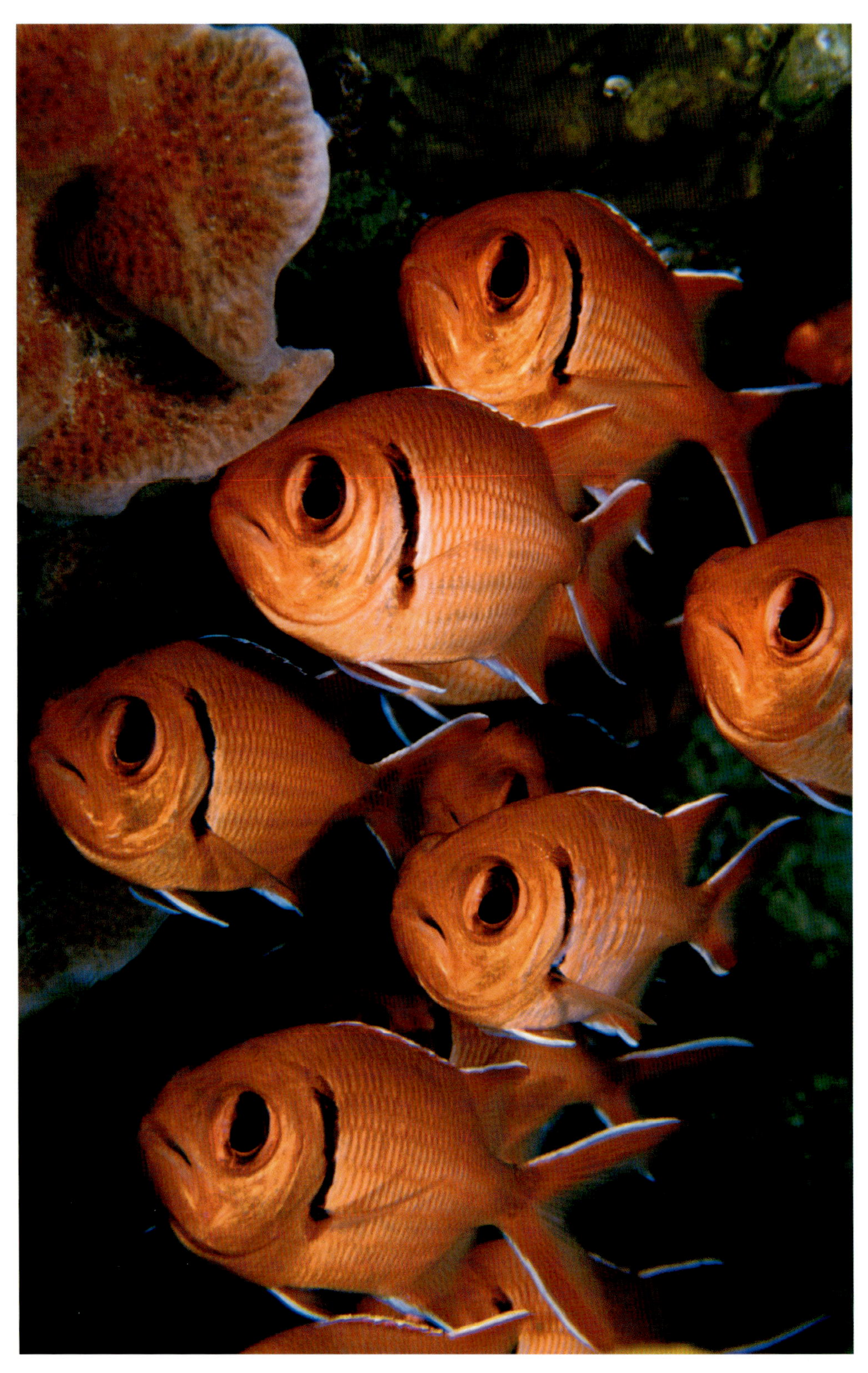

BLACKBAR SOLDIERFISH

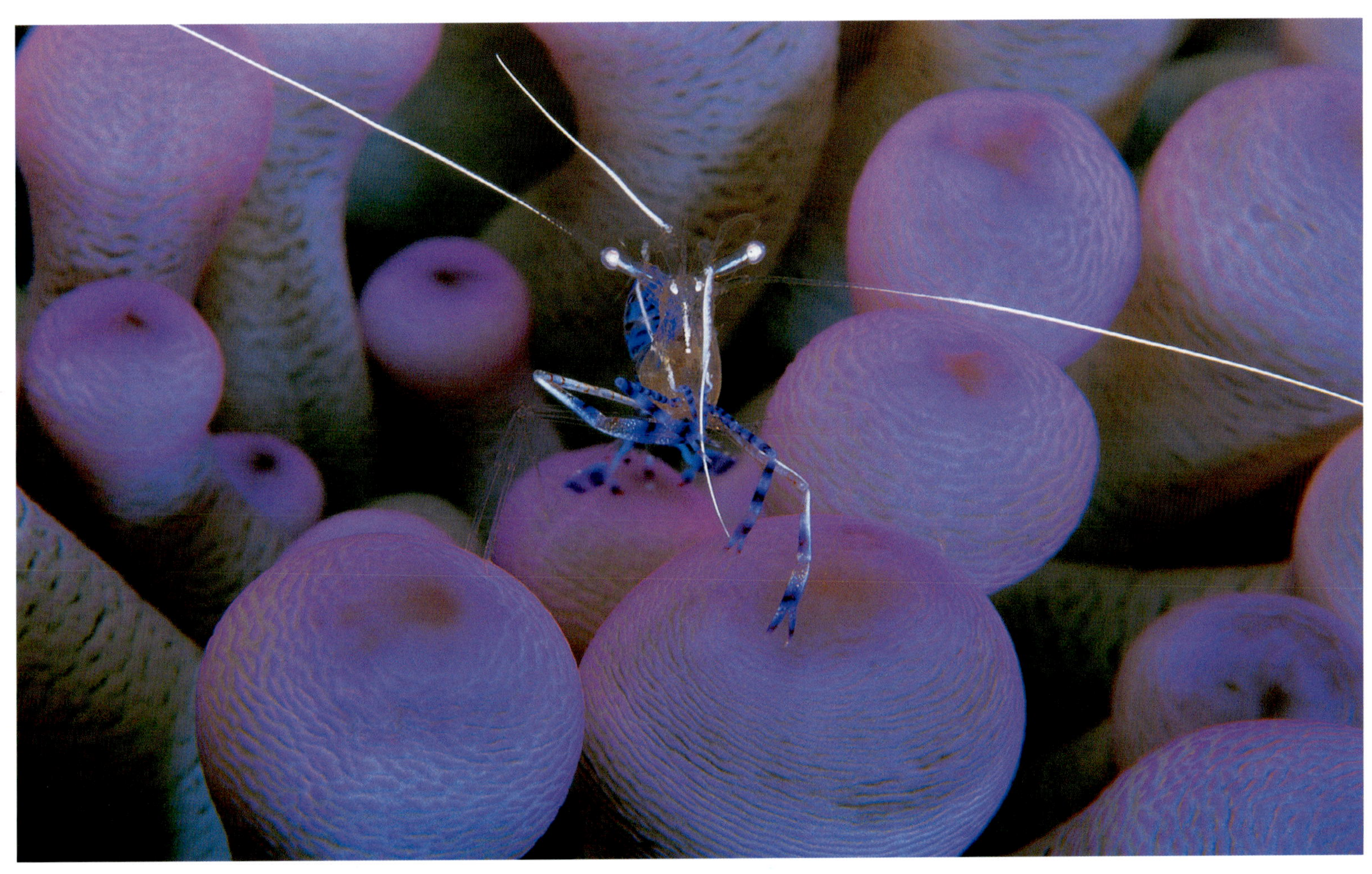

PEDERSONS SHRIMP ON ANEMONE

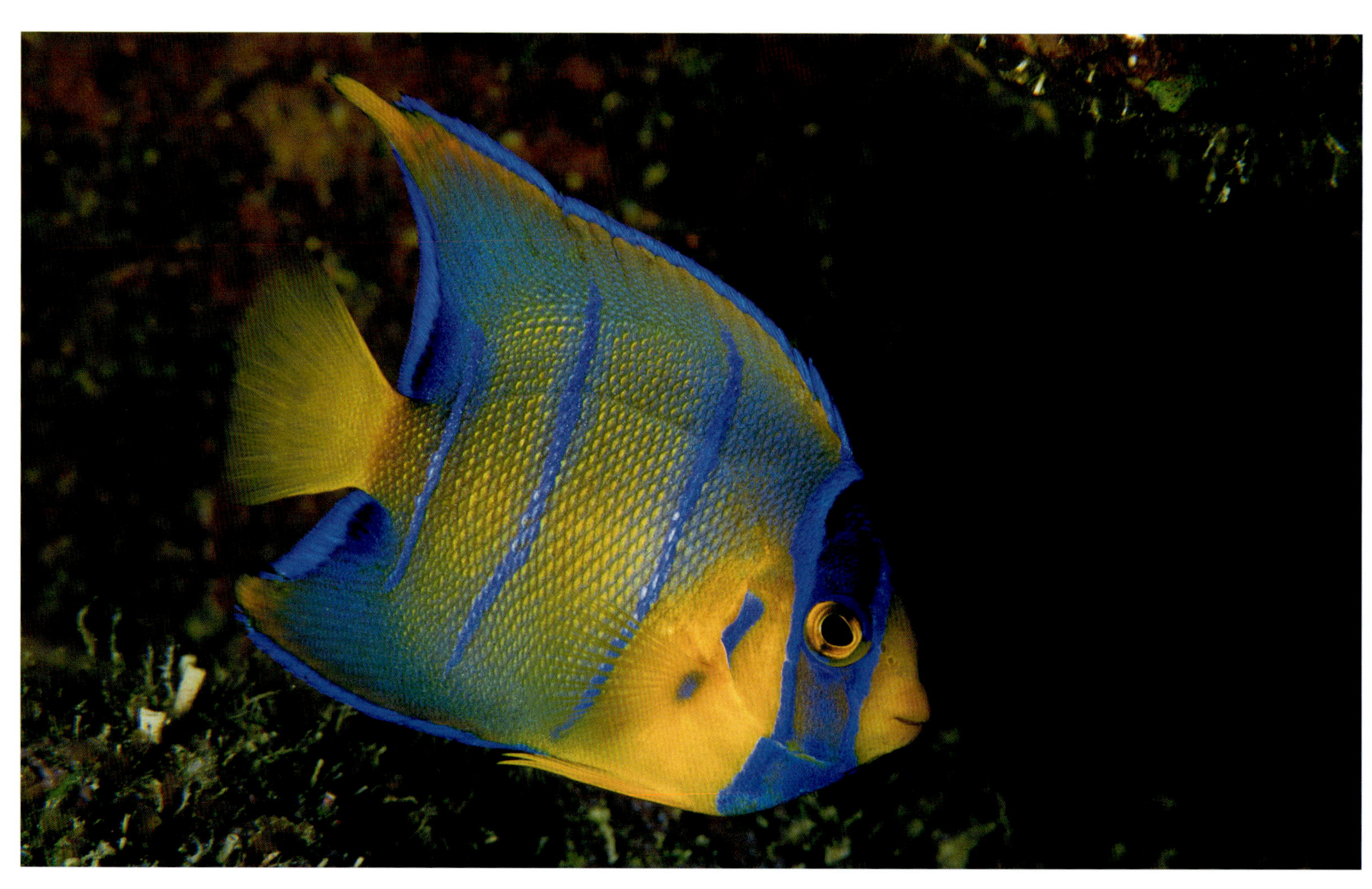

JUVENILE QUEEN ANGELFISH

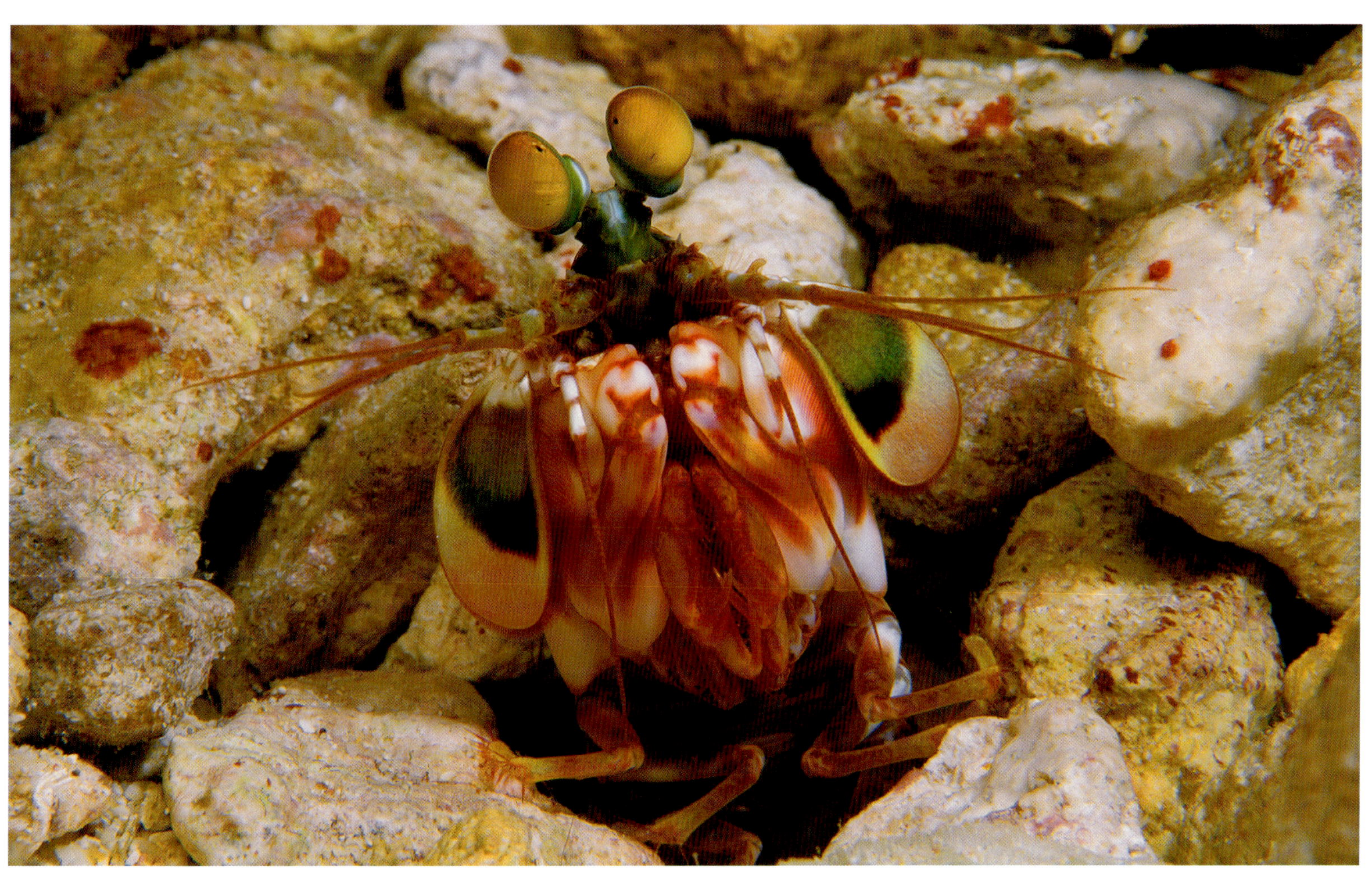

MANTIS SHRIMP

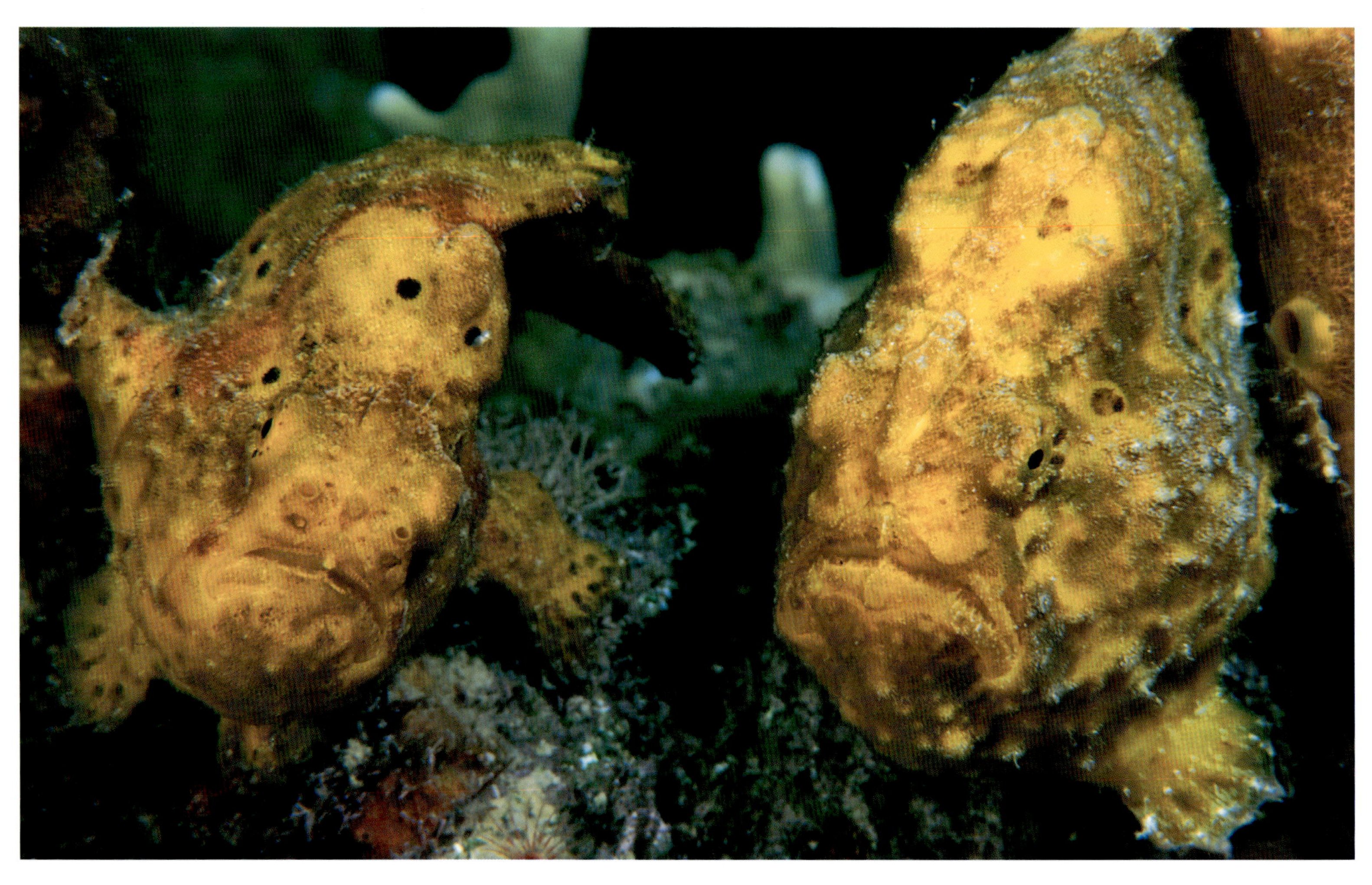

LONGLURE FROGFISH

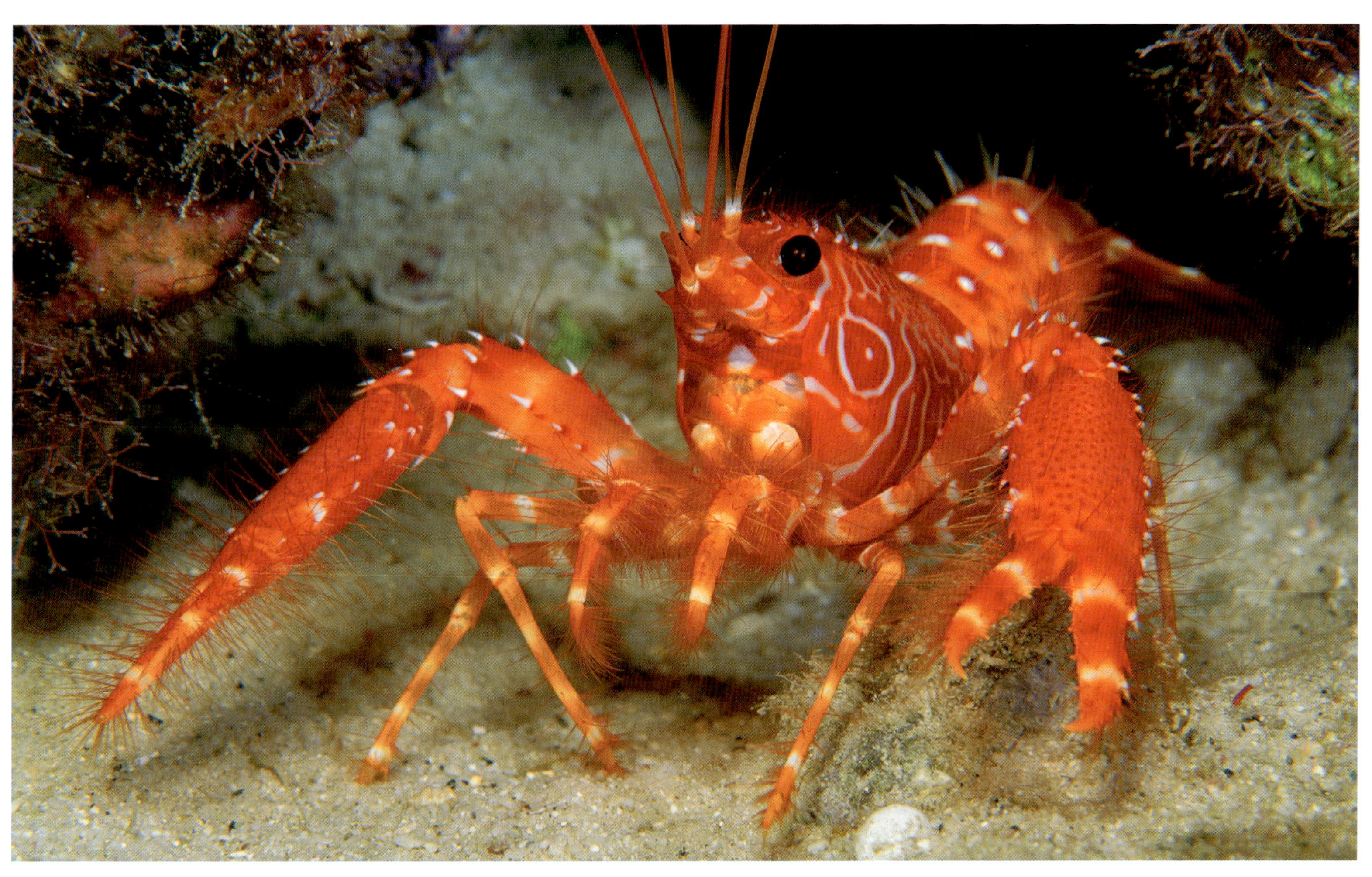

BULLSEYE LOBSTER

Borneo - Malaysia

Borneo - Malaysia

Just say the word Borneo and exotic adventure immediately comes to mind. This remarkable destination is Disney World for naturalists. The best diving in Borneo-Malaysia is off the Northeast coast where the Sulu Sea meets the Celebes Sea. A small group of islands offer sanctuary for divers and feature a parade of unusual marine life on the surrounding coral reefs. These reefs have, in the past, been victimized by overfishing and dynamiting. In recent years, however, the Malaysian government and the local diving community have begun to police these areas in an effort to reduce environmental damage. The results have been promising. Islands like Sipaden and Mabul offer world-class diving at your doorstep. You simply step out of your room and onto the reef. While the reefs may not be as pristine or as colorful as those in Fiji or Papua New Guinea, they make up for it with an astounding array of marine life. Underwater photographers feel like kids in a candy store when visiting these reefs. The list of subjects seems endless and the local divemasters know where to find them.

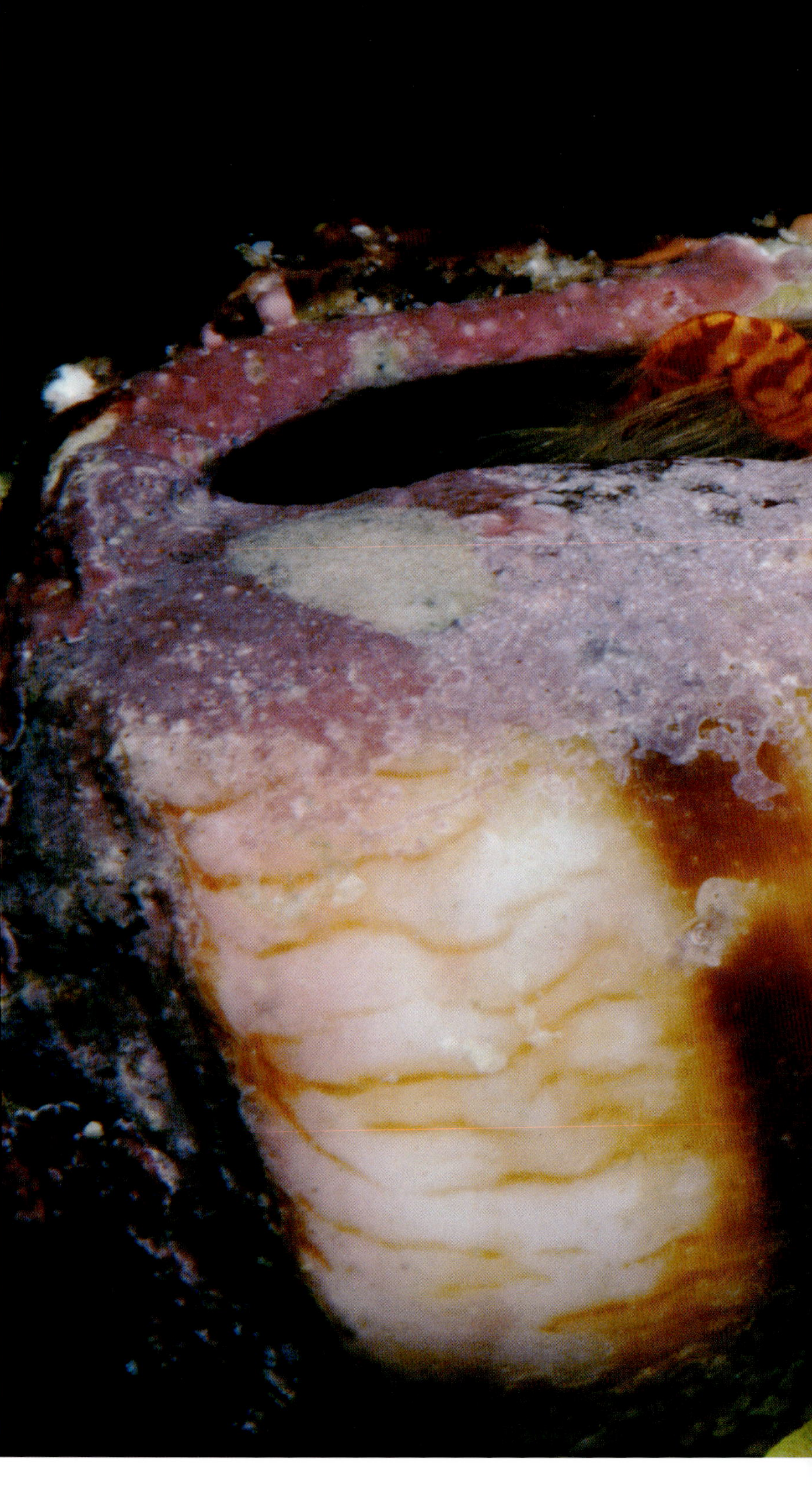

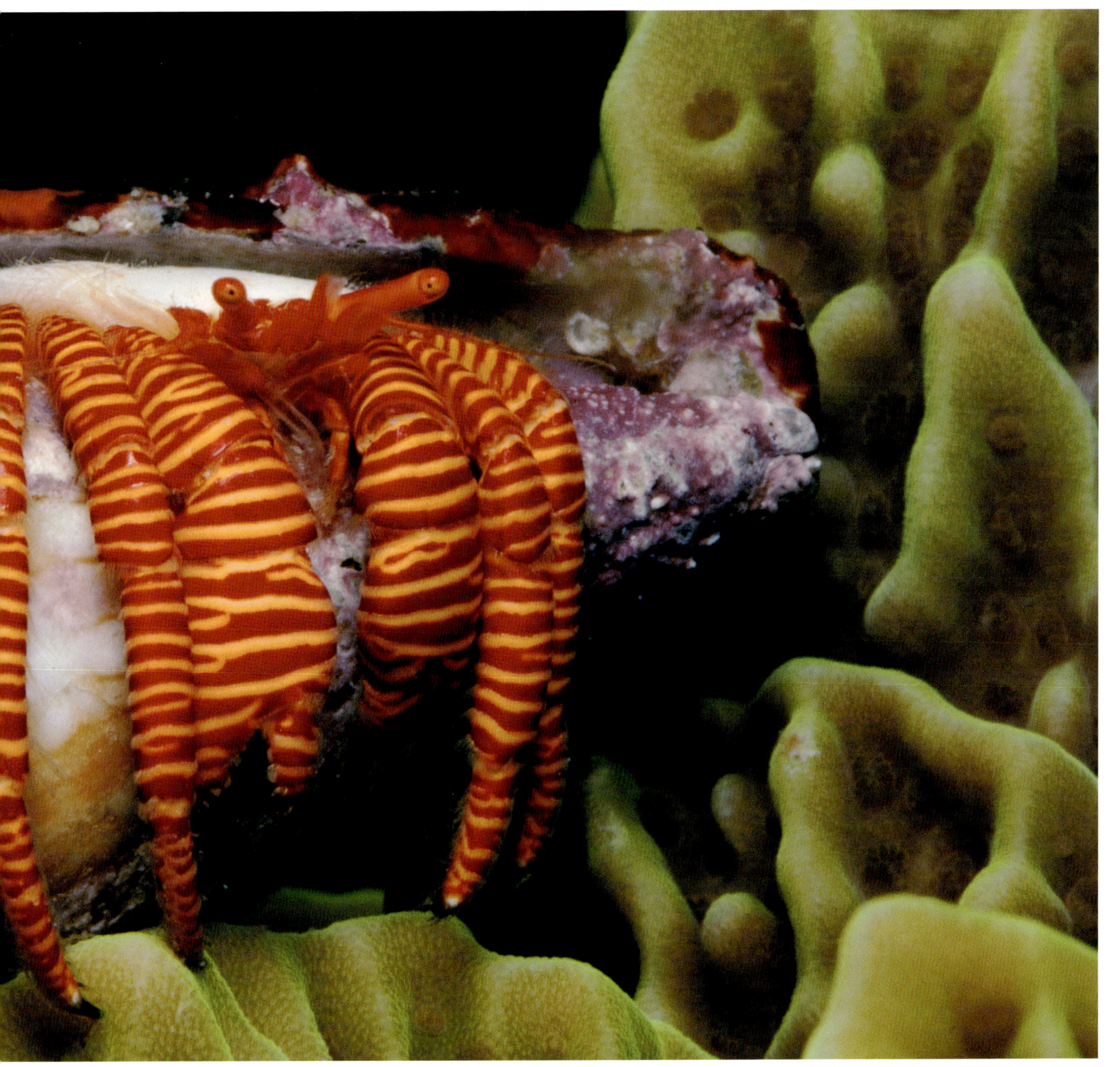

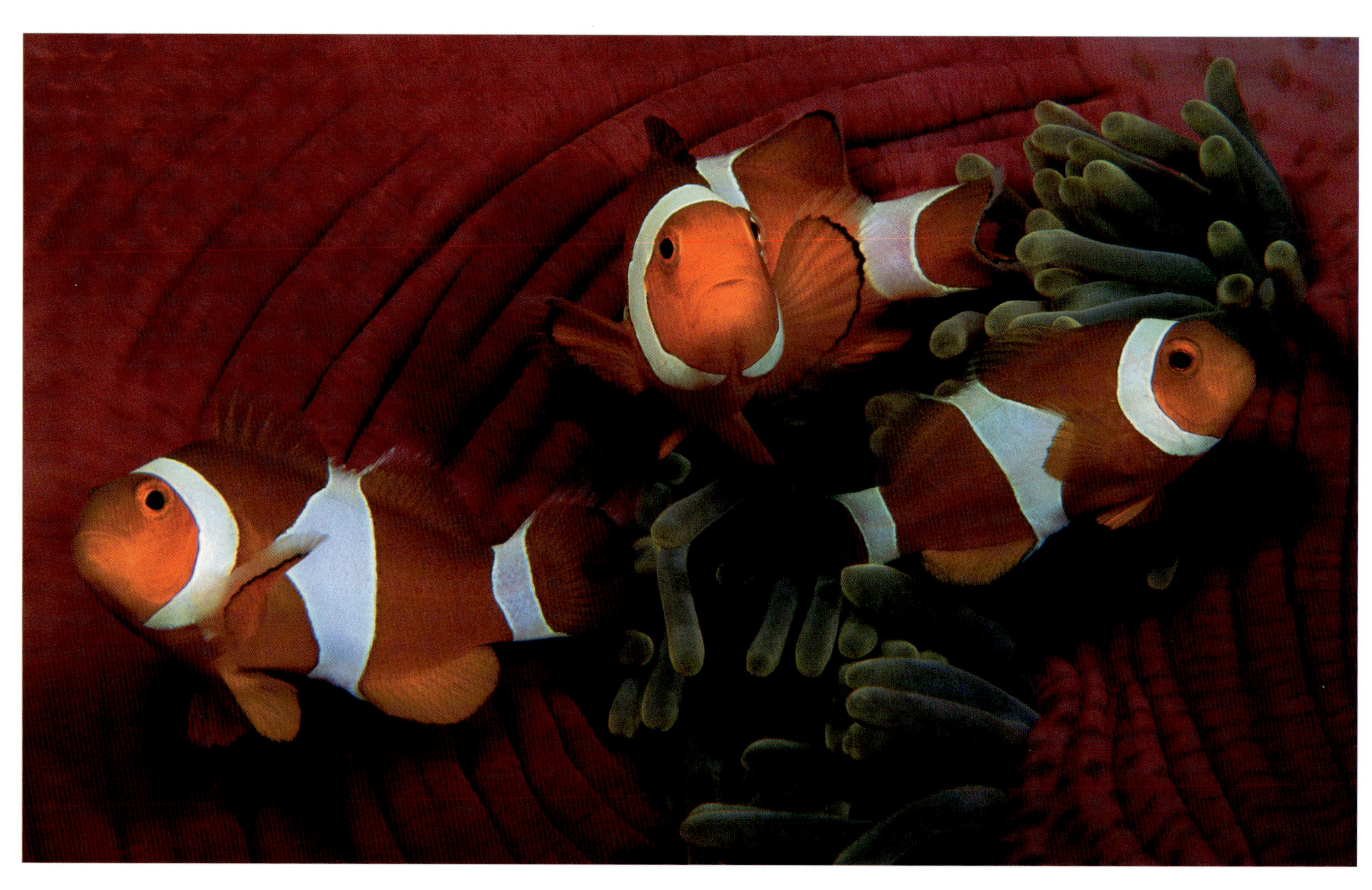

WESTERN CLOWNFISH AND ANEMONE

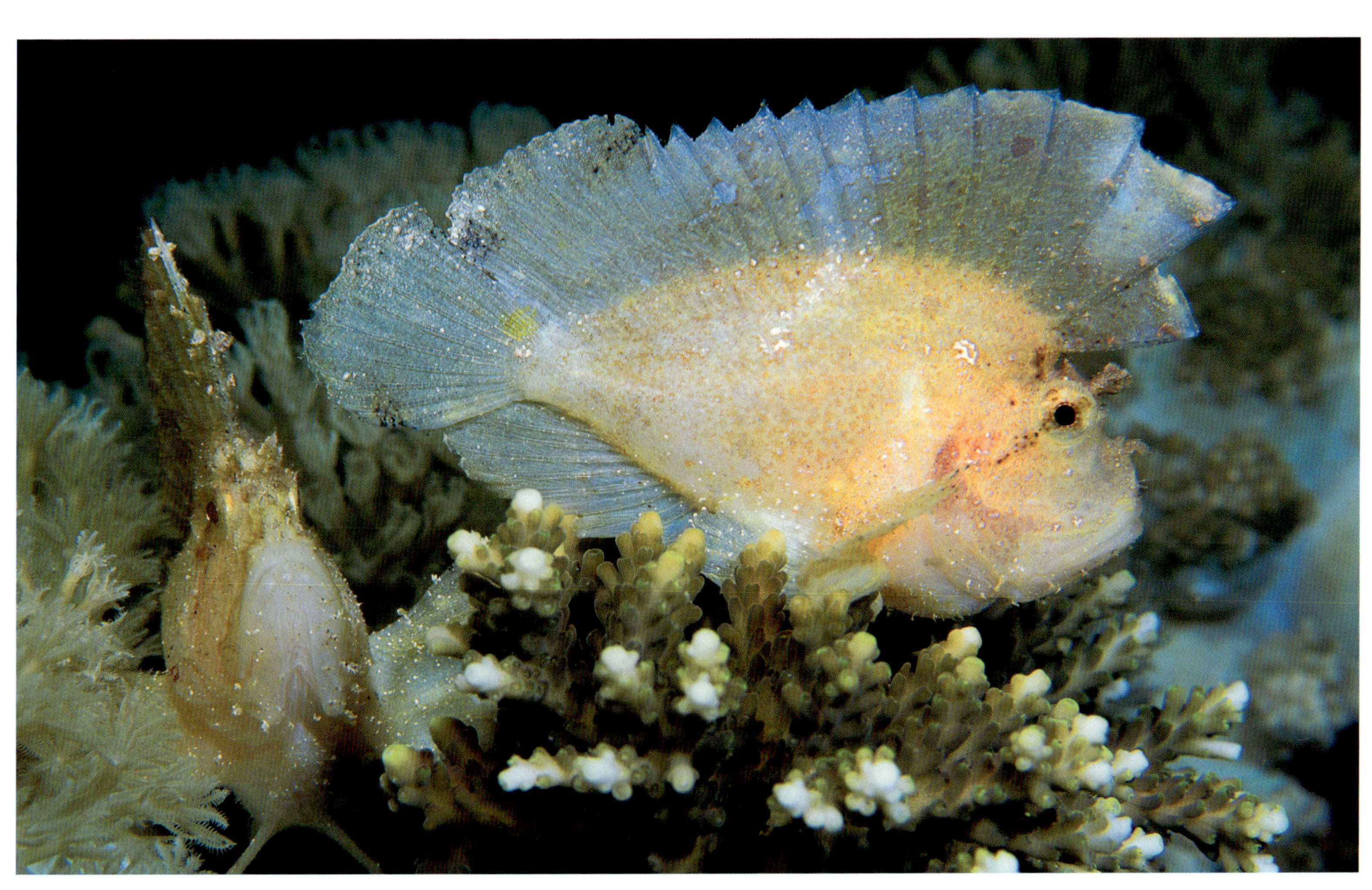

PAIR OF SAILFIN LEAF FISH

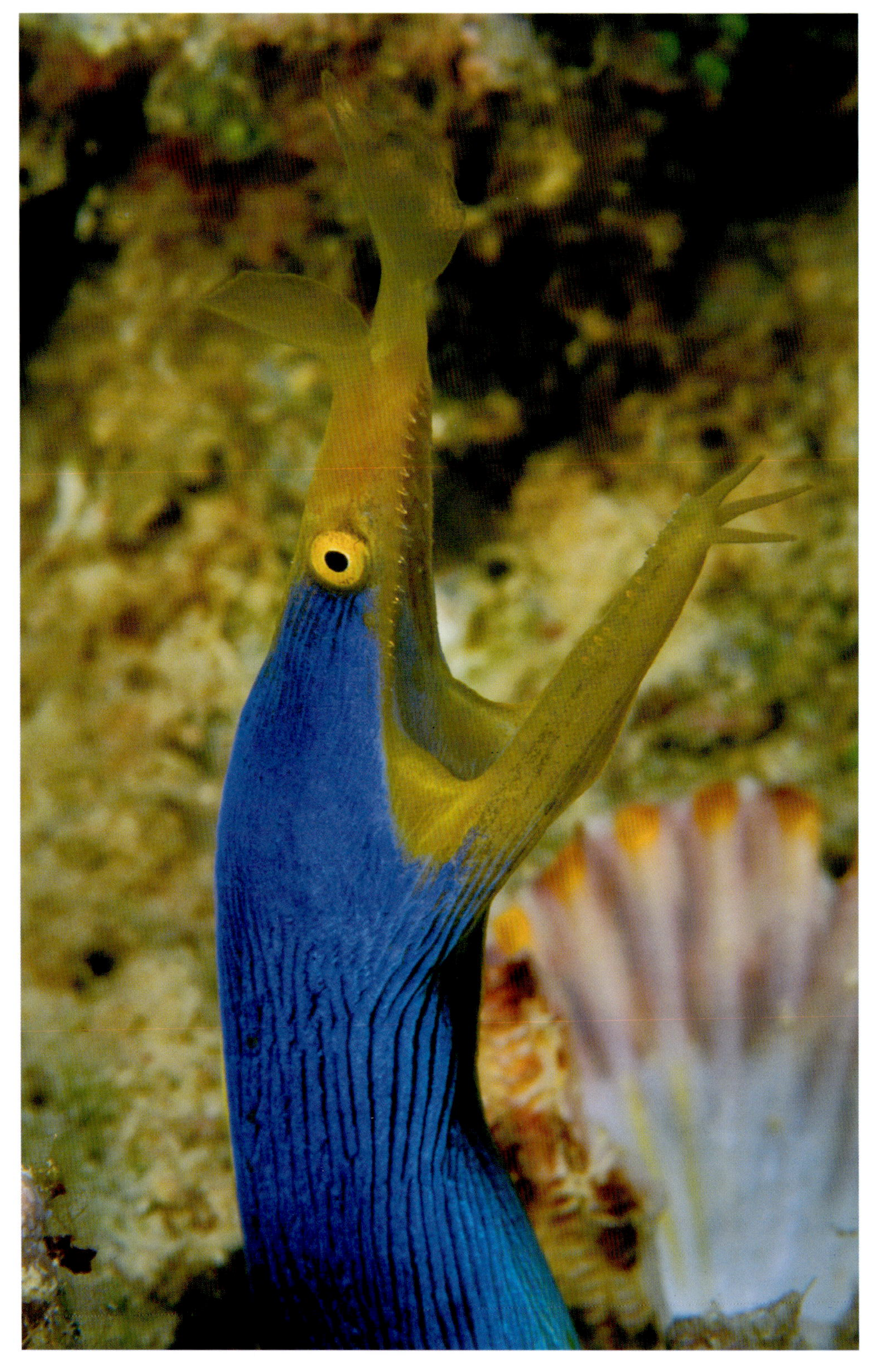

RIBBON EEL

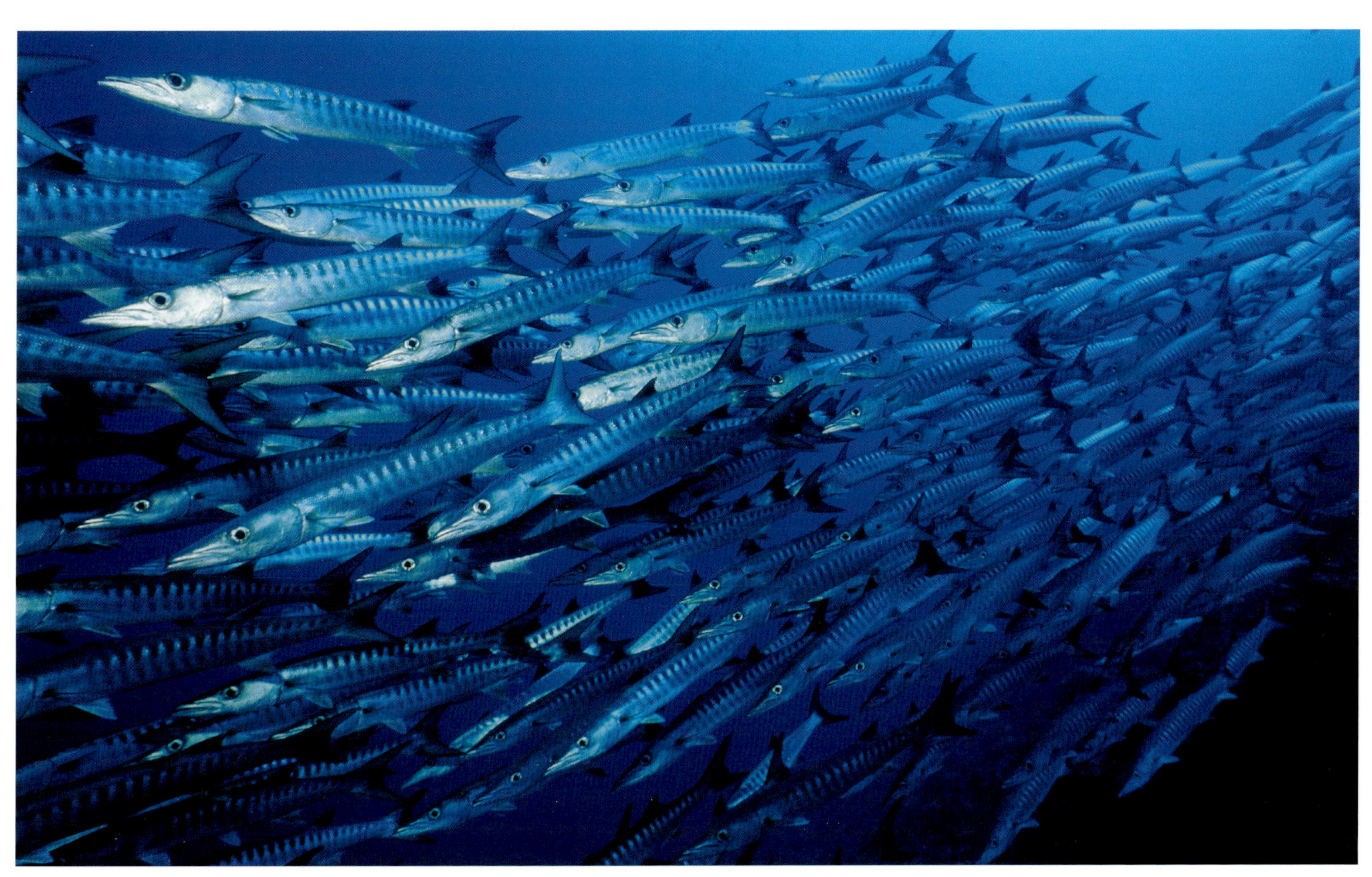

CHEVRONED BARRACUDA

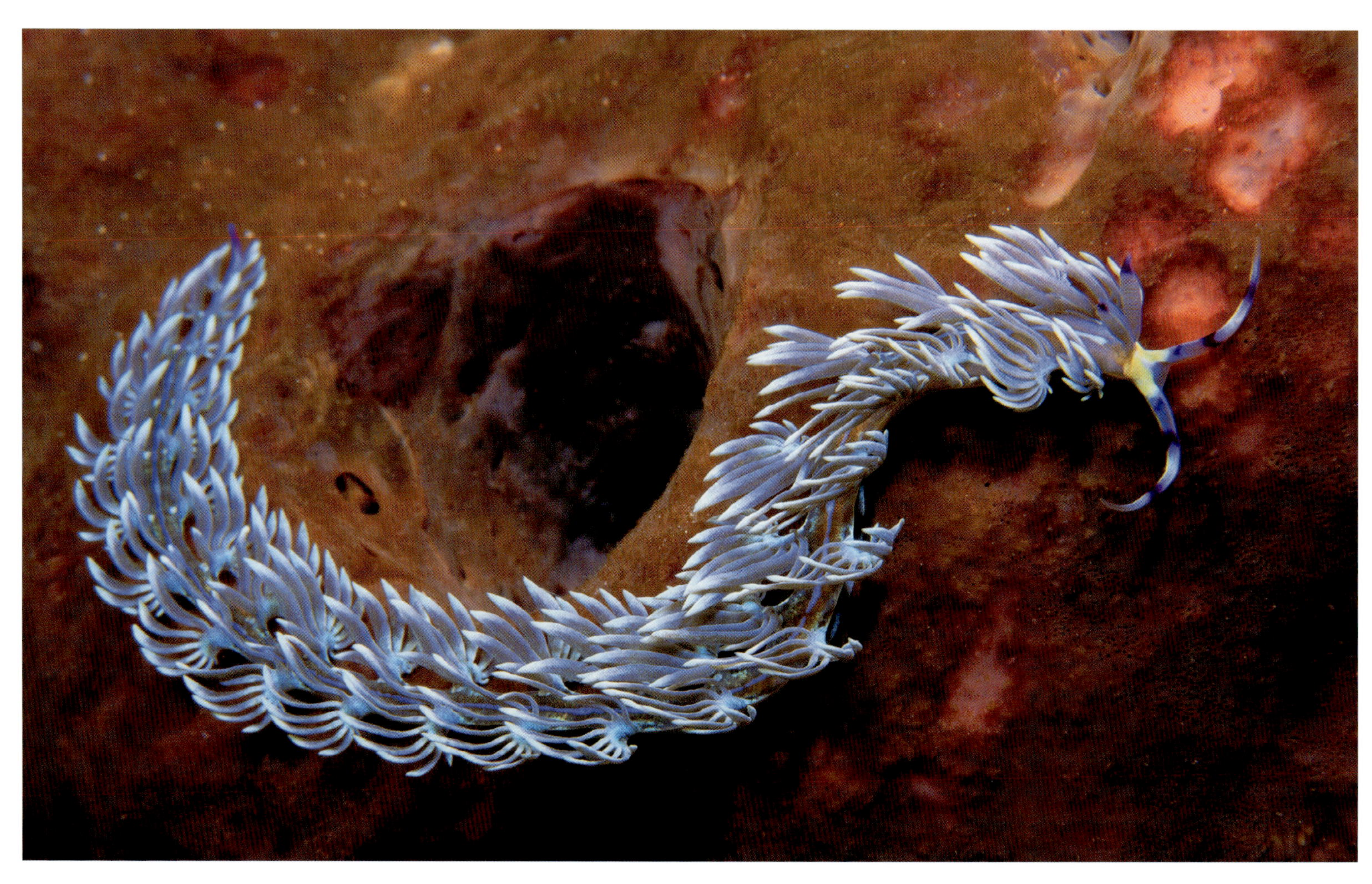

AEOLID NUDIBRANCH

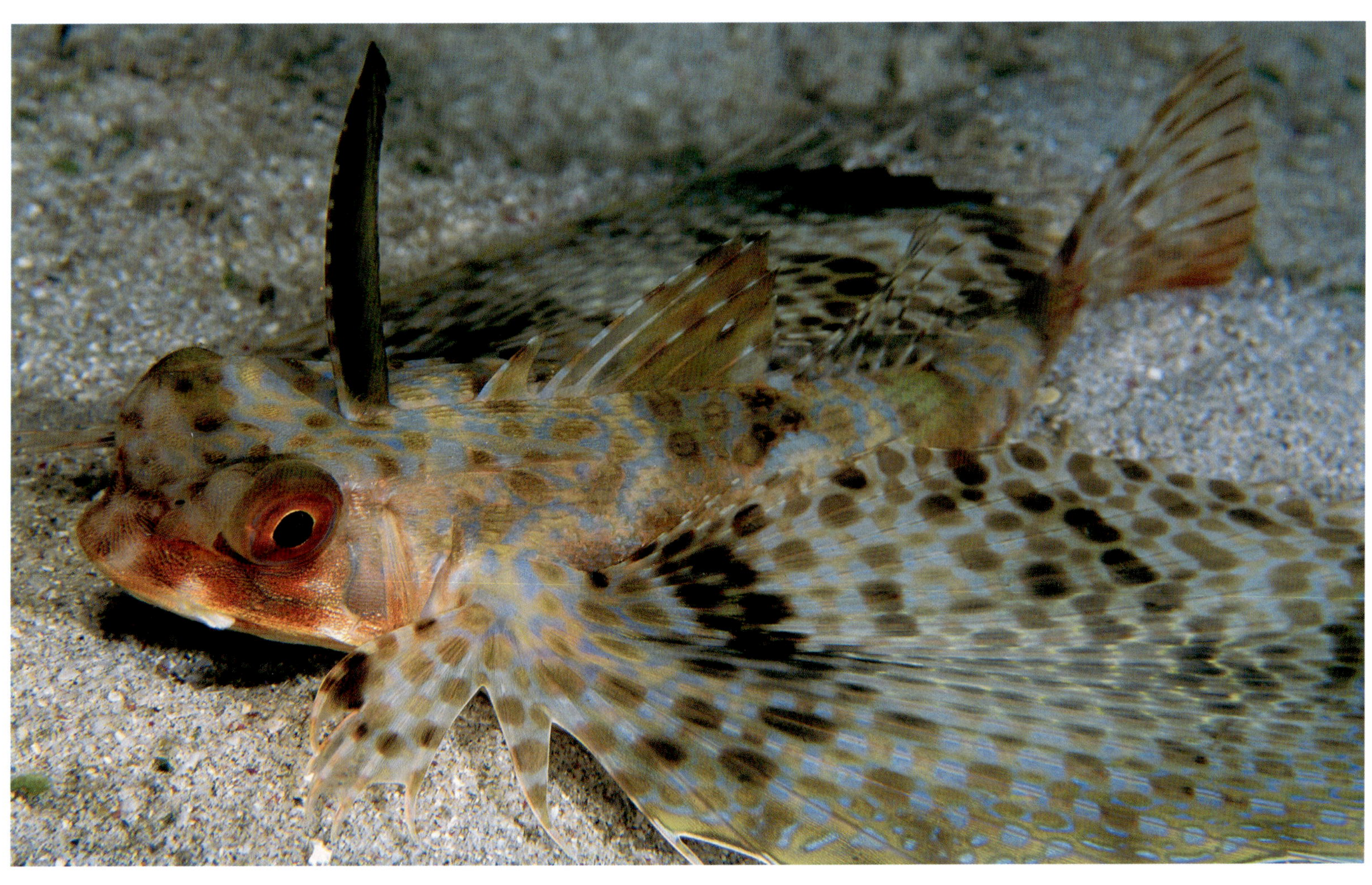

FLYING GURNARD

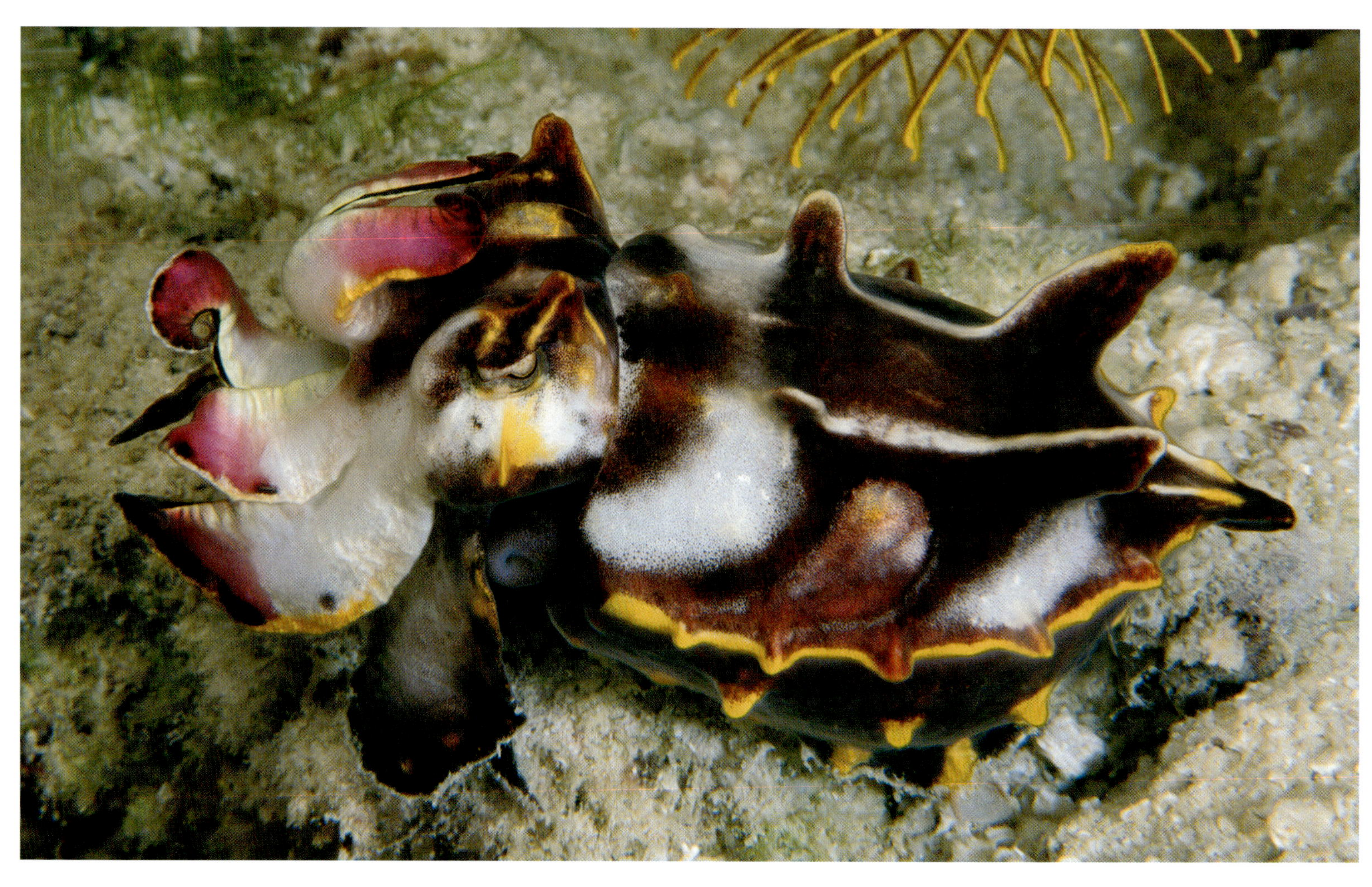

FLAMBOYANT CUTTLEFISH

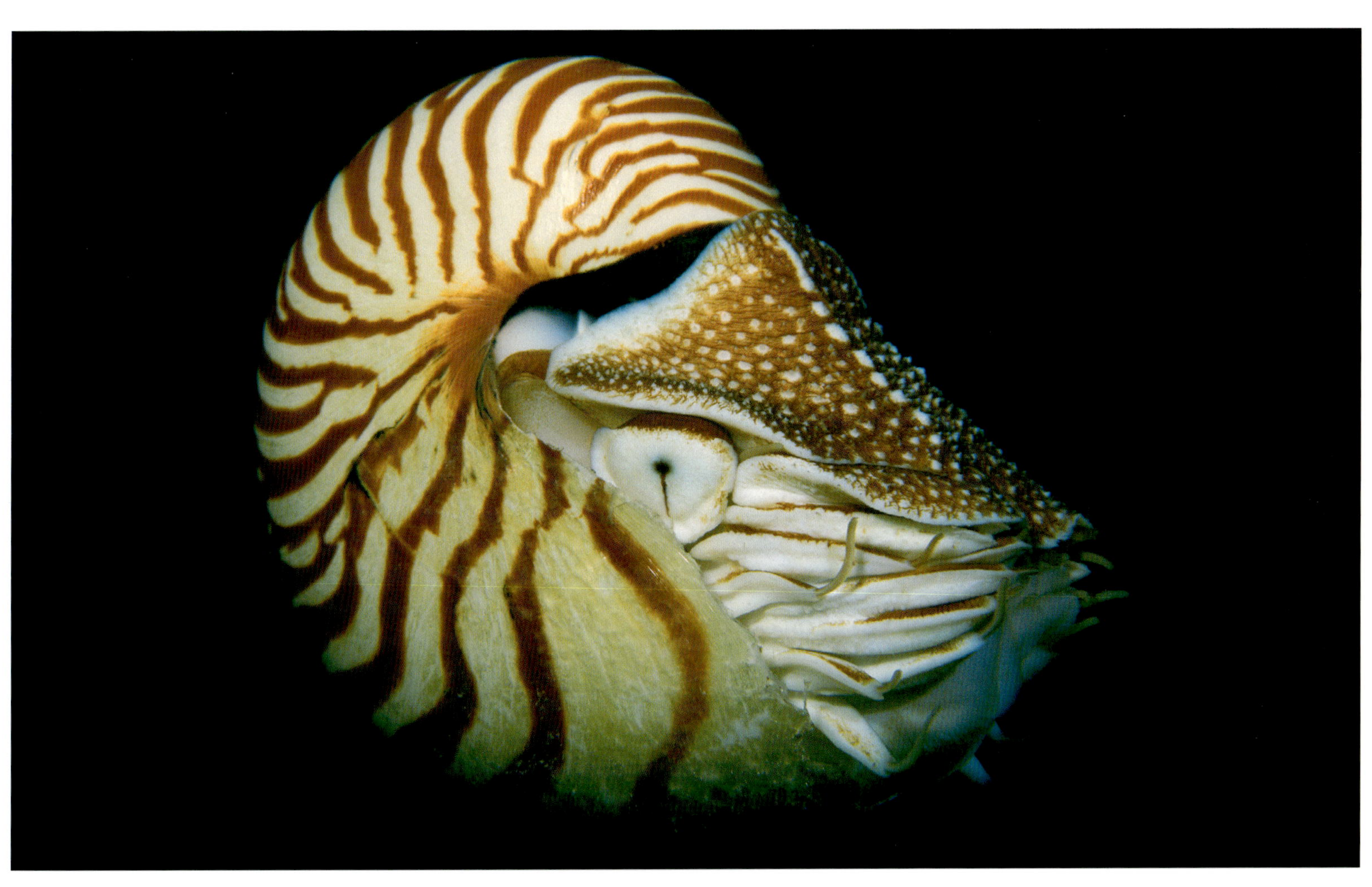

NAUTILUS

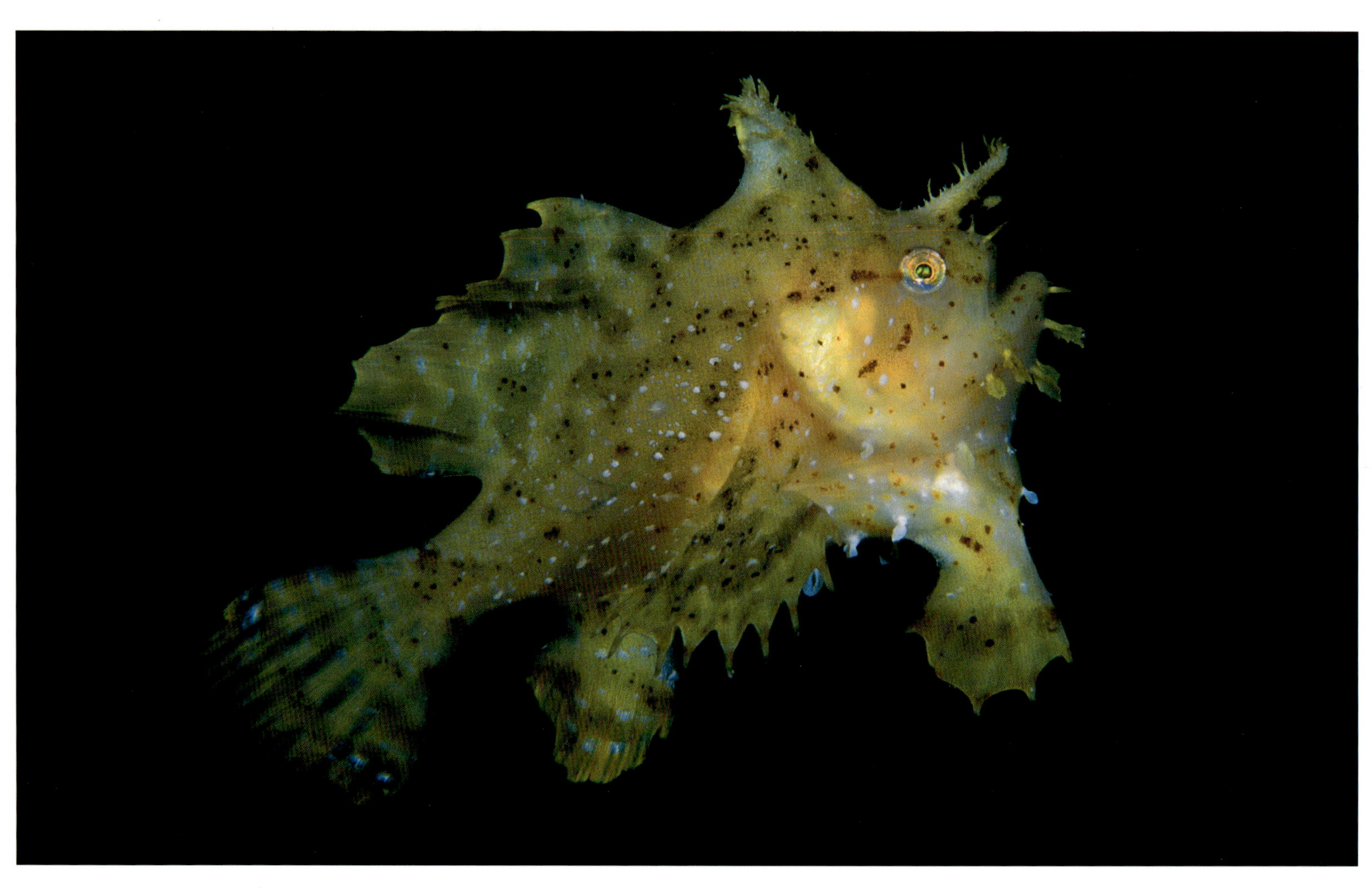

SARGASSUM ANGLERFISH

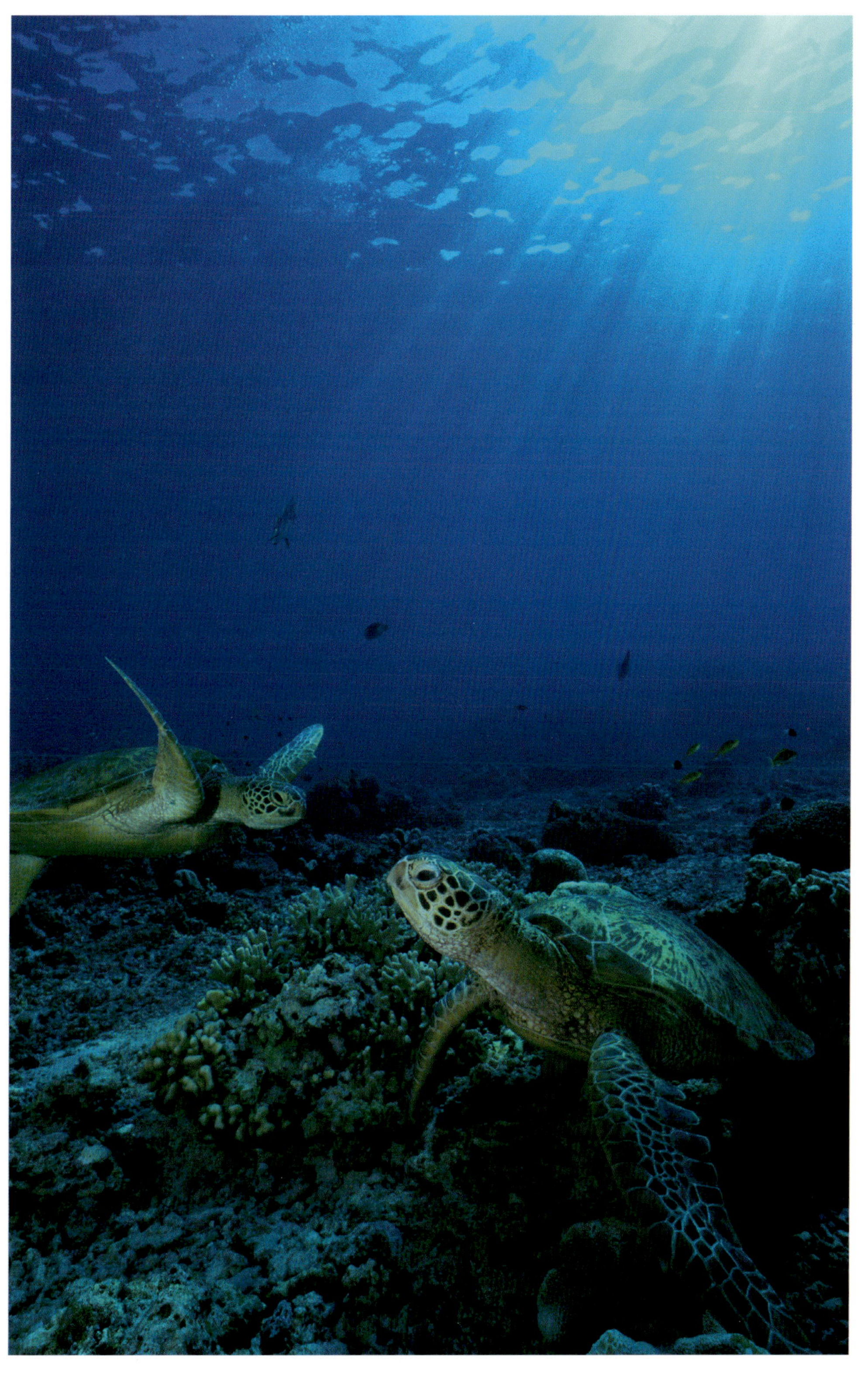

GREEN SEA TURTLES

Indonesia

Ocean of Fire, Land of the Dragon

I n d o n e s i a

Indonesia is an exotic, mystical island nation where coral reef diversity reaches its zenith. Here lies the epicenter of coral development, the mother lode of living aquatic treasures. Here, too, exists a burgeoning human population that relies heavily on these surrounding reef resources. Both politically and geologically, Indonesia represents islands in a constant flux. Both renewal and destruction seem to be the order of the day. On remote islands in the Celebes Sea, I have explored coral wonder worlds where the diving was the stuff of dreams, a fantasy bought to life. They were simply the most incredible reefs I have ever seen. Only miles away from these pristine coral palaces, I entered the water to find decimated reefs, products of dynamite fishing.

In other areas of Indonesia, Asian fishing fleets have over-harvested food fish populations ranging from inshore species such as grouper to offshore apex populations such as shark and tuna. Ironically, Indonesia can offer to the underwater enthusiast both the best and the worst of diving experiences. It is already apparent that tourist dollars can and will continue to have a remarkable impact on the fate of large tracts of coral reefs in this region.

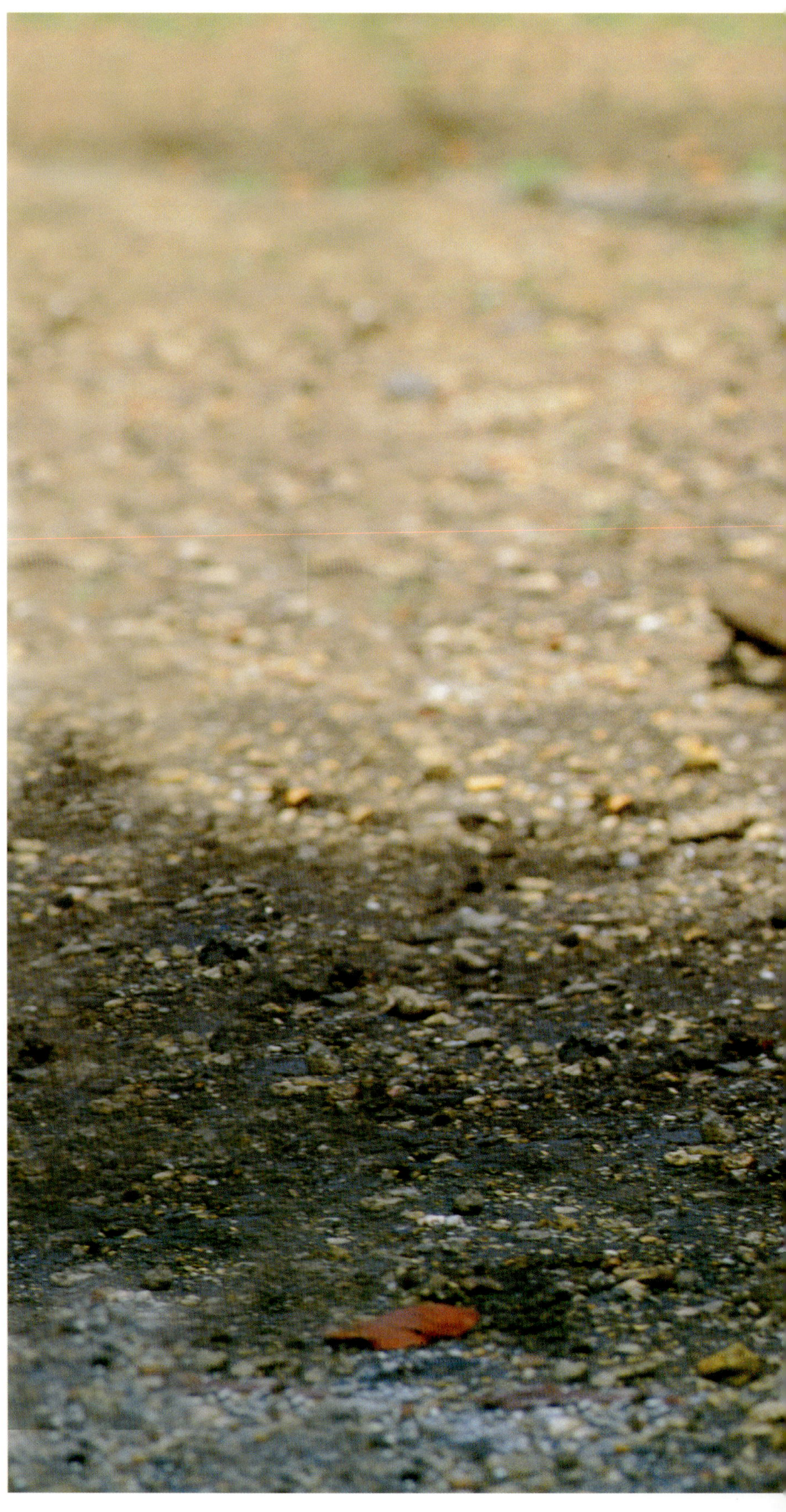

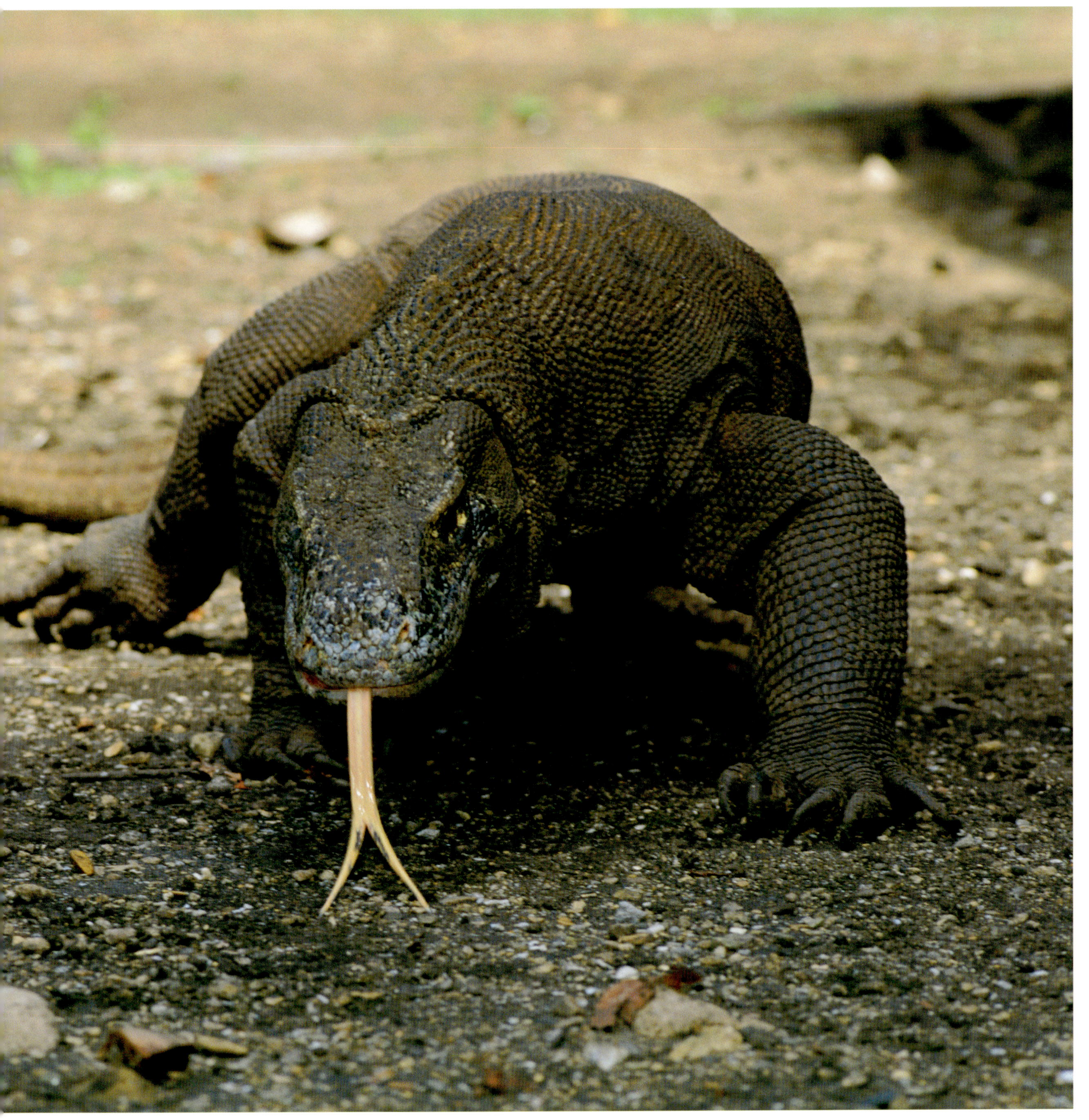

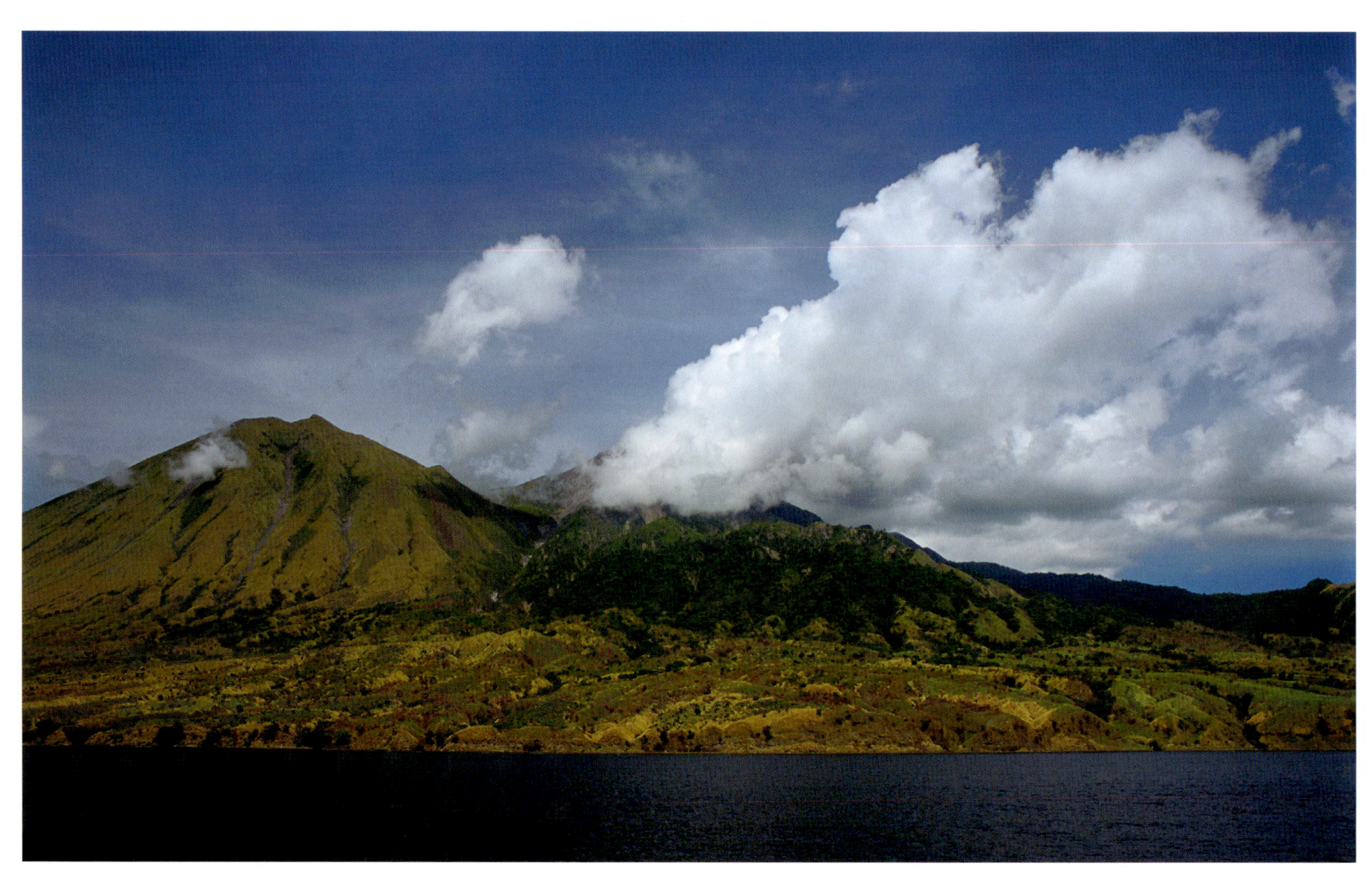

SANGIANG ISLAND

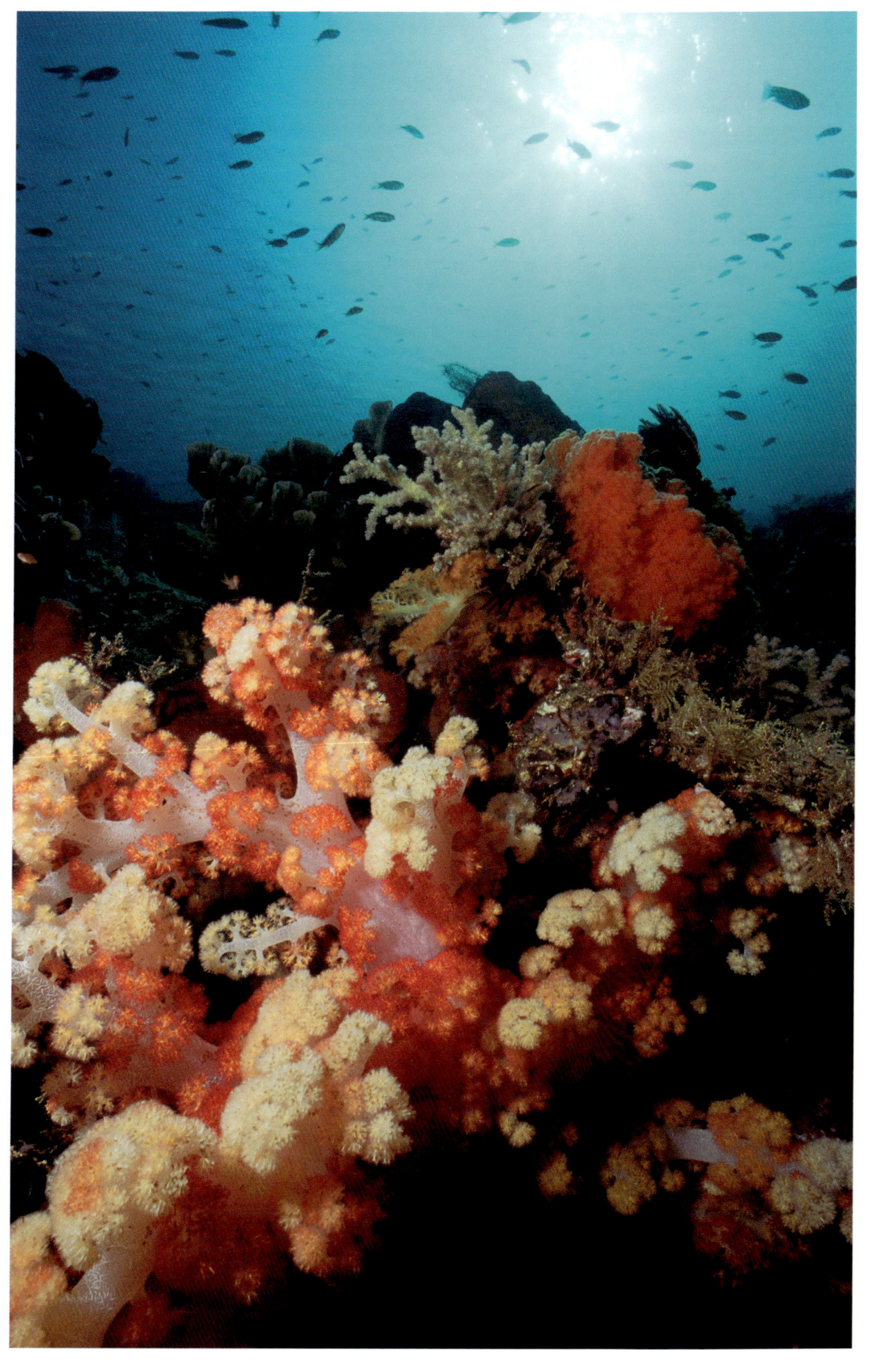

SOFT CORAL

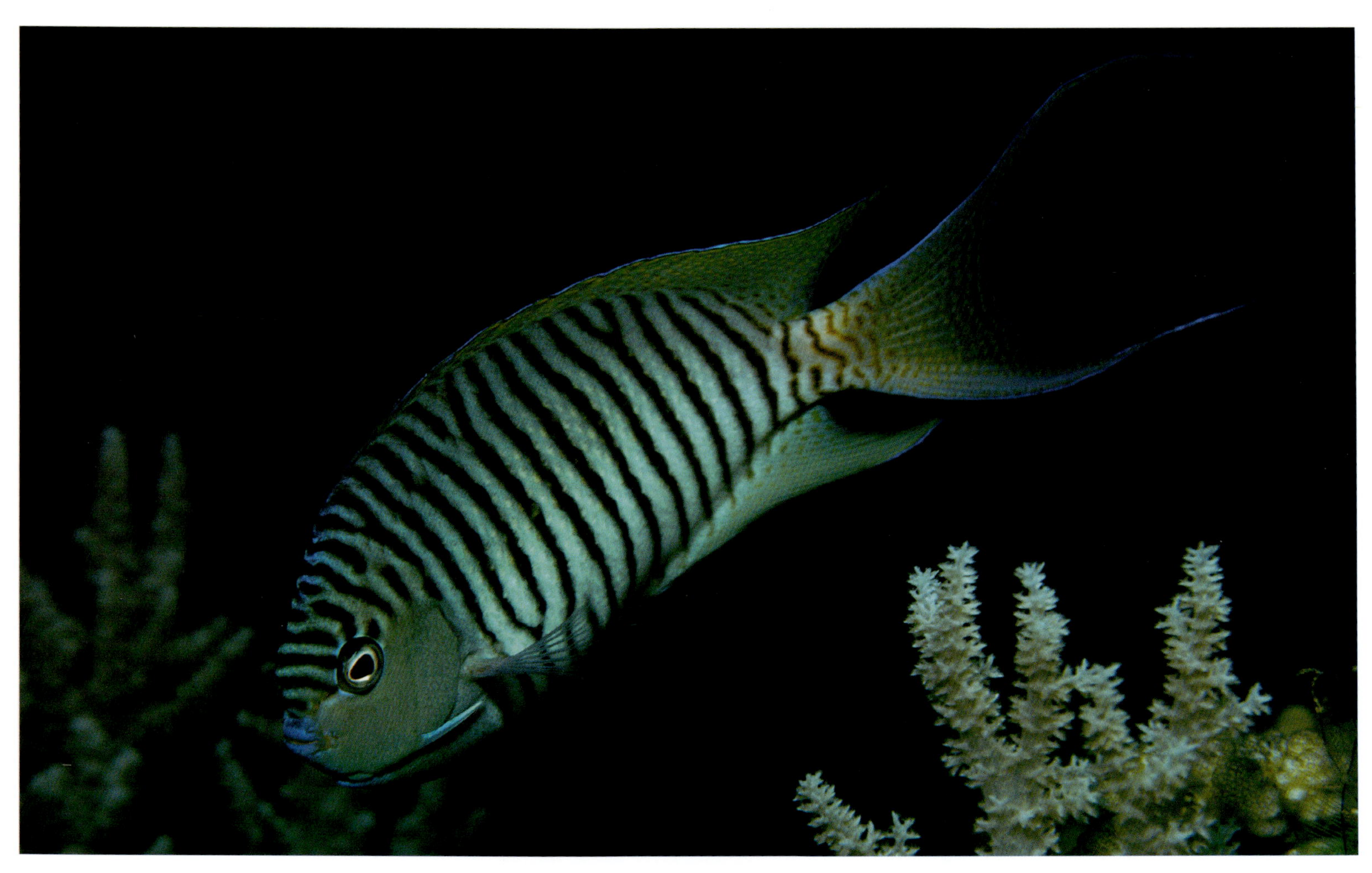

LYRETAIL ANGELFISH

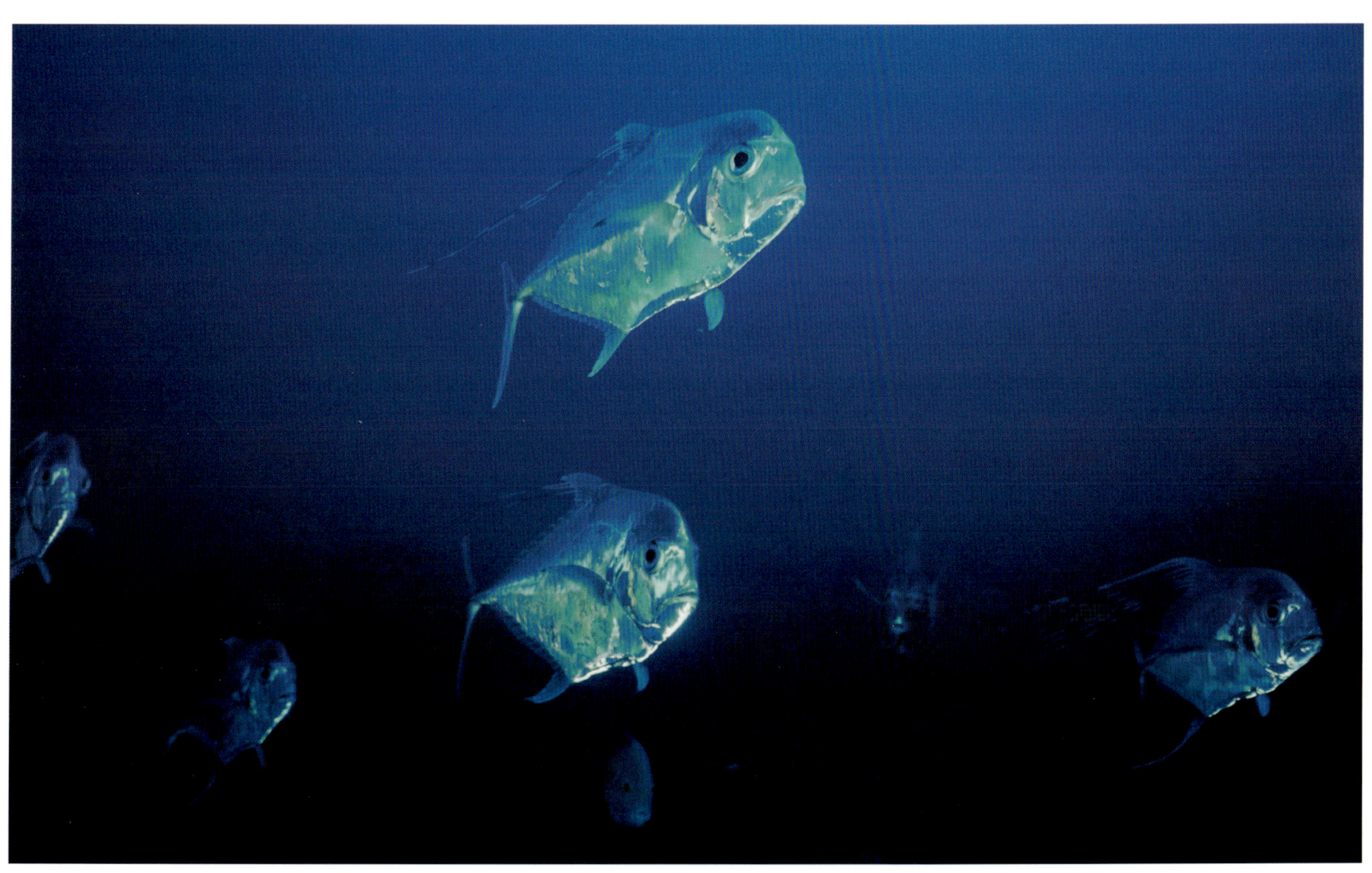

JUVENILE AFRICAN POMPANO

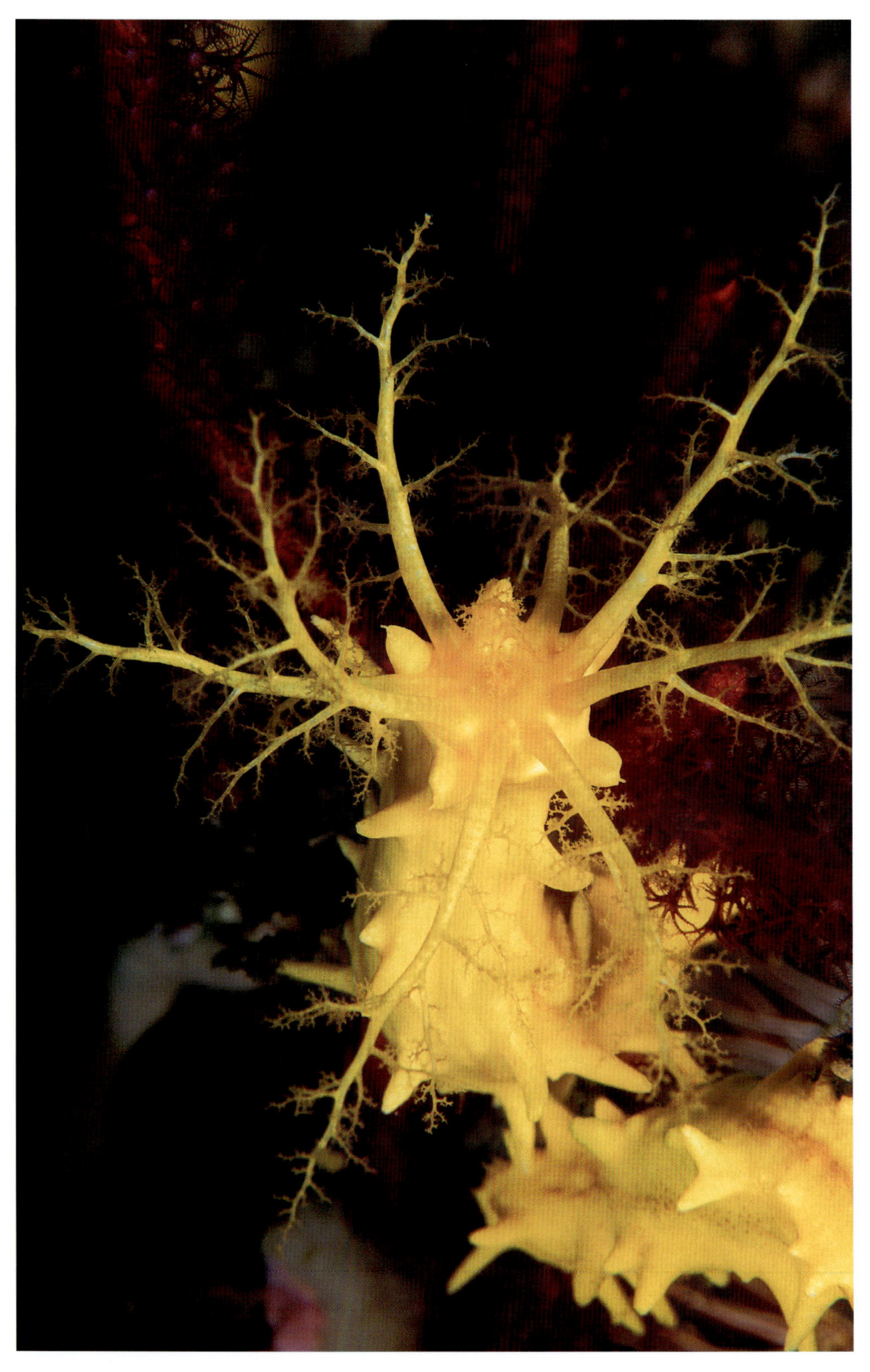

SEA CUCUMBER

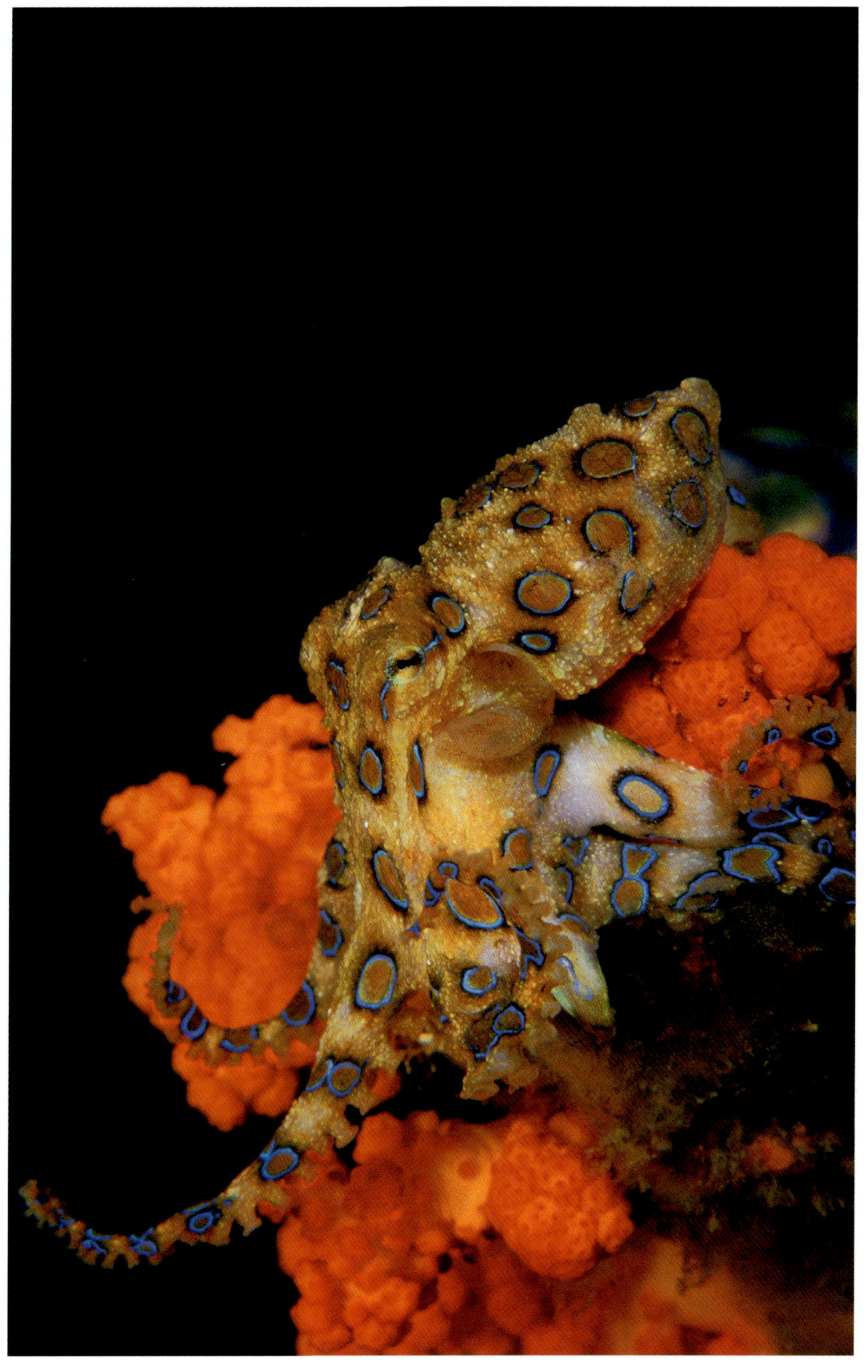

BLUE RING OCTOPUS

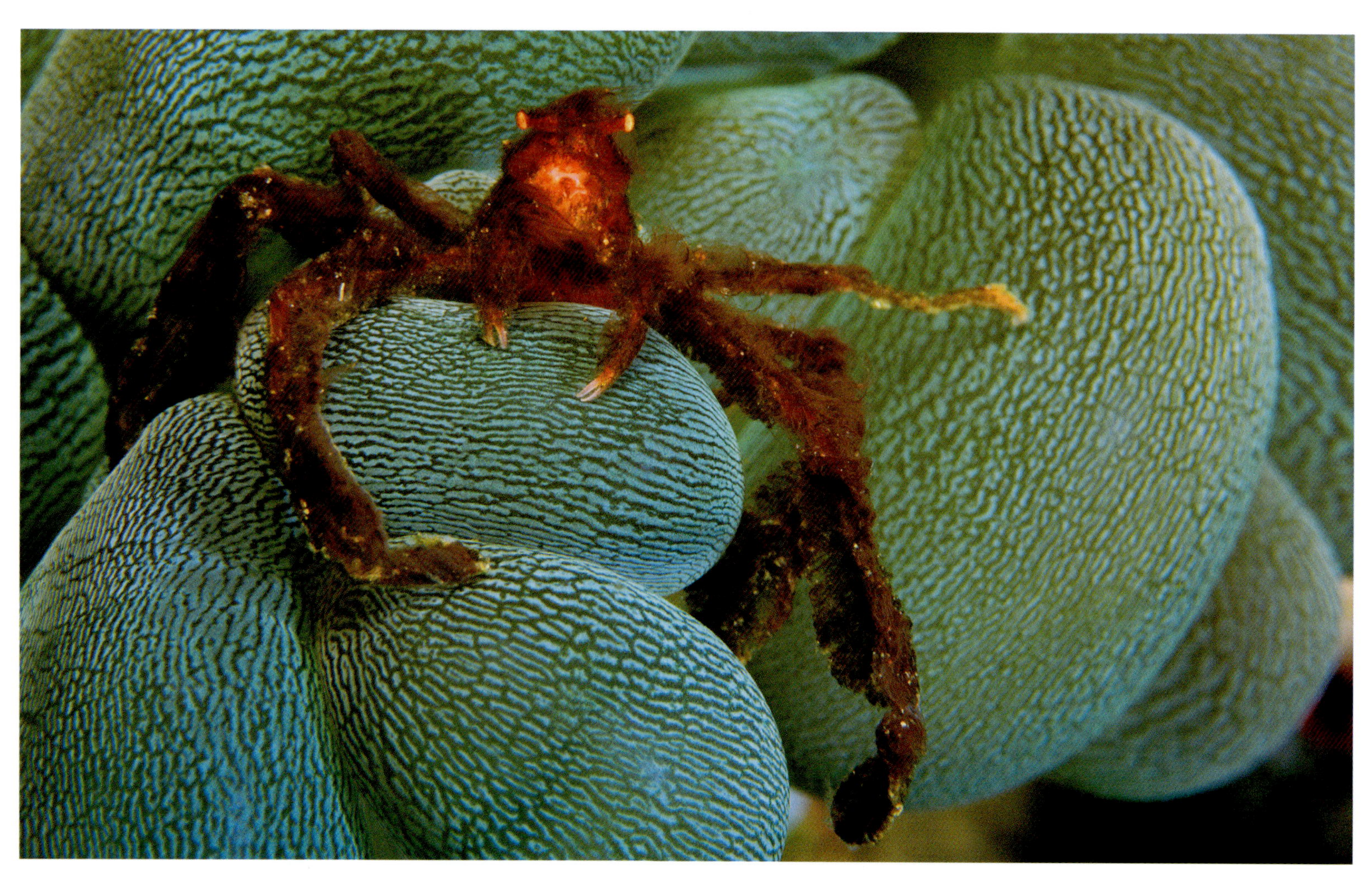

ORANGUTAN CRAB ON BUBBLE CORAL

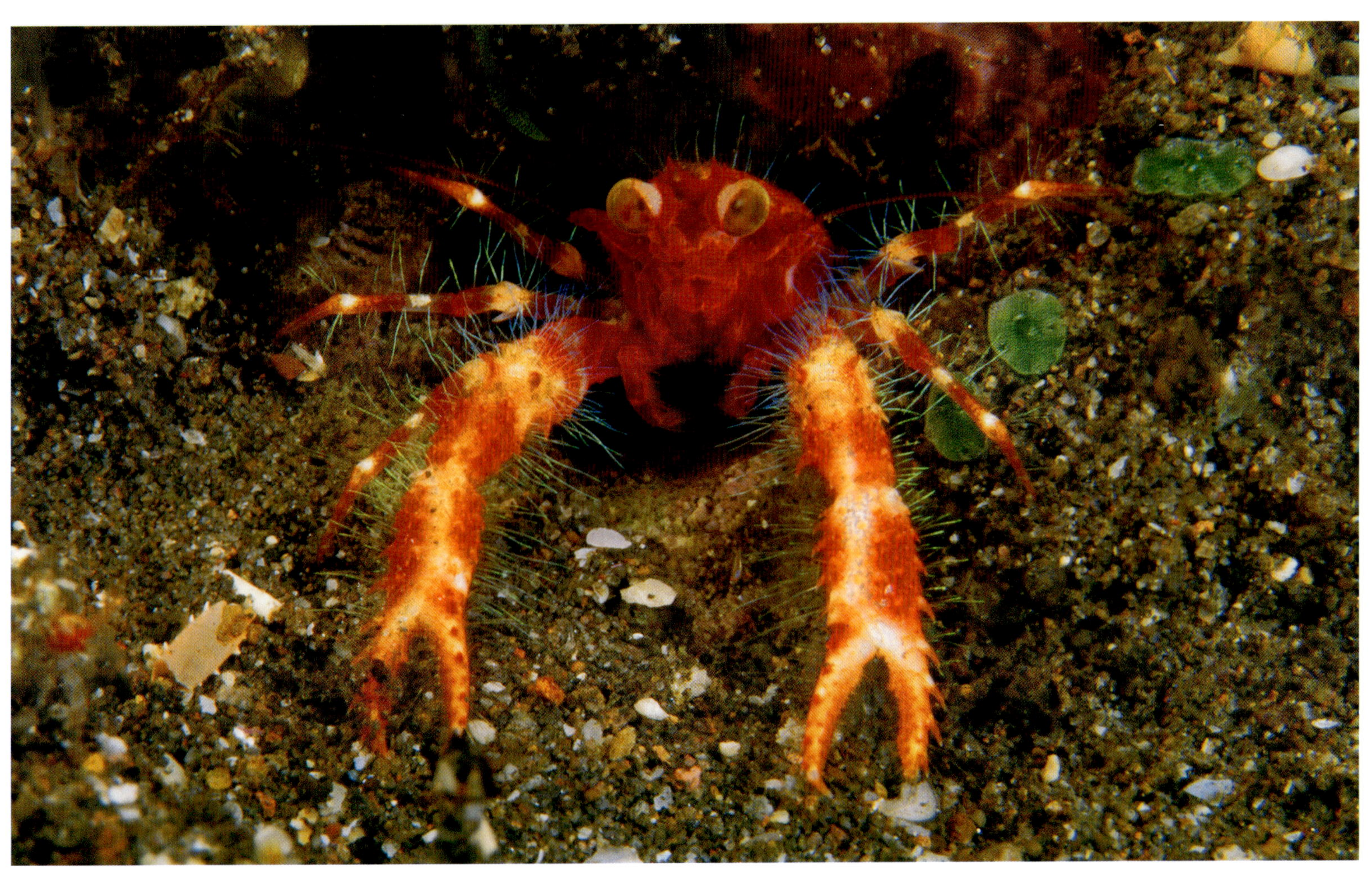

SQUAT LOBSTER

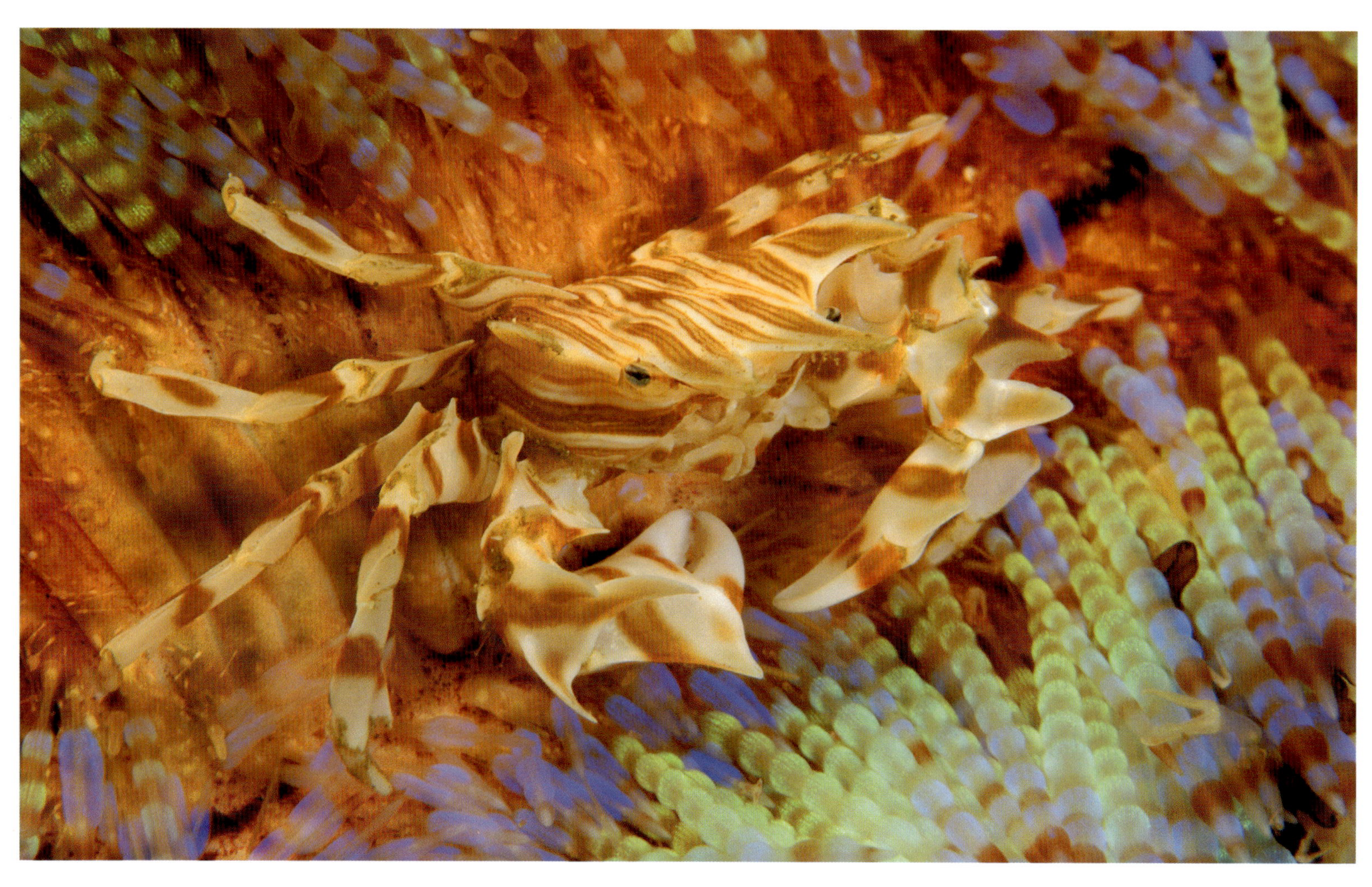

ZEBRA CRAB ON FIRE URCHIN

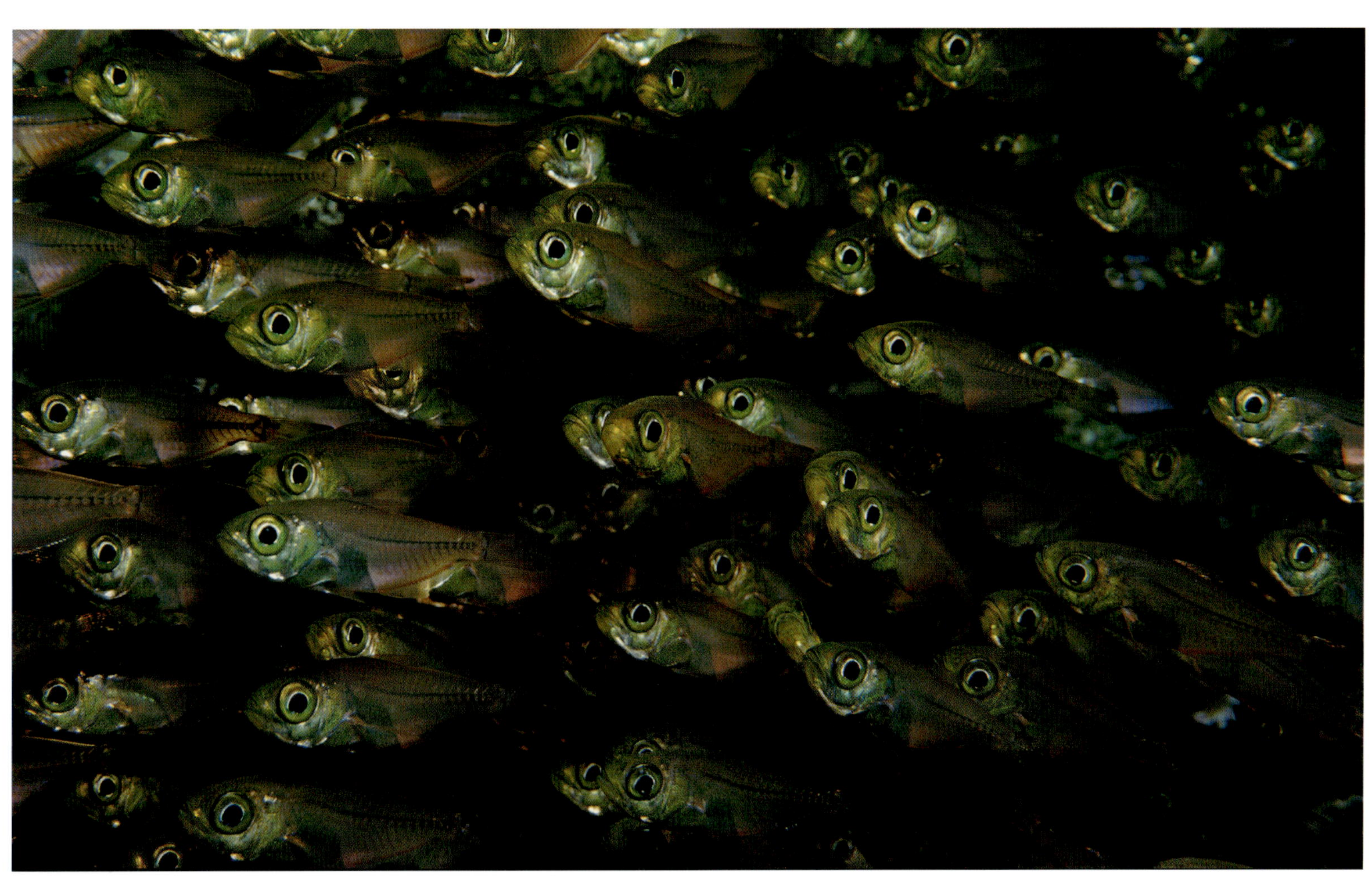

GLASSY SWEEPERS

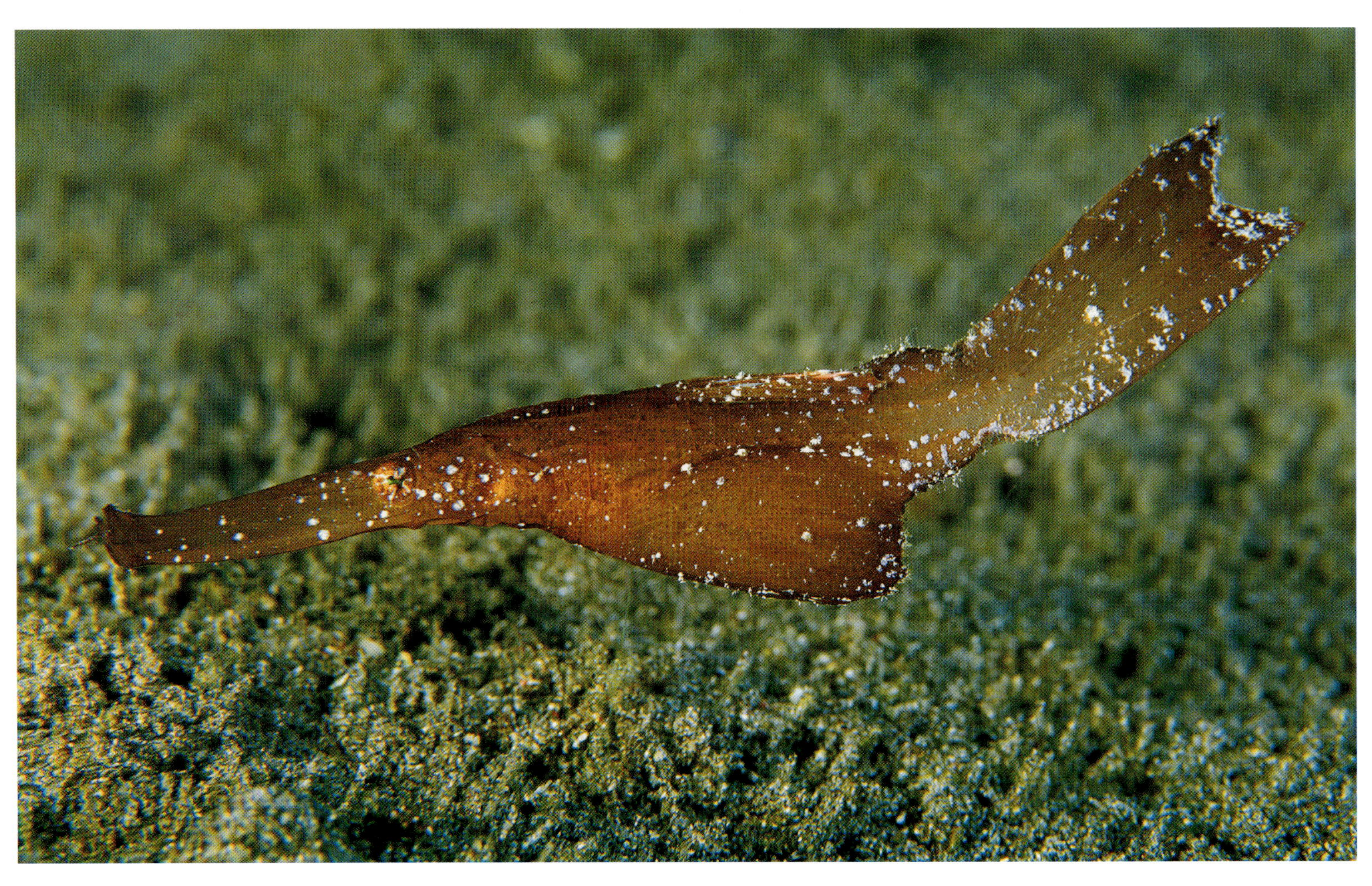

LEAF GHOST PIPEFISH

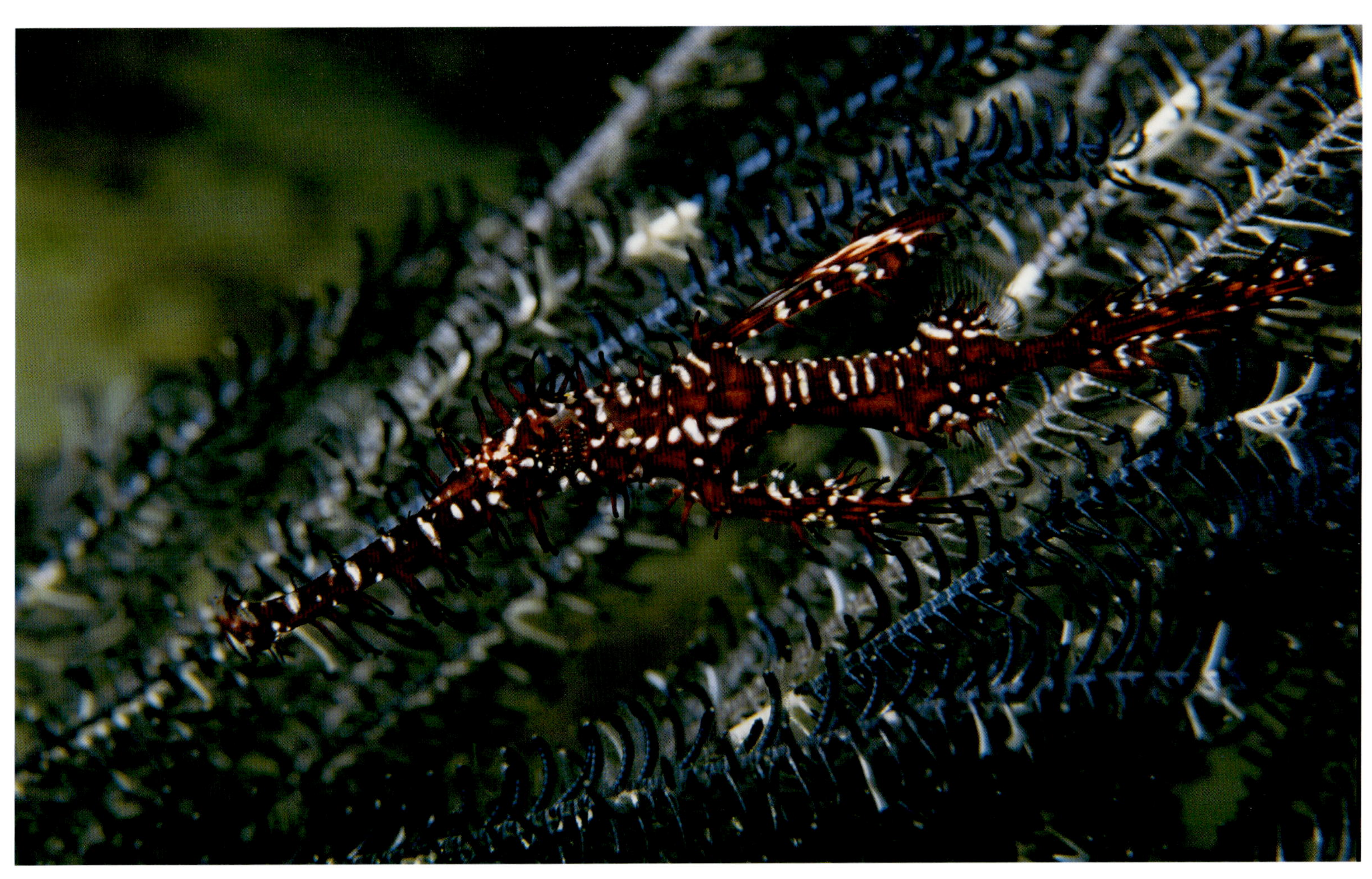

ORNATE GHOST PIPEFISH

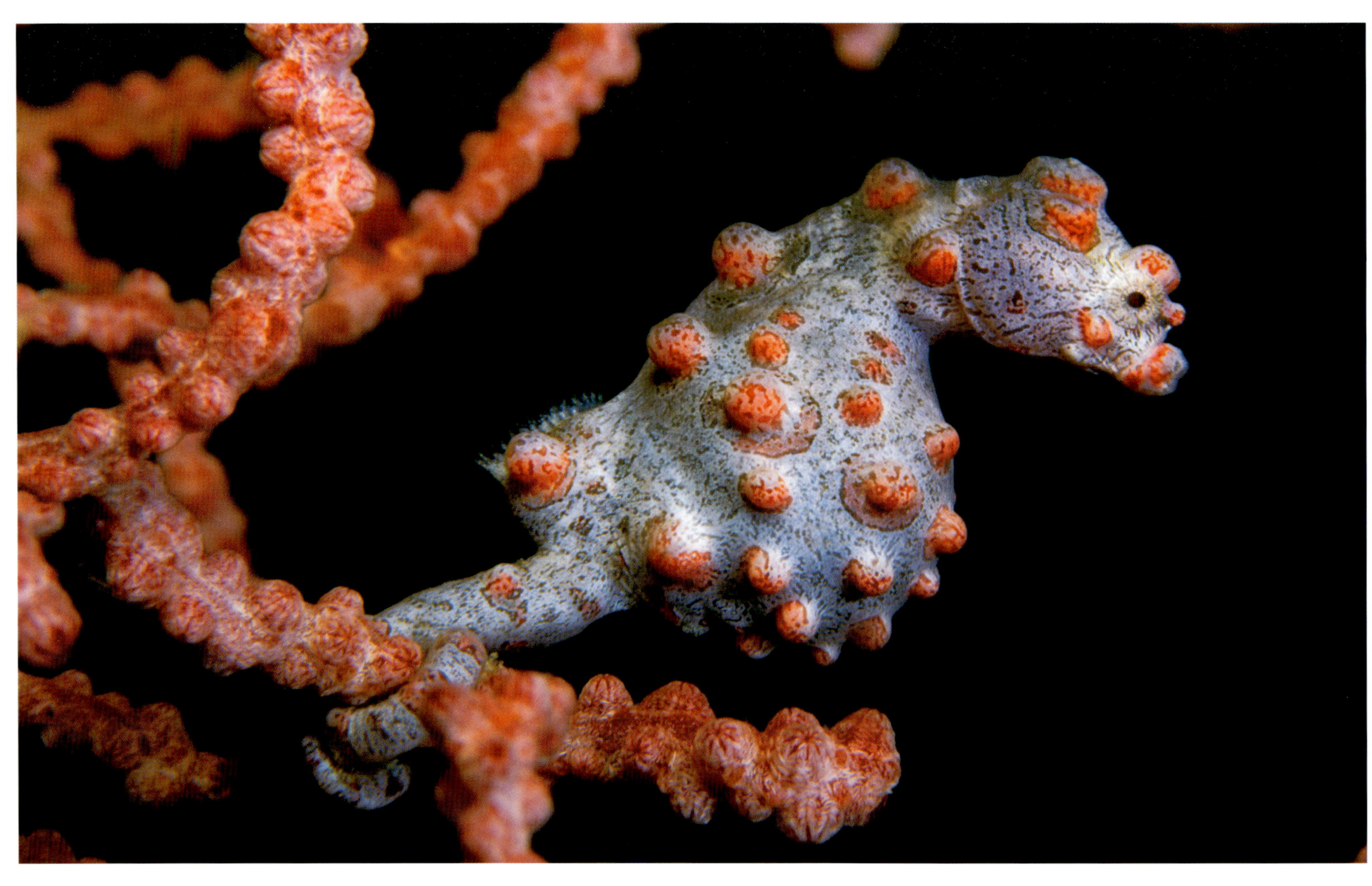

PYGMY SEAHORSE

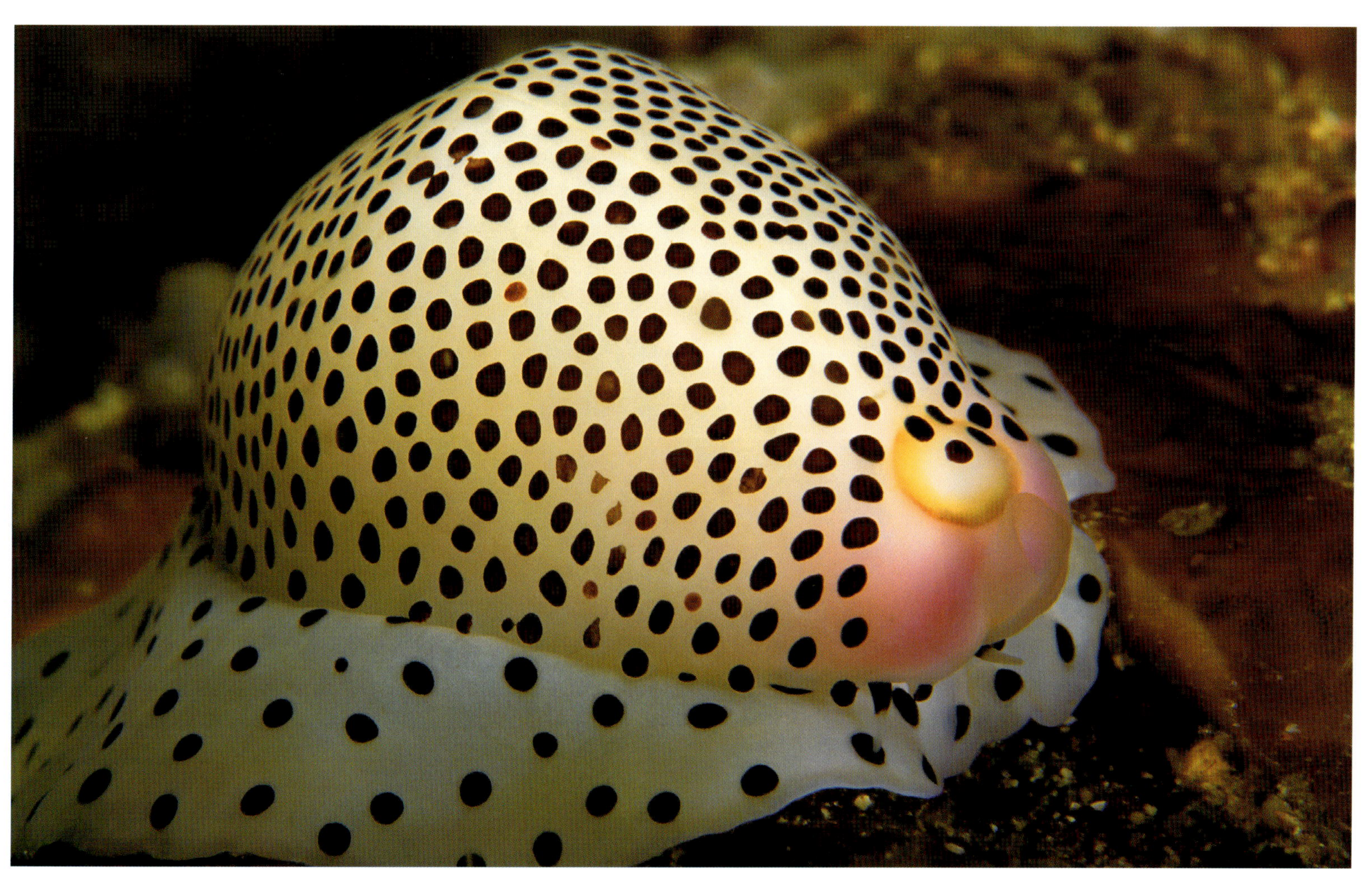

SPOTTED EGG COWRY

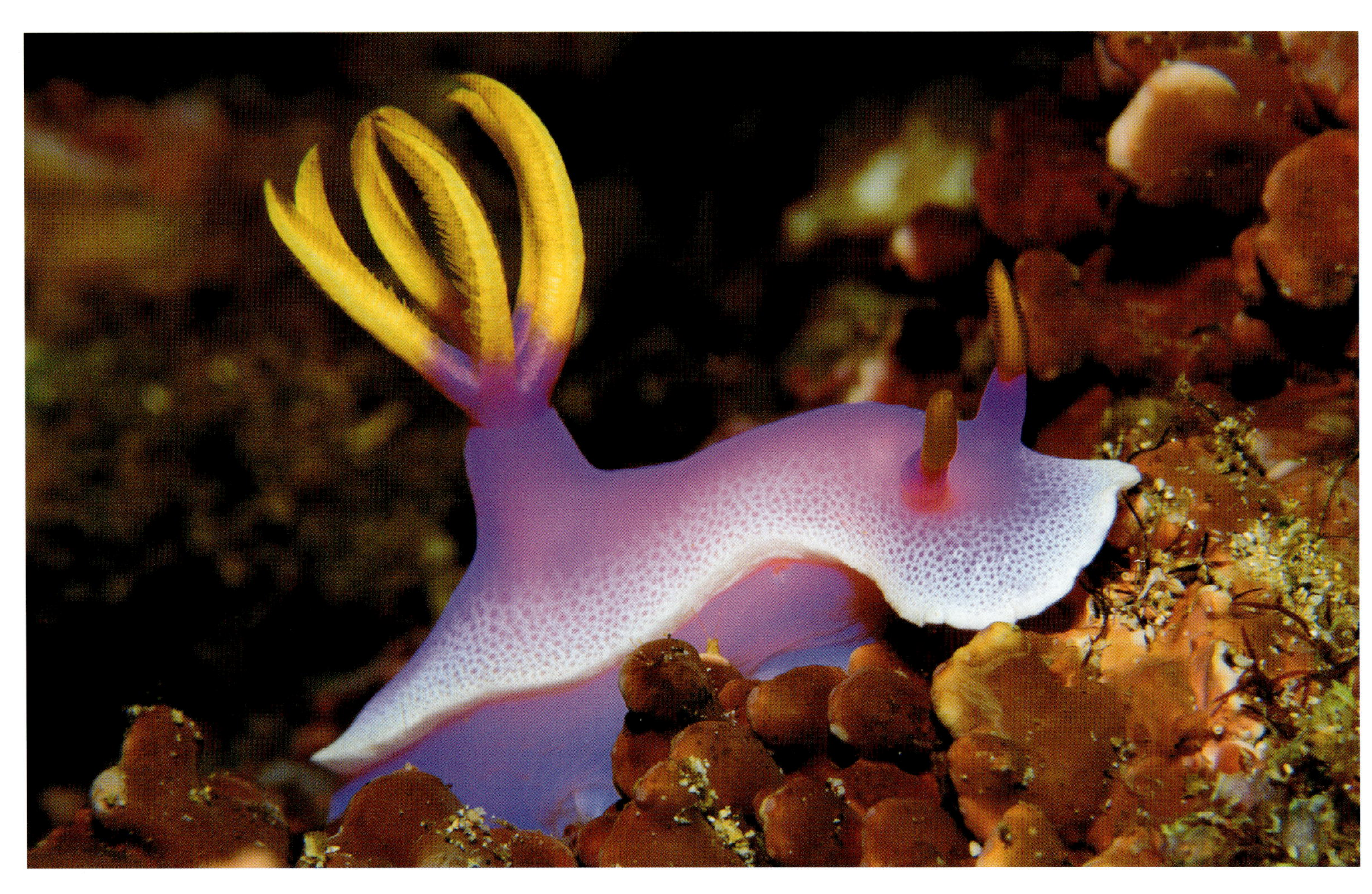

CHROMODORID NUDIBRANCH

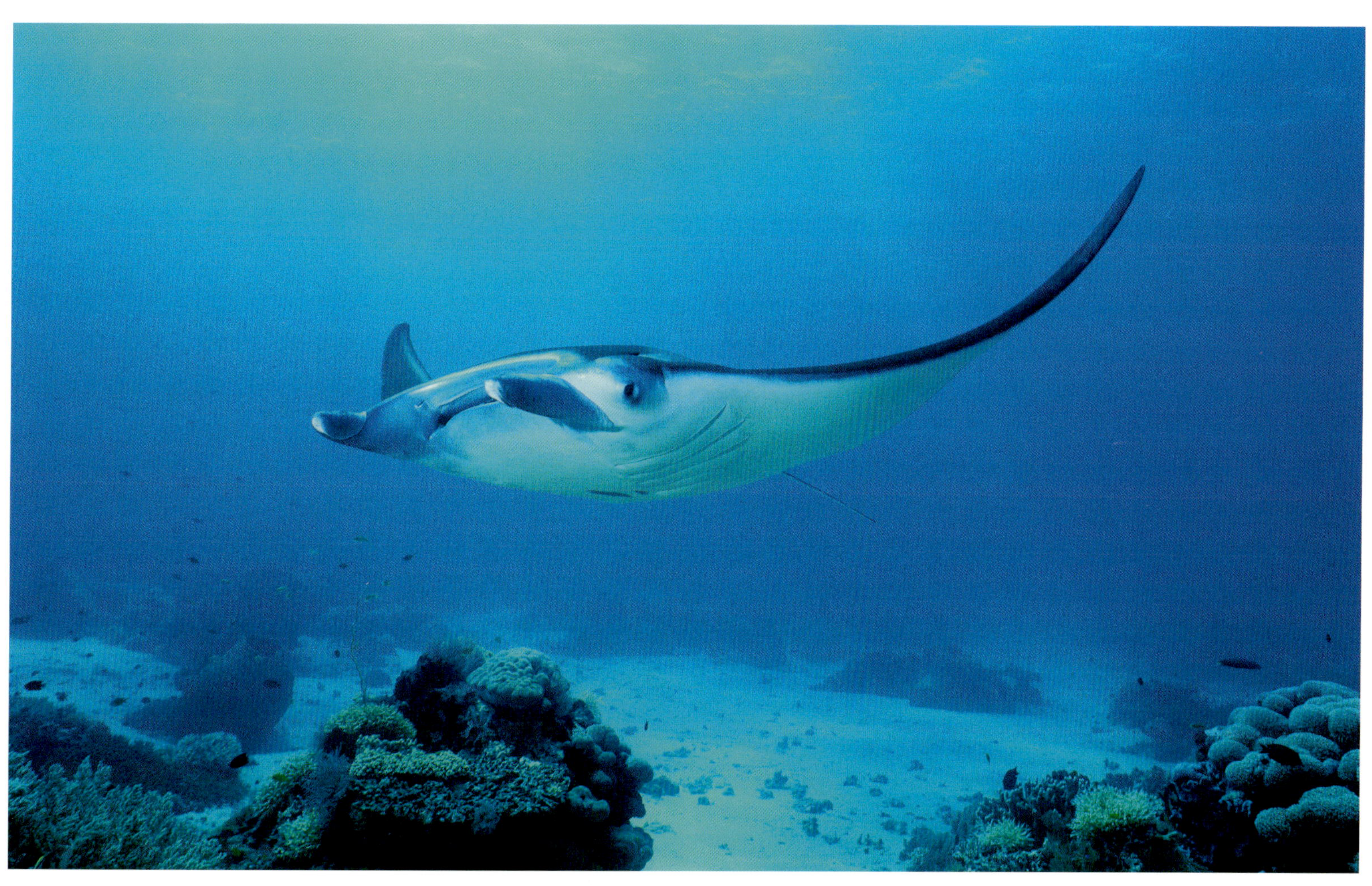

MANTA RAY

Papua New Guinea

Welcome To The Jungle

Another perfect dive had reached its conclusion all too soon. I broke the surface of a tropical sea awash in a surreal glow. The sky was a primordial canvas painted in pastel pink and blaze orange. Violet clouds were spaced across the horizon like alien craft migrating en masse to conquer unknown worlds. Backlit by a brilliant setting sun, I wondered if perhaps I had surfaced in another place, perhaps another time. The ocean was tepid and the waves had taken the evening off. I floated alone, watching the sun work its magic upon the earth and sky. And below me, through the ocean window, yet another world of splendor was unfolding. I was a spellbound traveler, drifting between worlds. The onset of darkness merged the two worlds and a curtain of stars fell over the dreamscape. Nightfall had come to Papua New Guinea.

Papua New Guinea (PNG) is the second largest island on Earth. Above, in the verdant rainforests and below, among the prolific reefs, PNG is still "The Land That Time Forgot." By any measure, when you're here, you're in the jungle. And the coral reefs surrounding PNG are among the richest in the world, rivaling those of Indonesia. To this day, many of the reefs remain pristine and largely unexplored. True adventure is alive in PNG. Its waters will, no doubt, give our species a final glimpse of an undisturbed reef ecosystem.

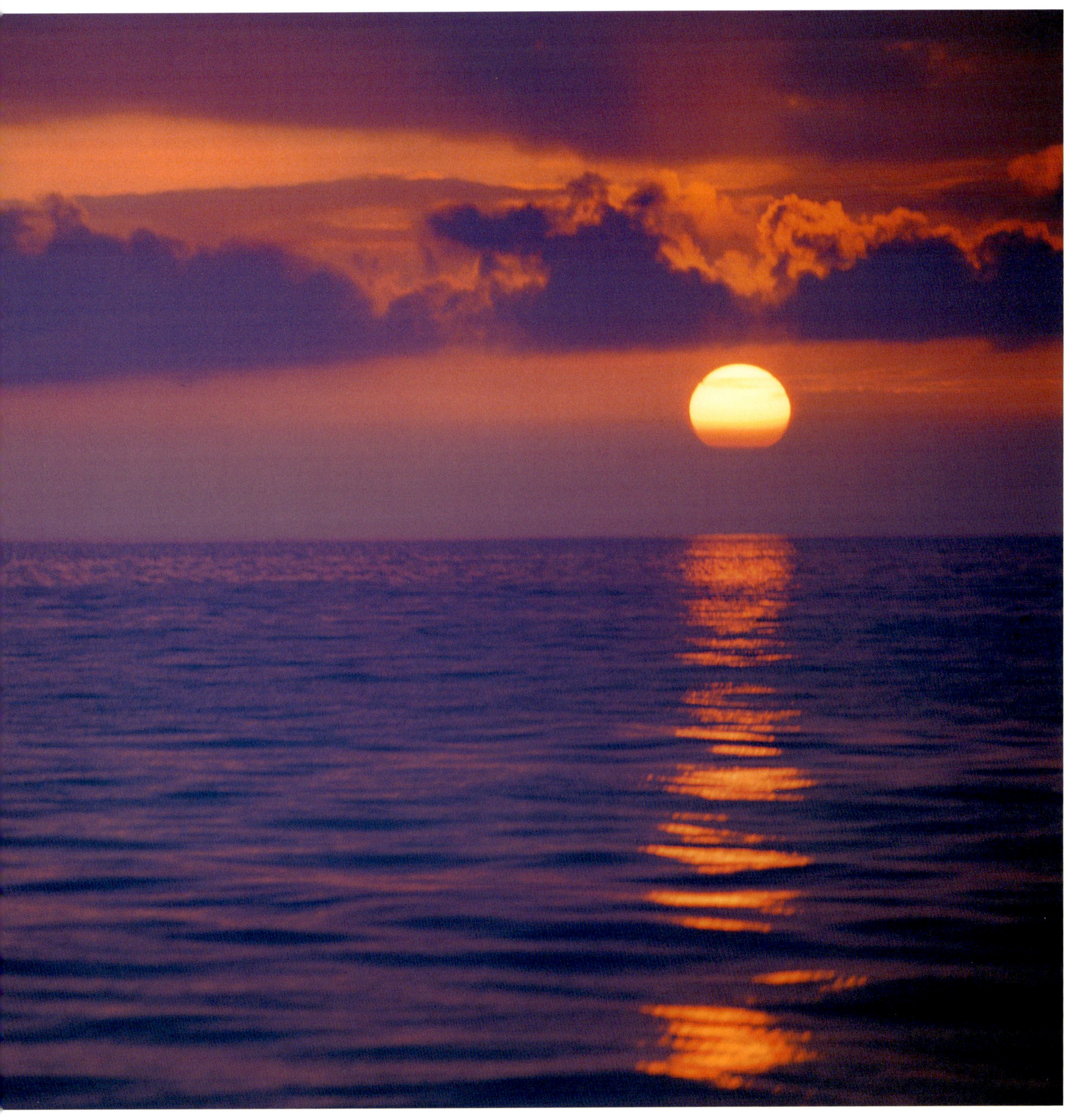

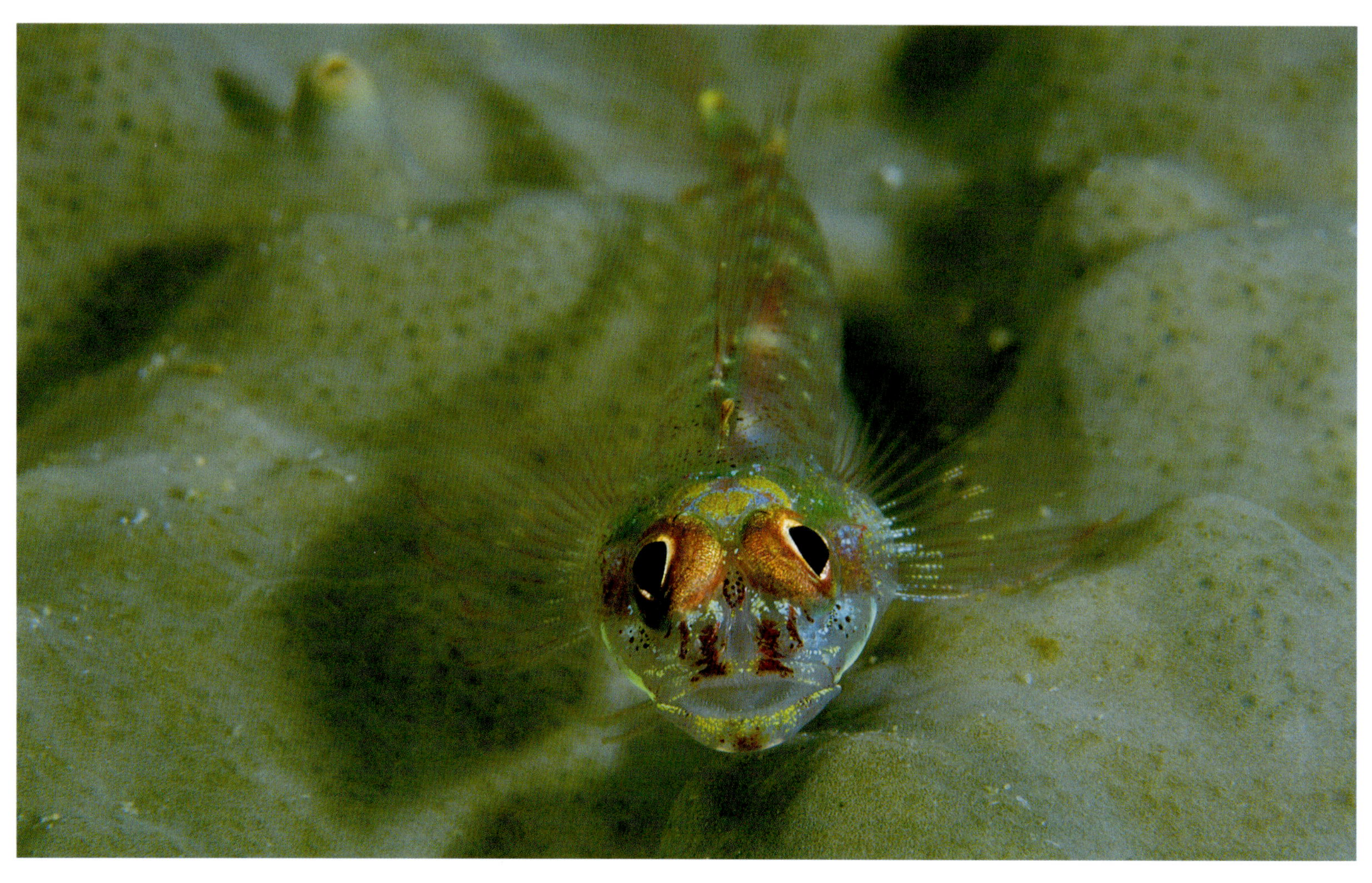

TRIPLEFIN

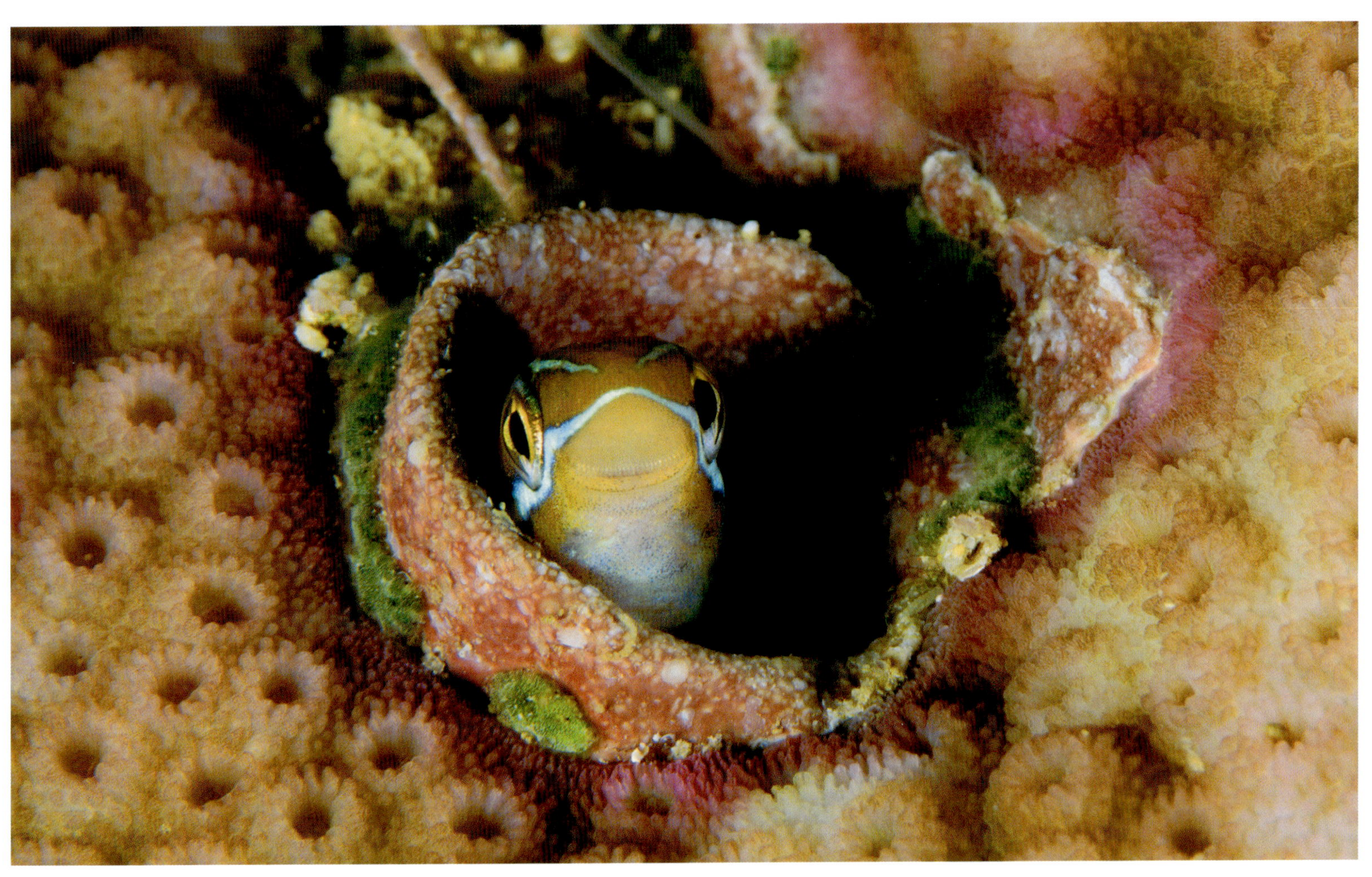

SABERTOOTH BLENNY

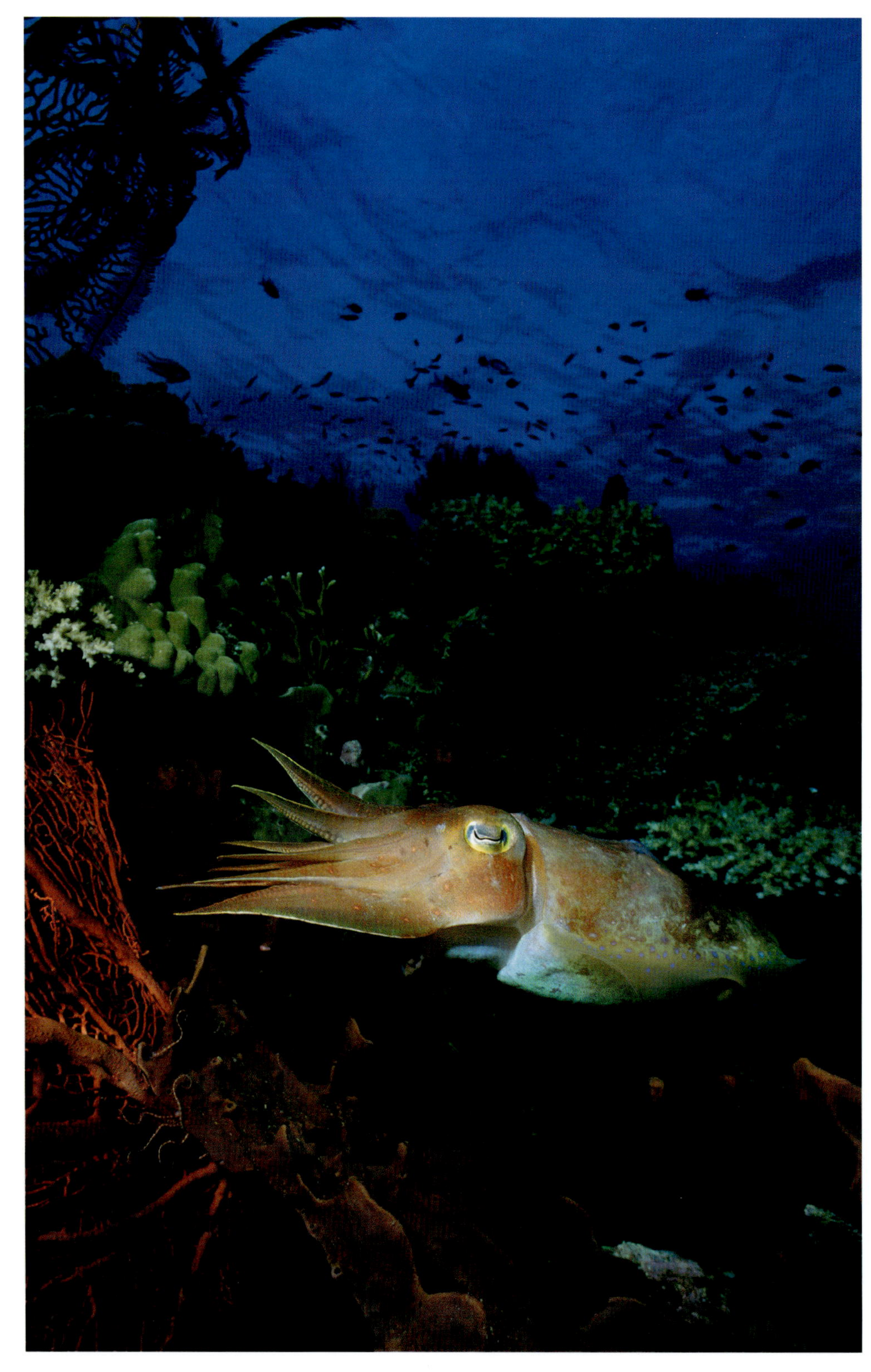

CUTTLEFISH

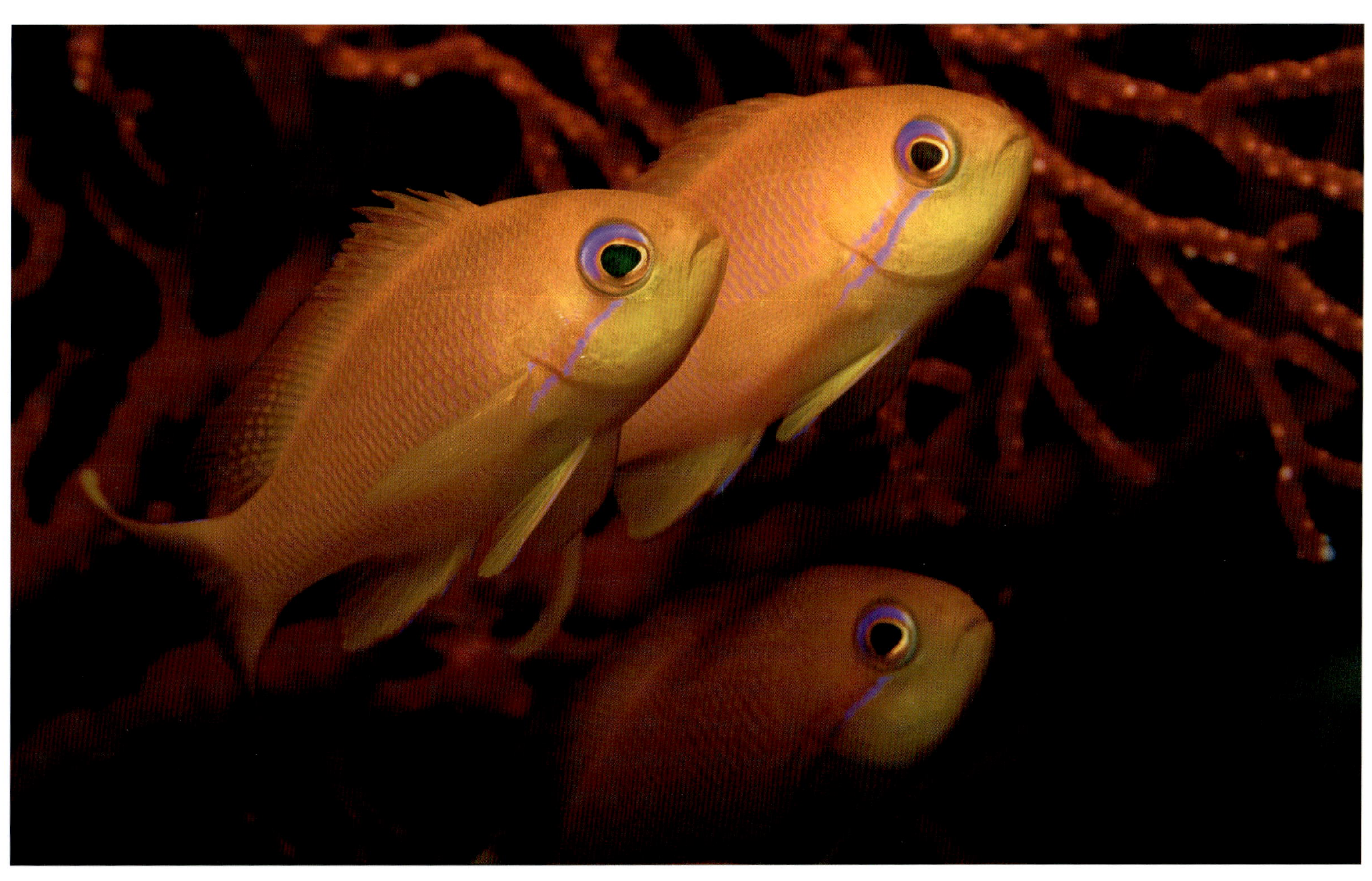

LYRETAIL BASSLETS

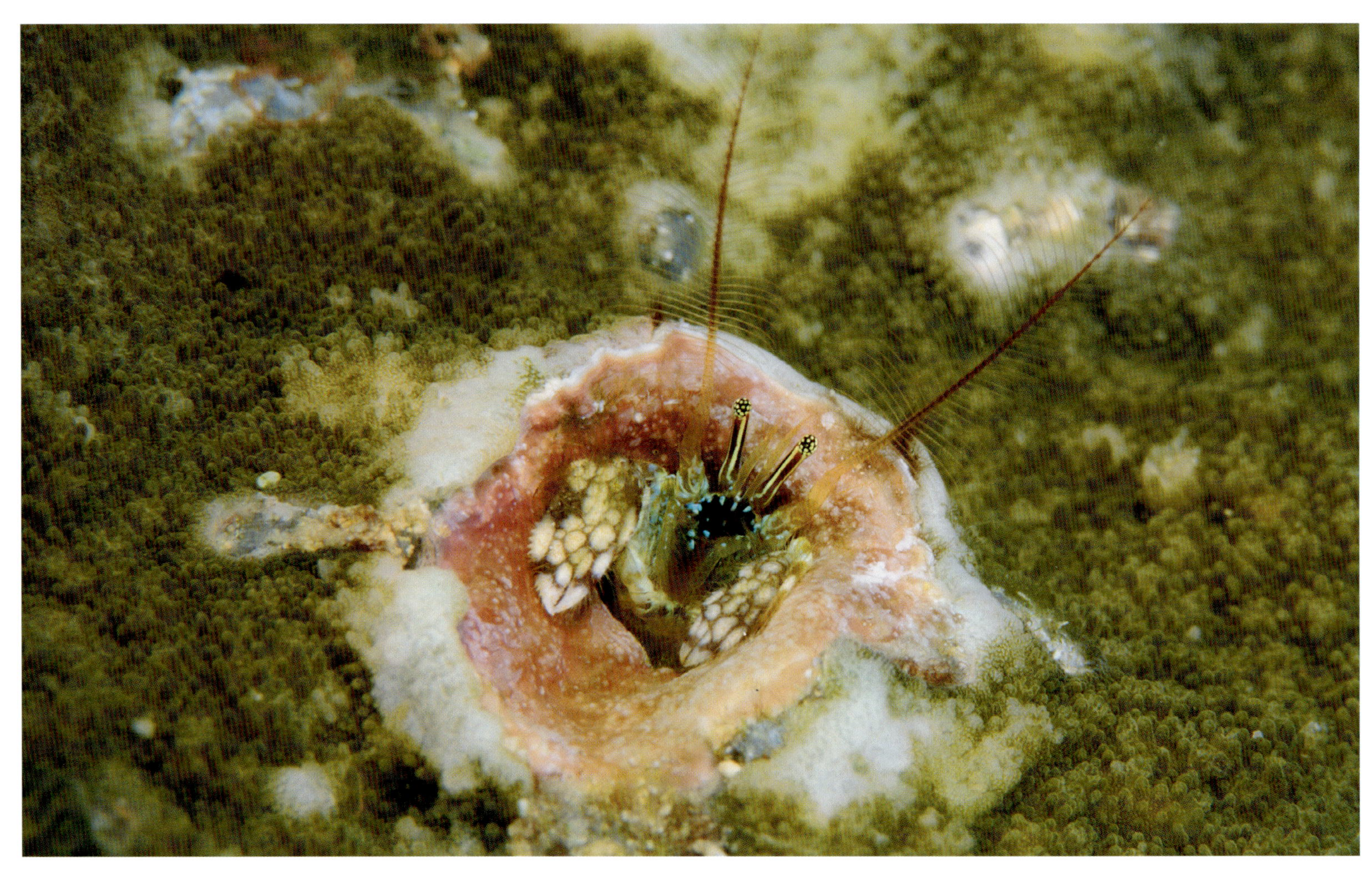

CORAL HERMIT CRAB

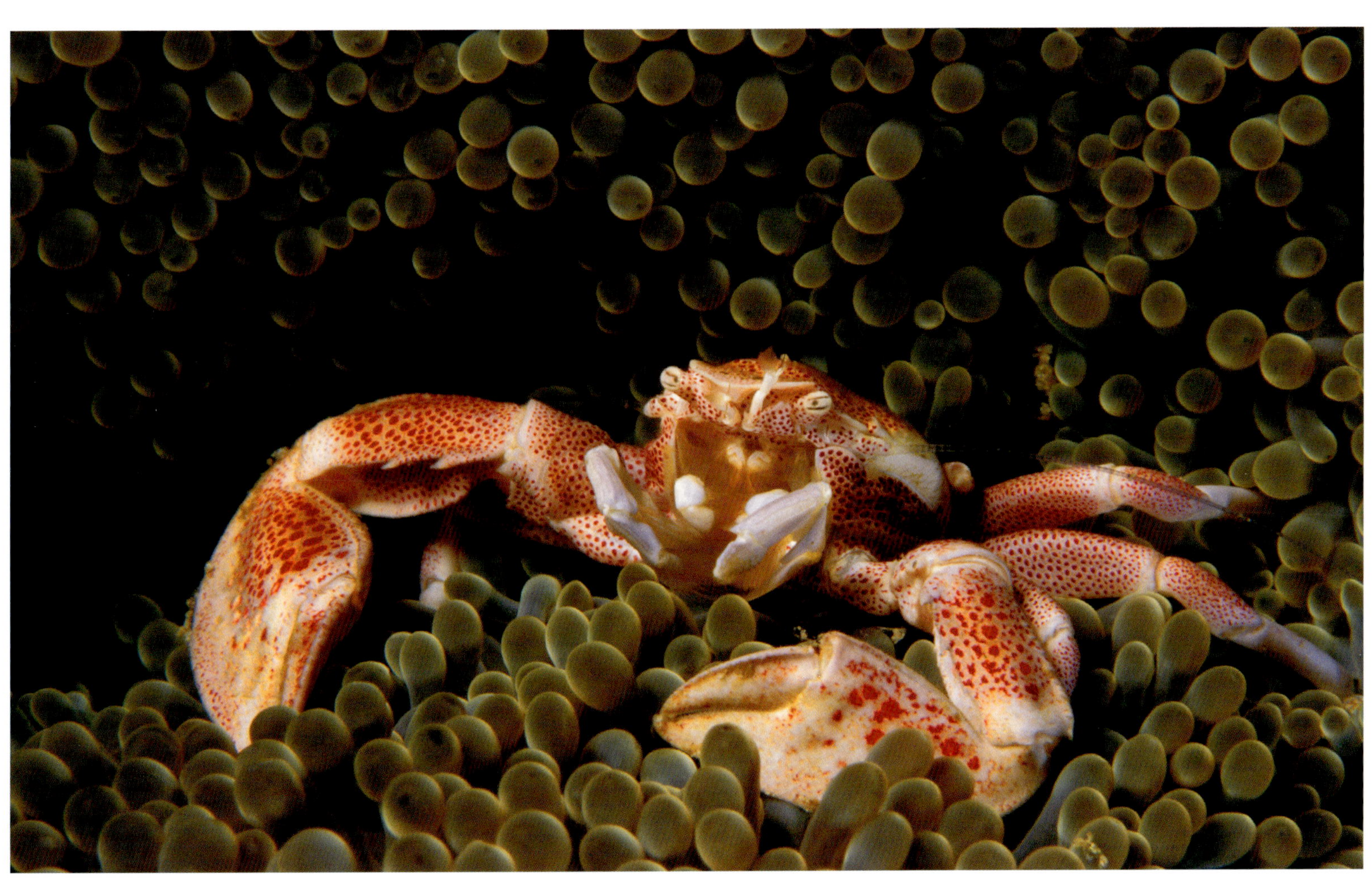

PORCELAIN CRAB

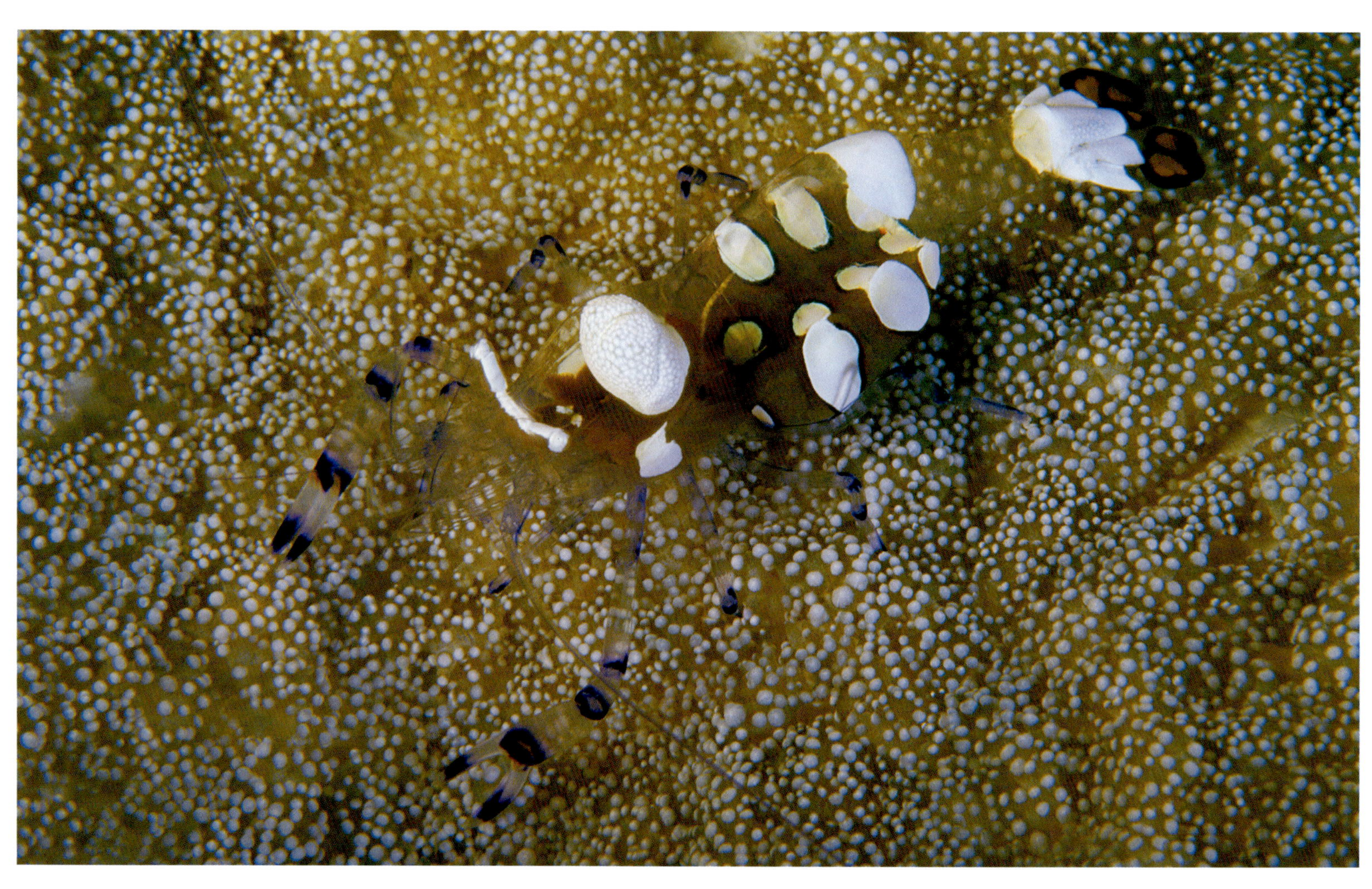

EGGSHELL SHRIMP

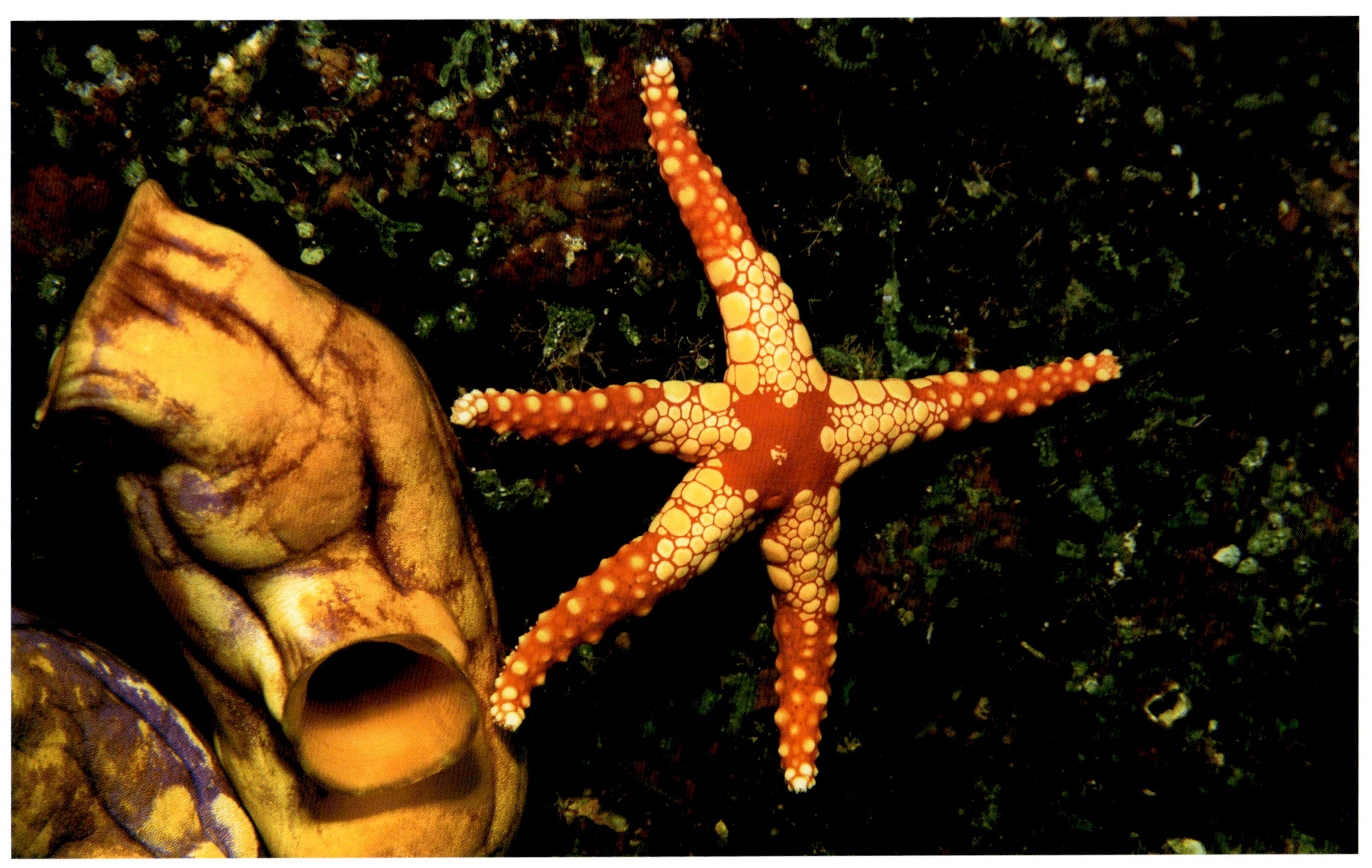

TUNICATE AND STARFISH

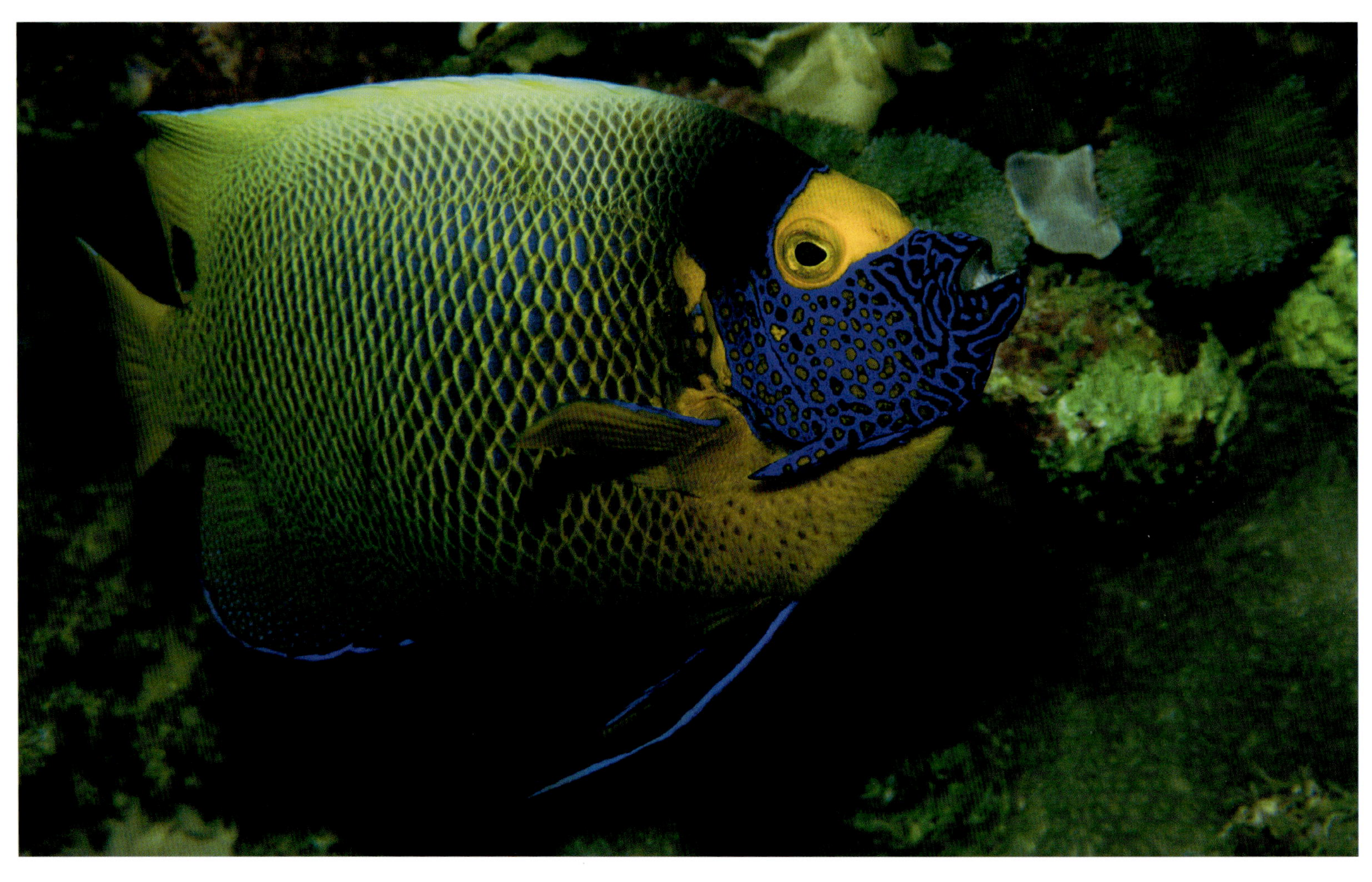

BLUE-FACE ANGELFISH

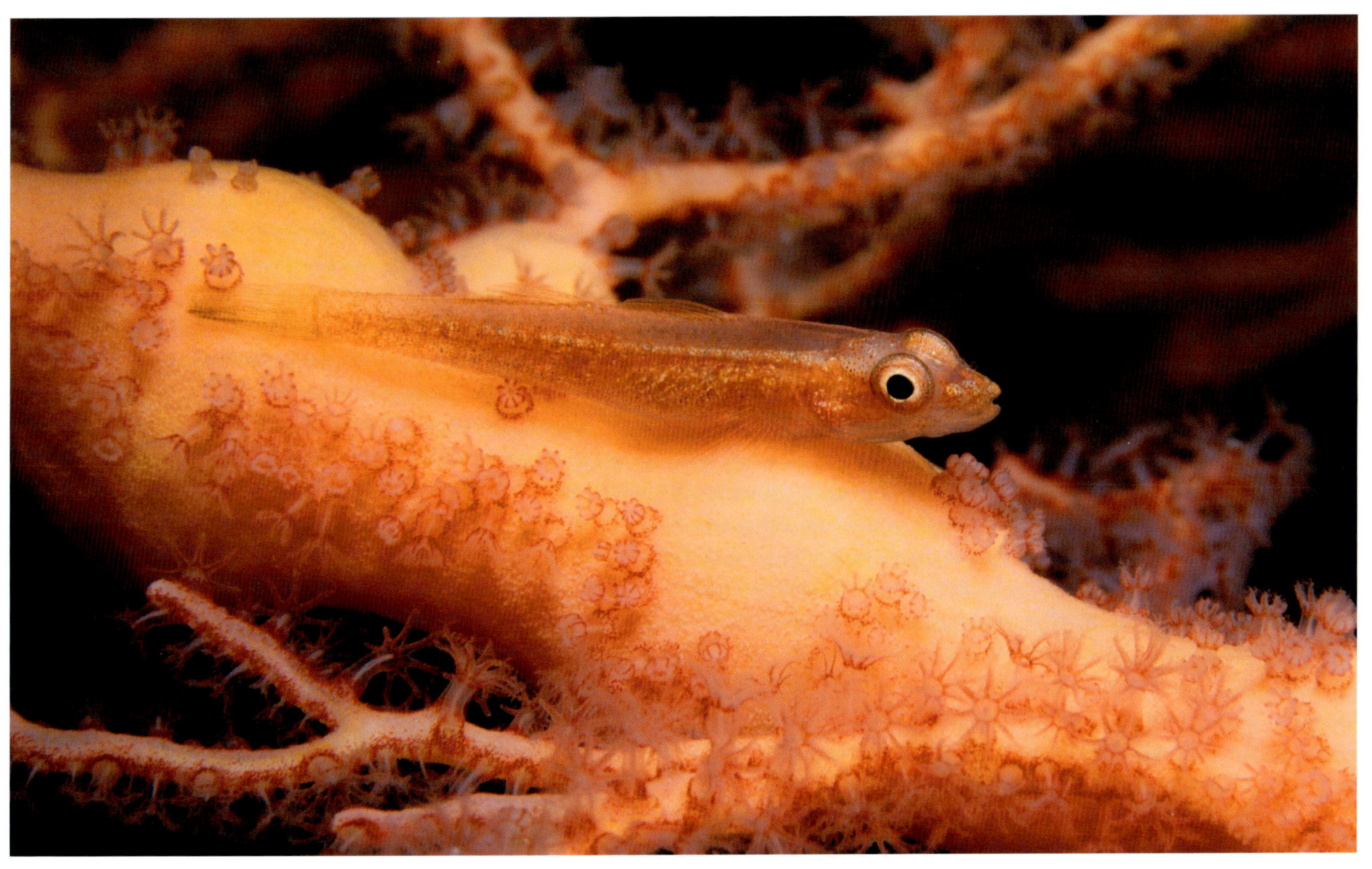

FAN GOBY

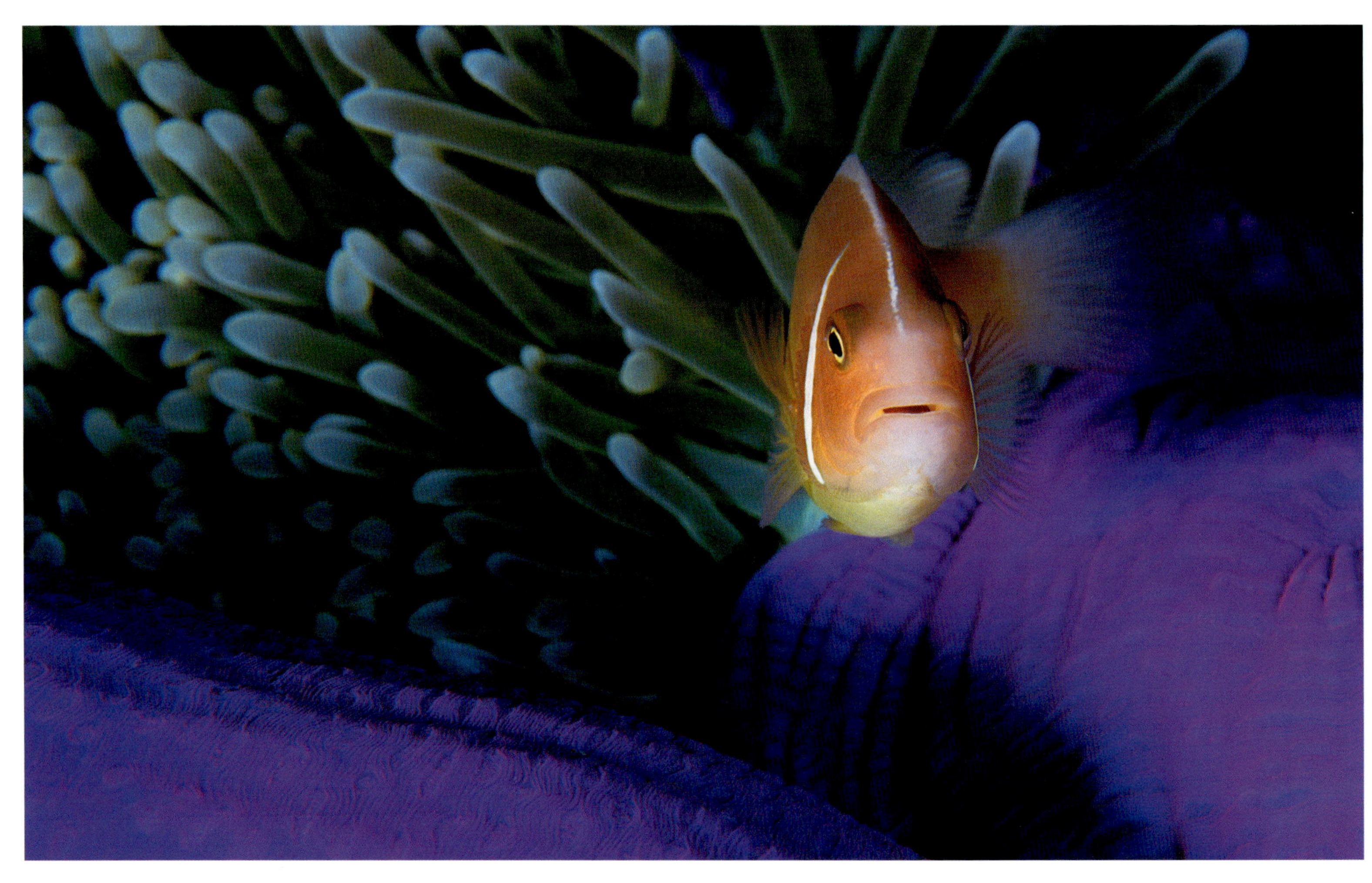

WHITE STRIPED ANEMONEFISH

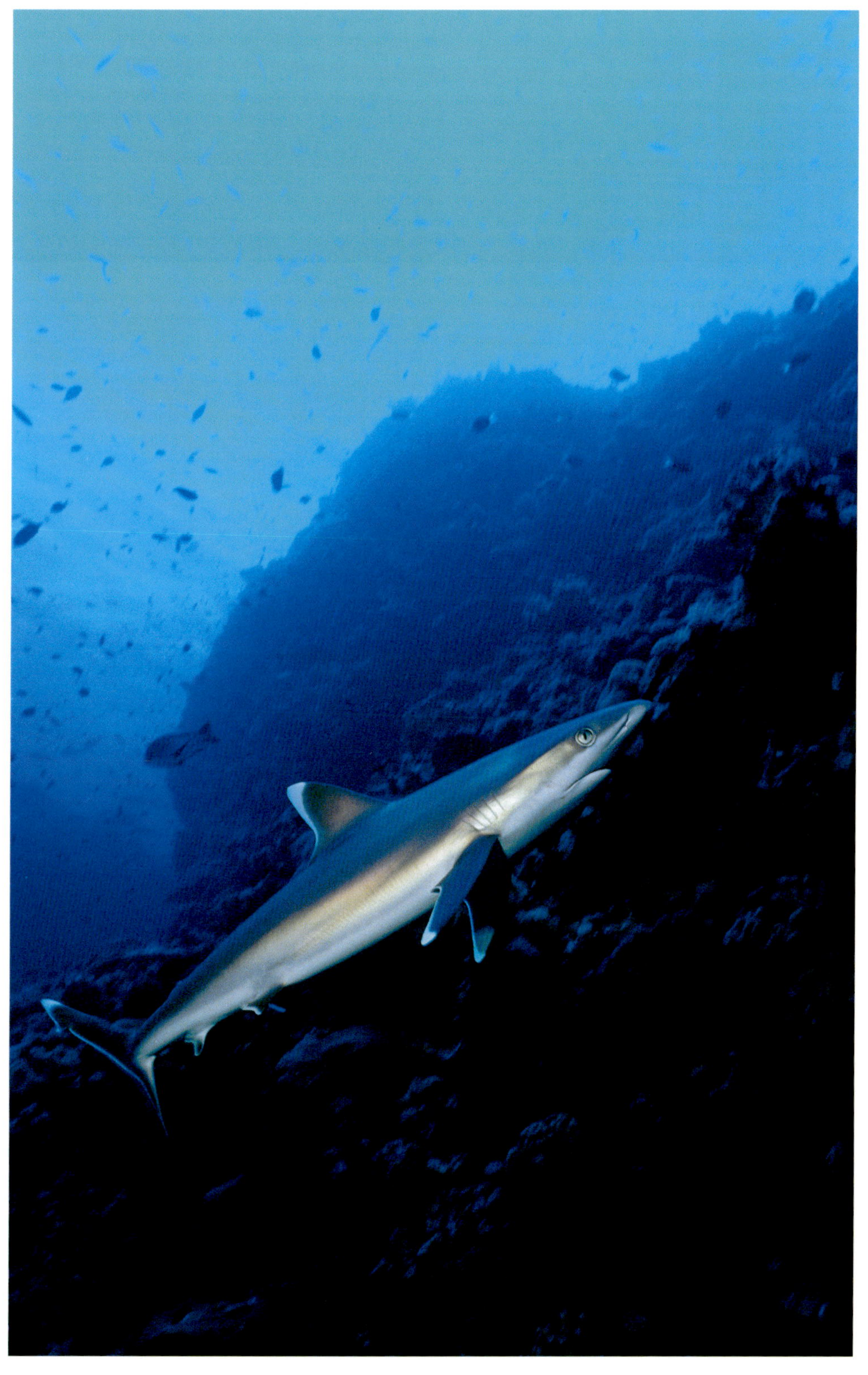

SILVERTIP REEF SHARK

Fiji Islands

Fiji Islands

Sere-Ni-Wai

These oceanic island jewels with their friendly people are the embodiment of the term "South Pacific Paradise." In 1985, I made my first dives in Fiji. Like so many others, I fell in love with the diving and the lifestyle. Whenever I return to these islands, I always feel like I am returning home. And whenever I get back "home," you can find me in the water.

Fiji is often called "The Soft Coral Capital of the World." The resplendent populations of hard and soft corals in Fiji create some of the most mesmerizing underwater vistas on the planet. A wealth of colorful fish and other invertebrates decorate these phenomenal reefs. Diving in Fiji is like listening to beautiful music. You never tire of it. With every visit, these magnificent islands seem to whisper an alluring, inspiring melody. It is the sound of gentle waves on an exotic shore coupled with the pulsing rhythms of the reef...a song of the sea.

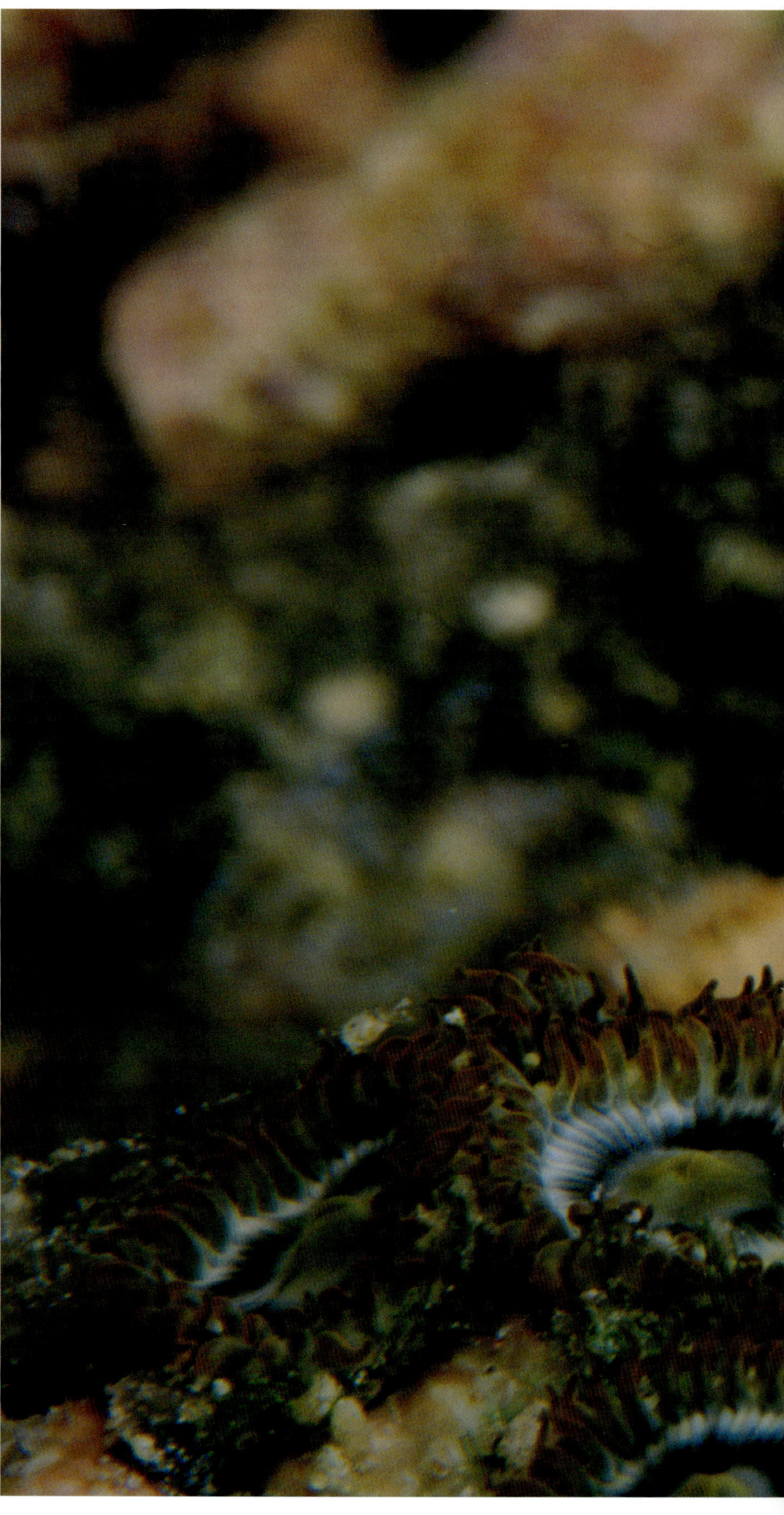

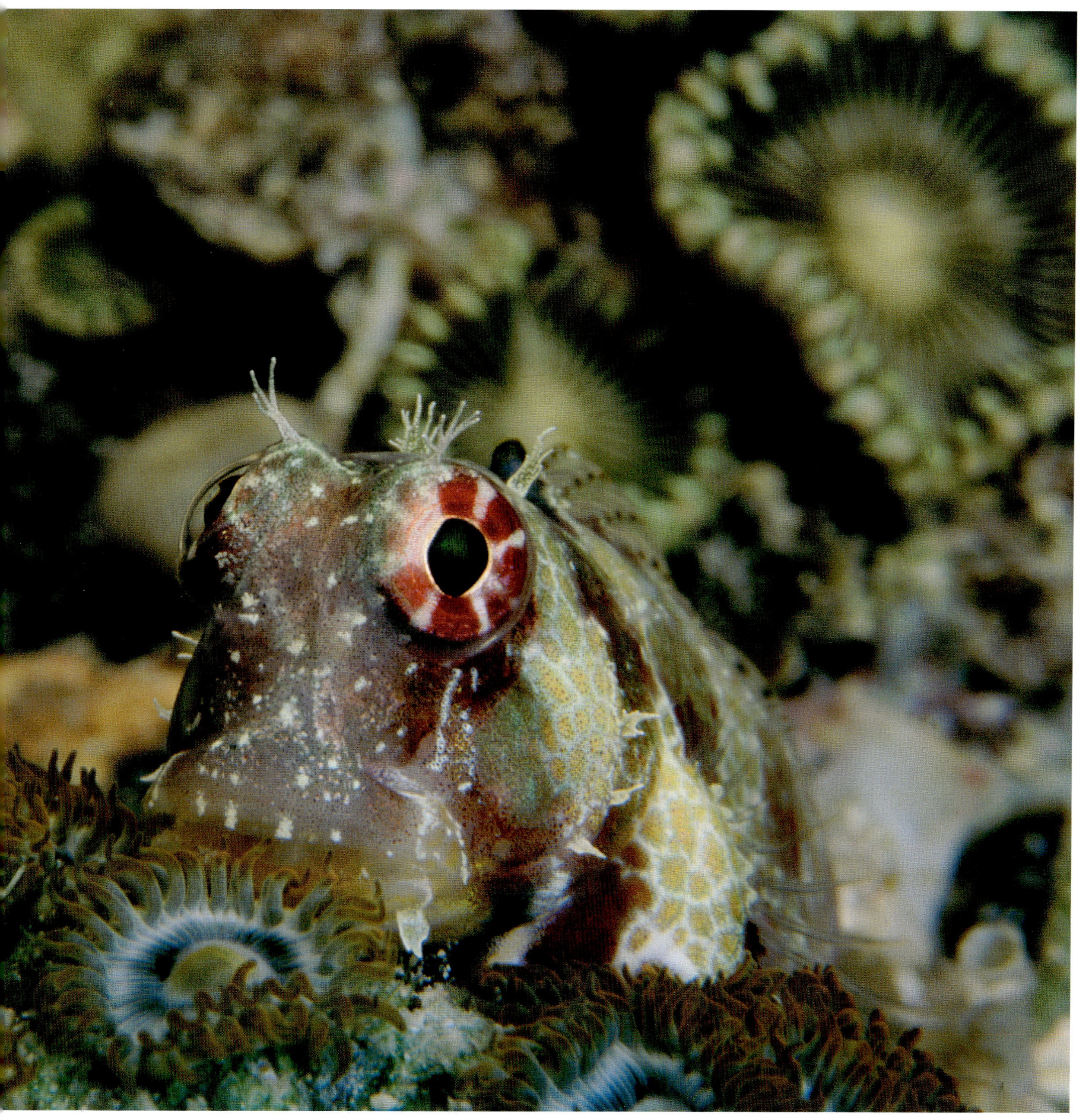

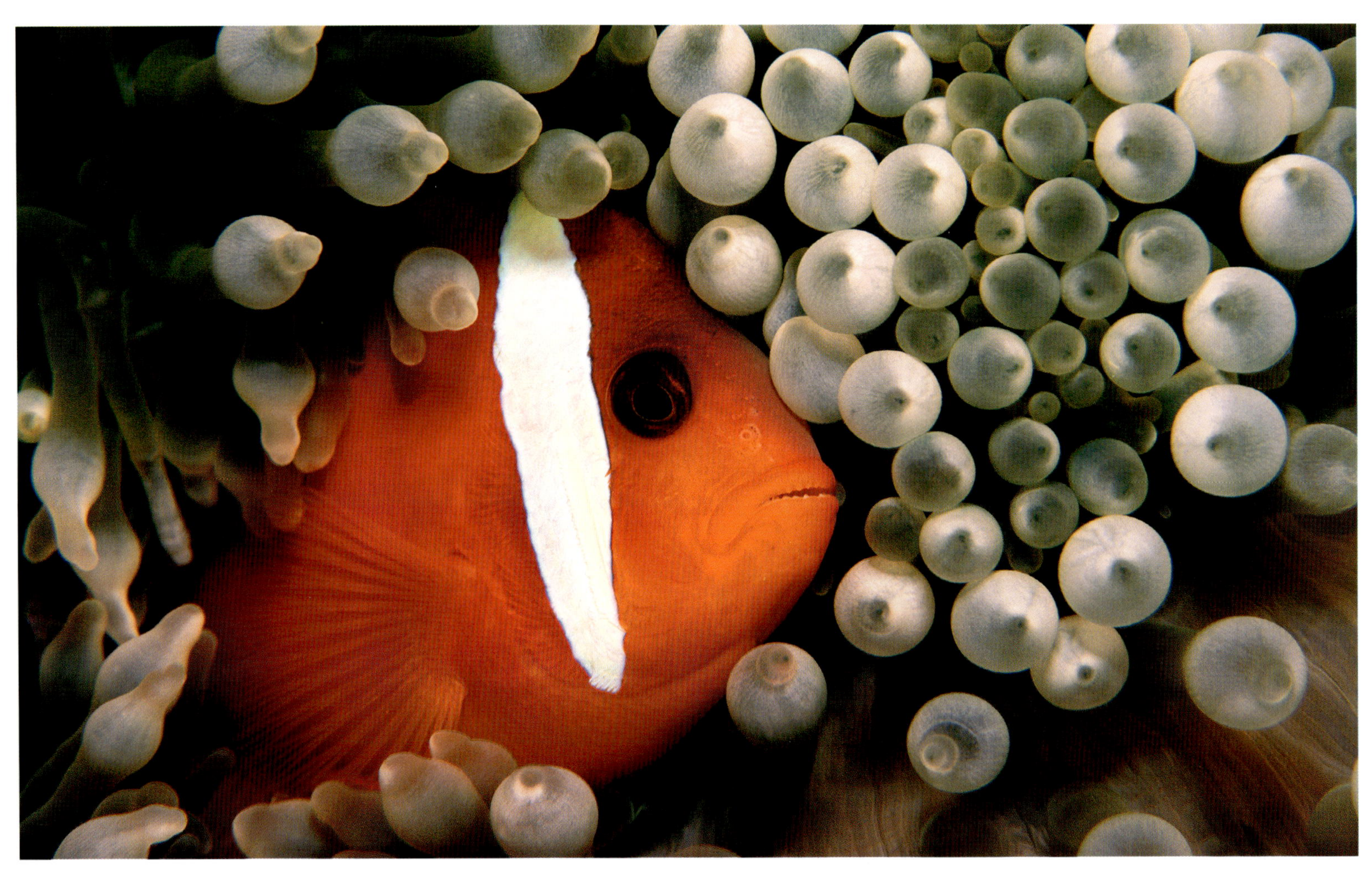

RED ANEMONEFISH

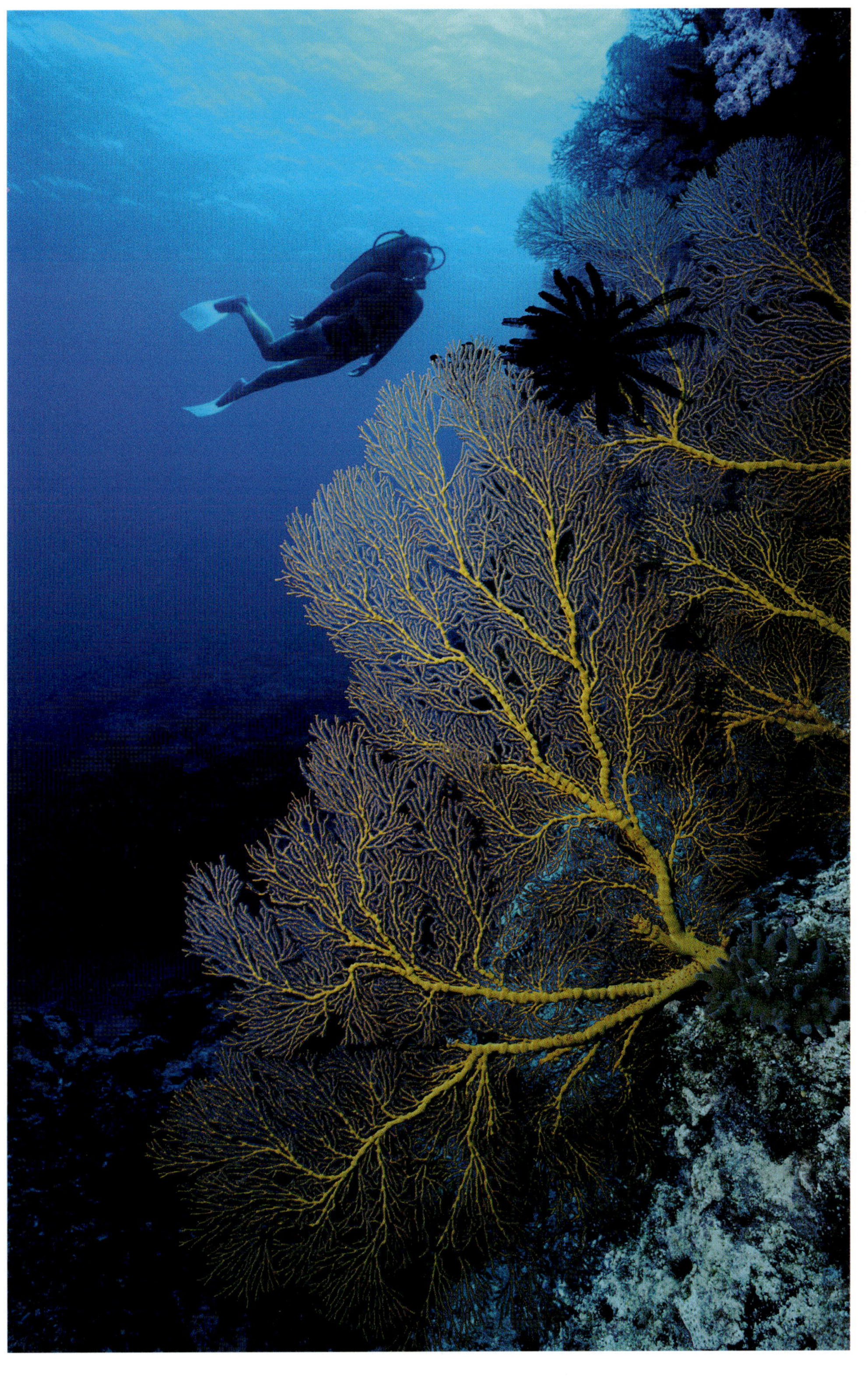

GIANT SEA FAN

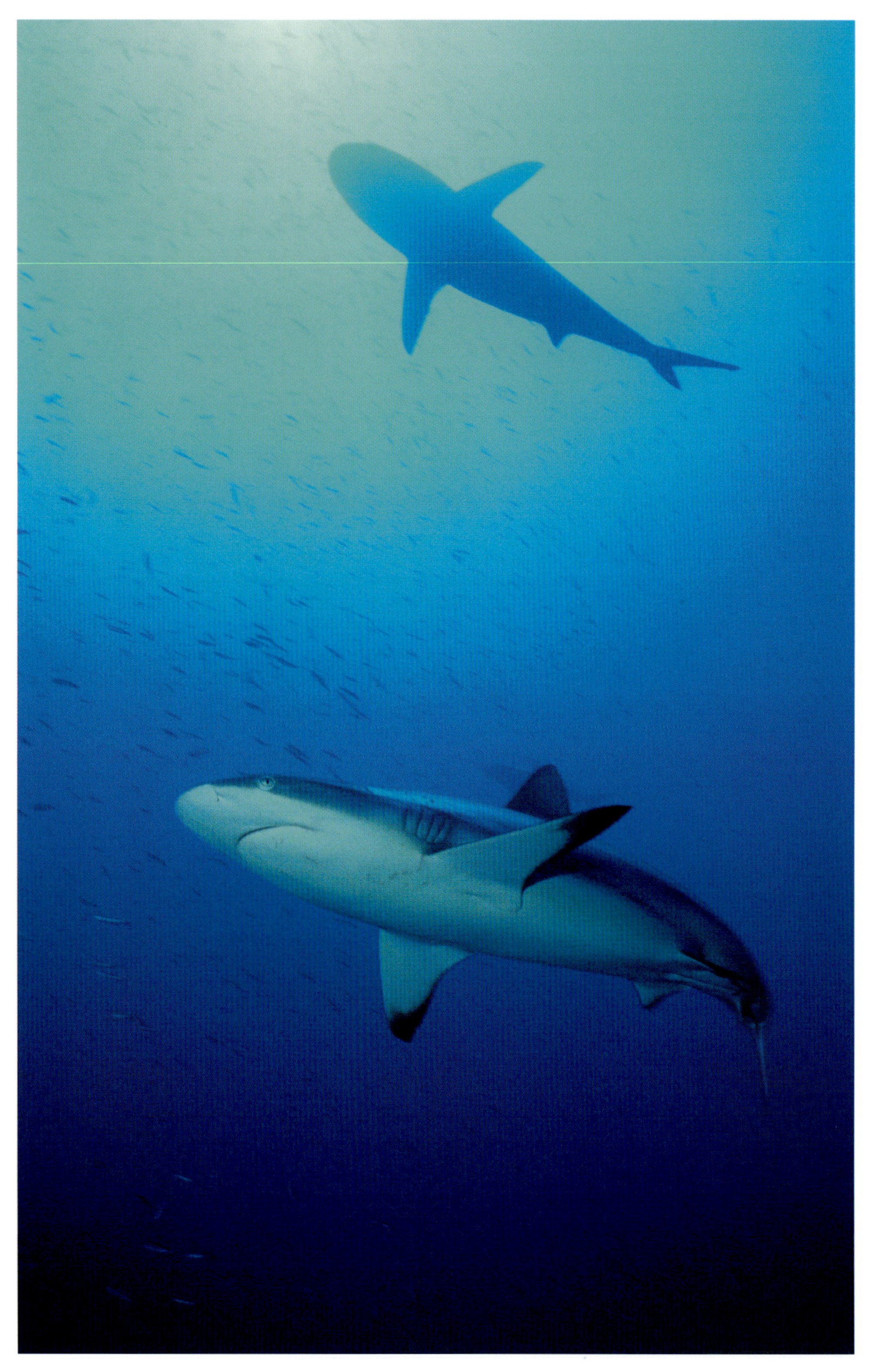

GRAY REEF SHARK

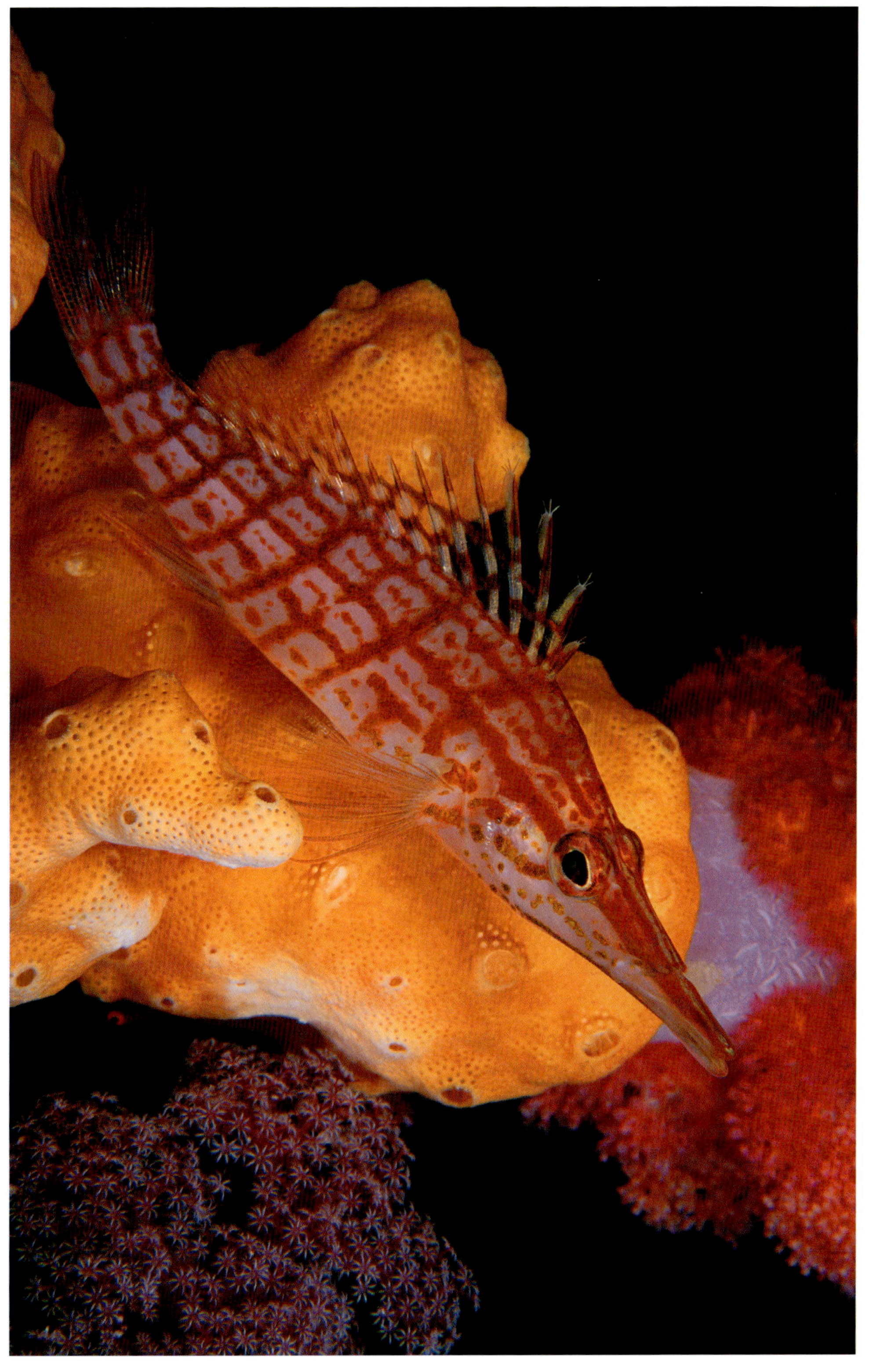

LONGNOSE HAWKFISH

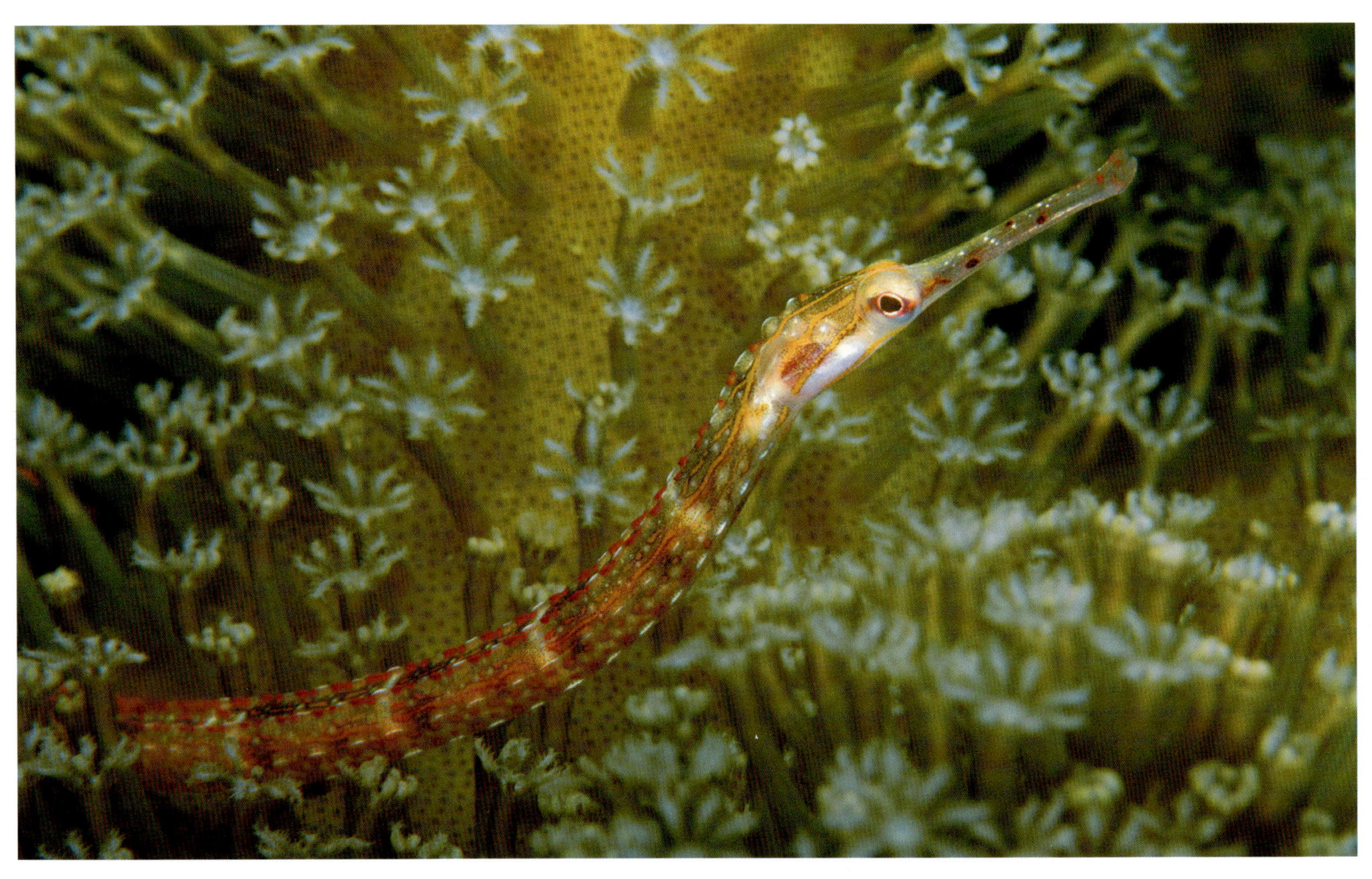

BANDED PIPEFISH

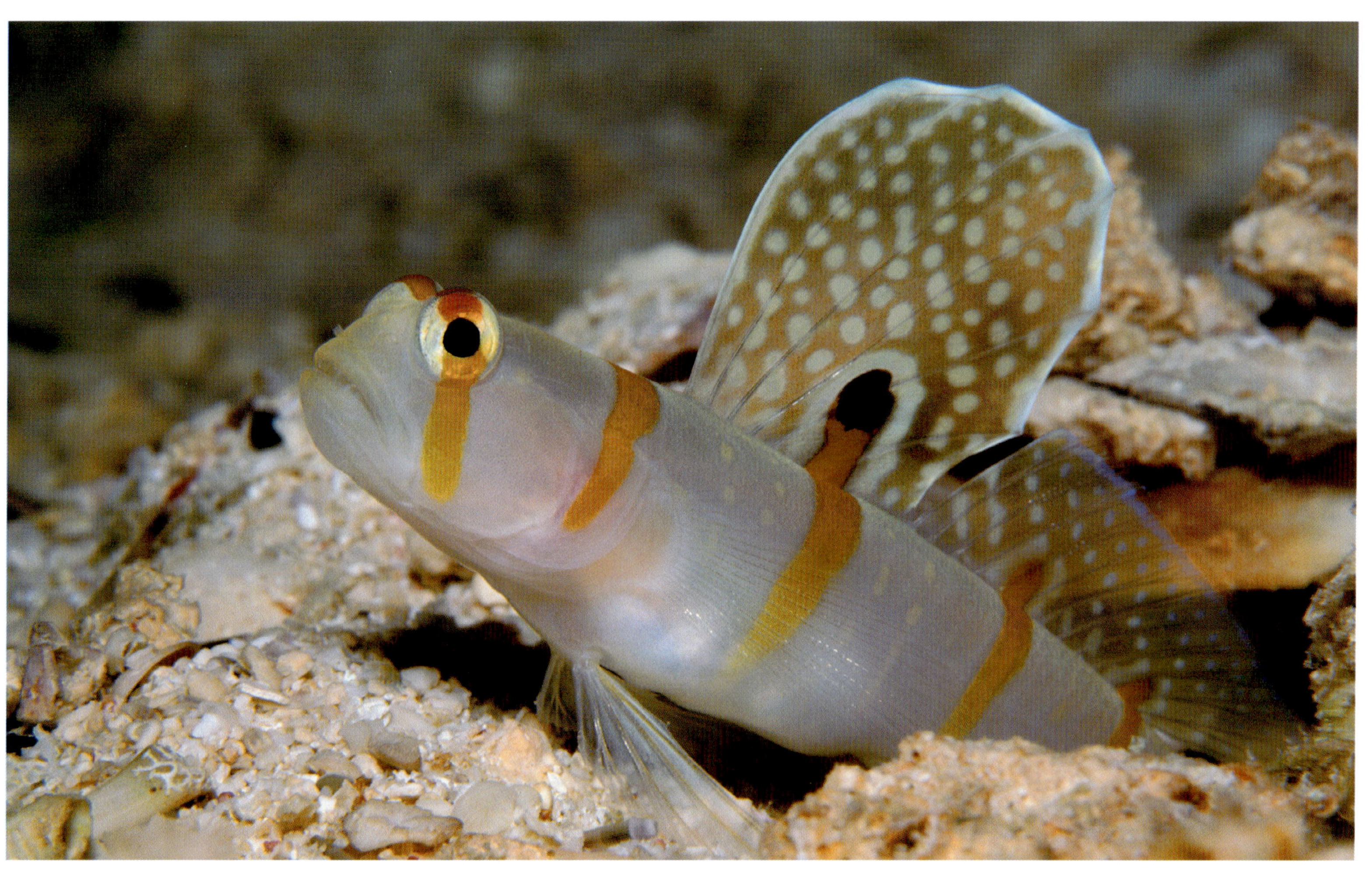

SAILFIN GOBY

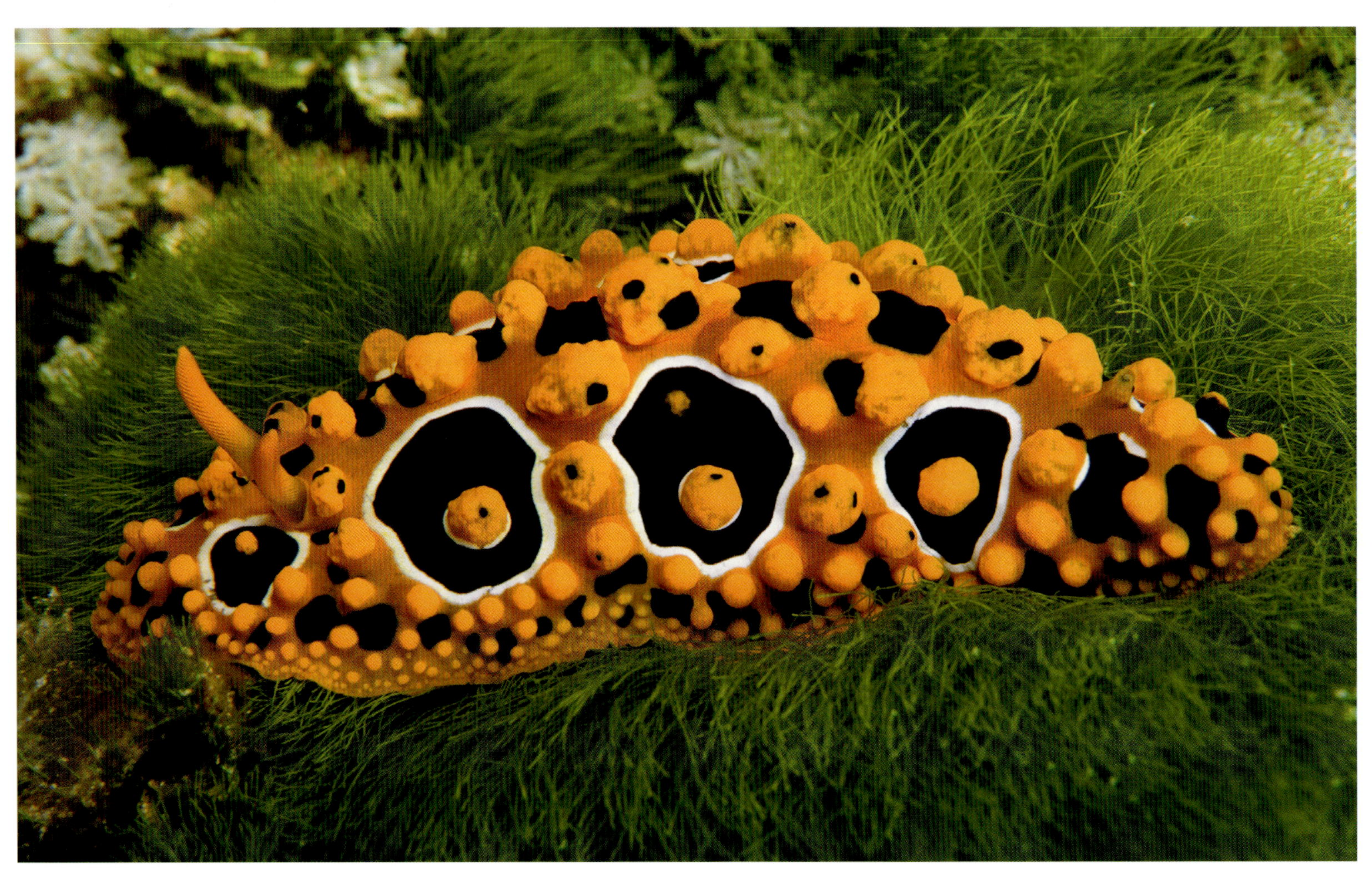

OCELLATED NUDIBRANCH

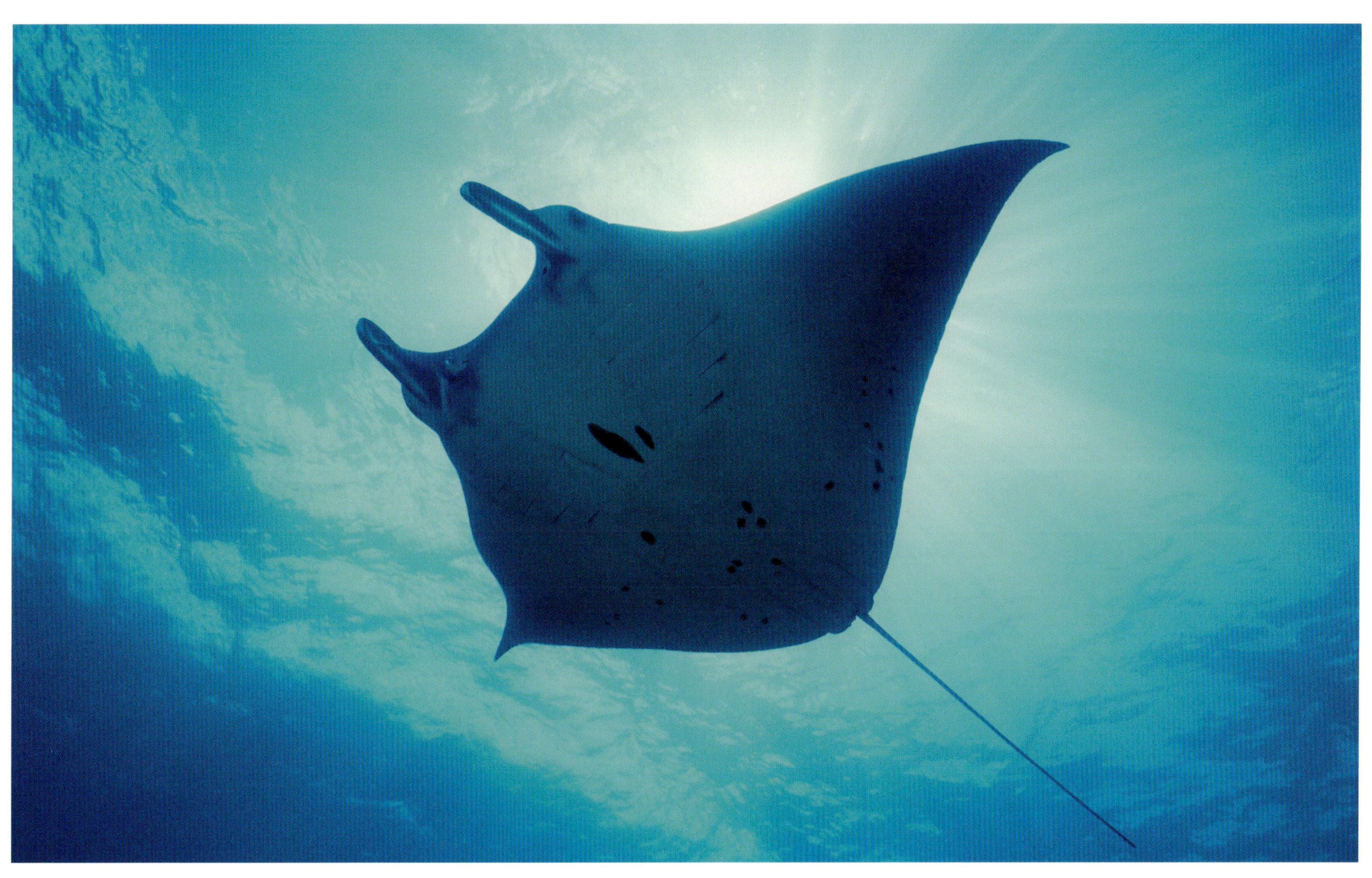

MANTA RAY

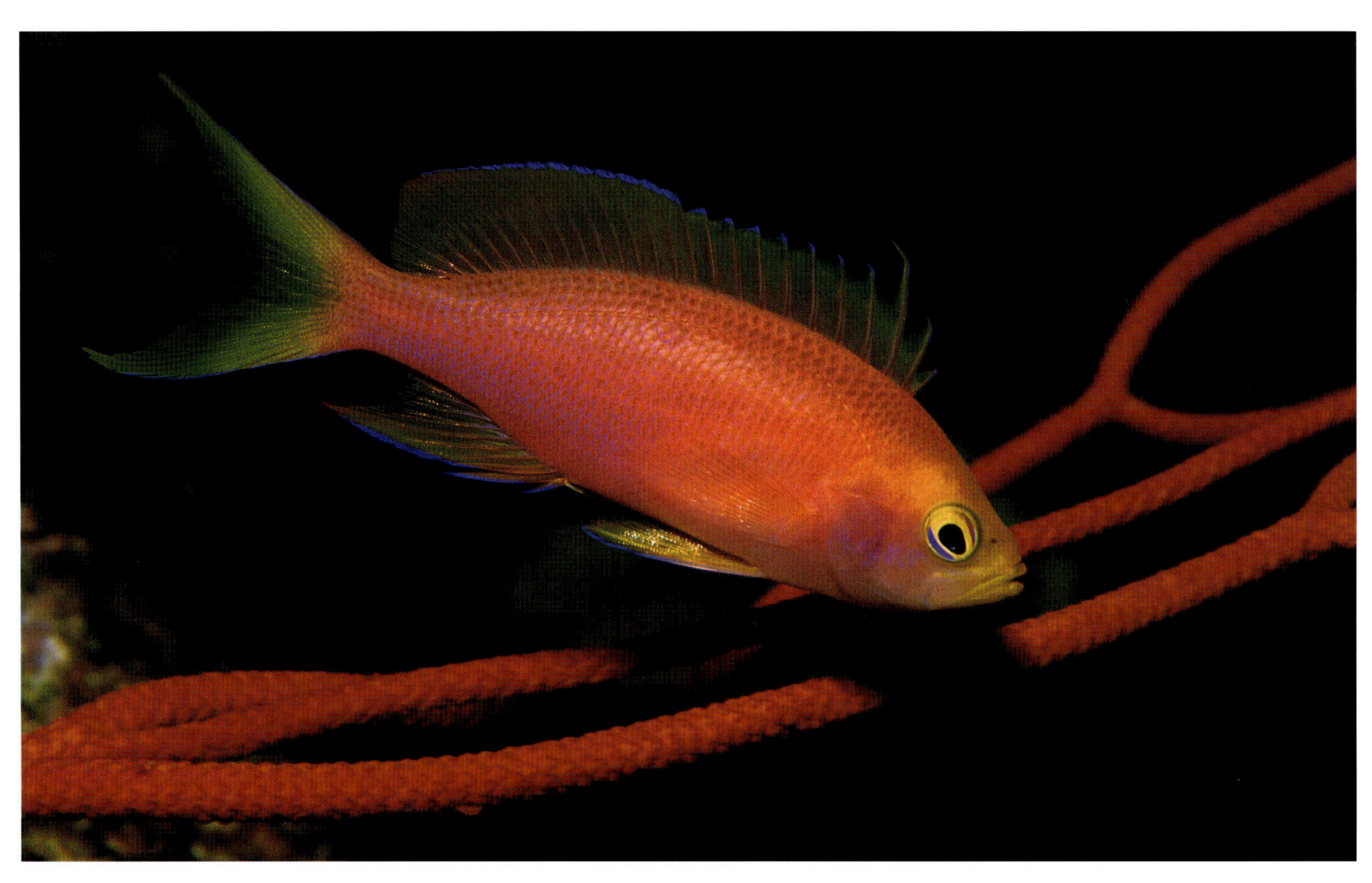

YELLOWTAIL BASSLET, FEMALE

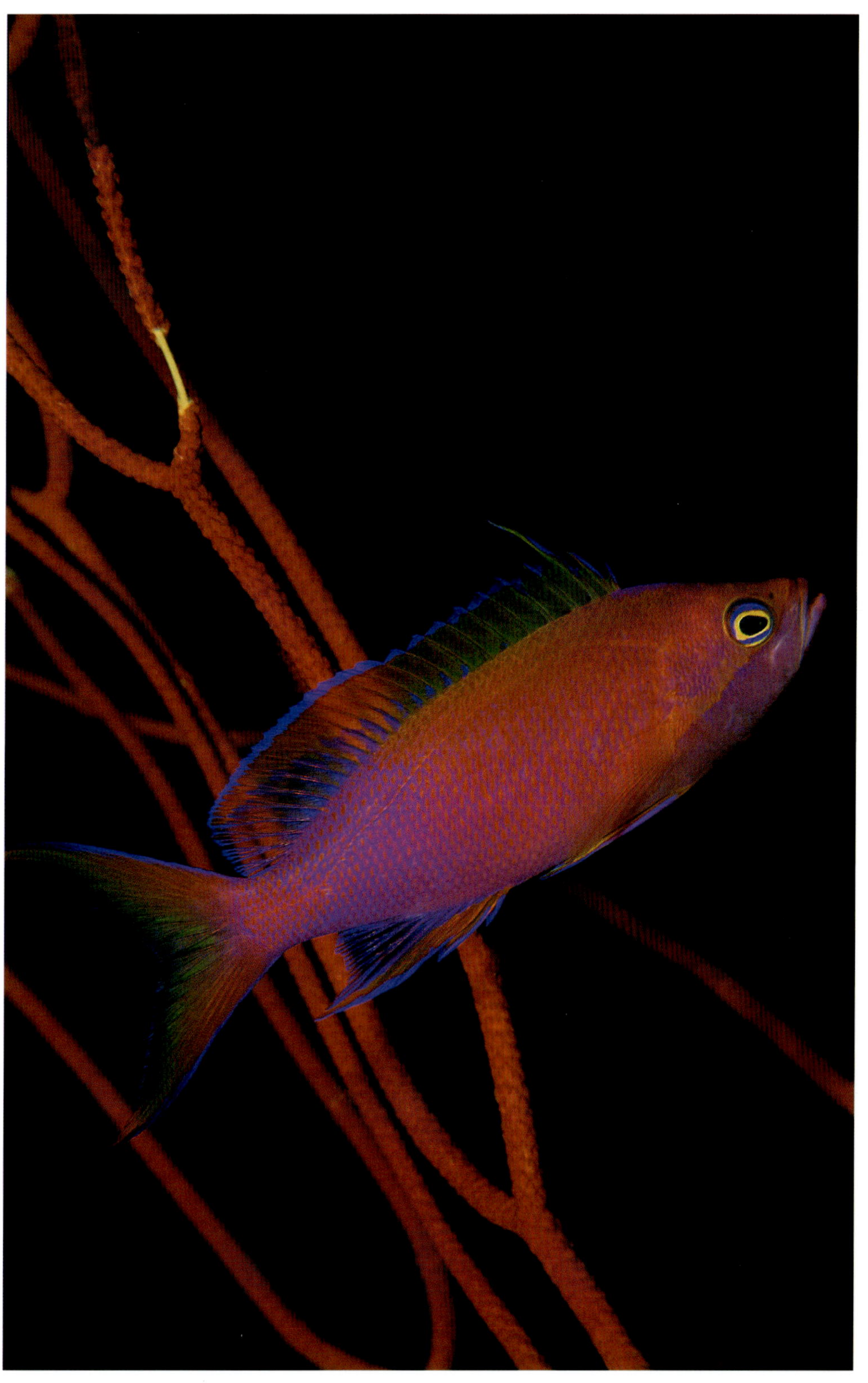

YELLOWTAIL BASSLET, MALE

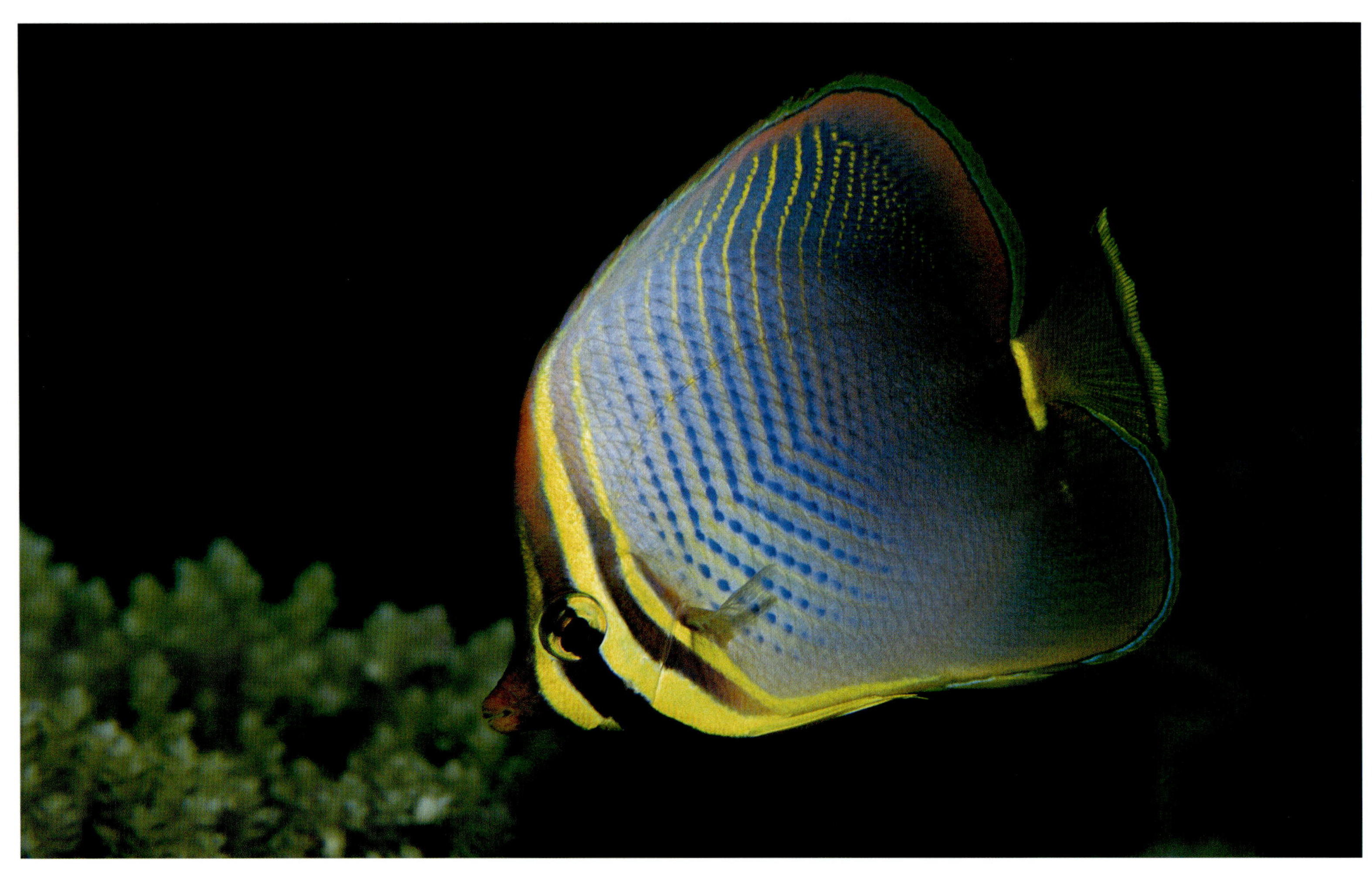

BARONESS BUTTERFLYFISH

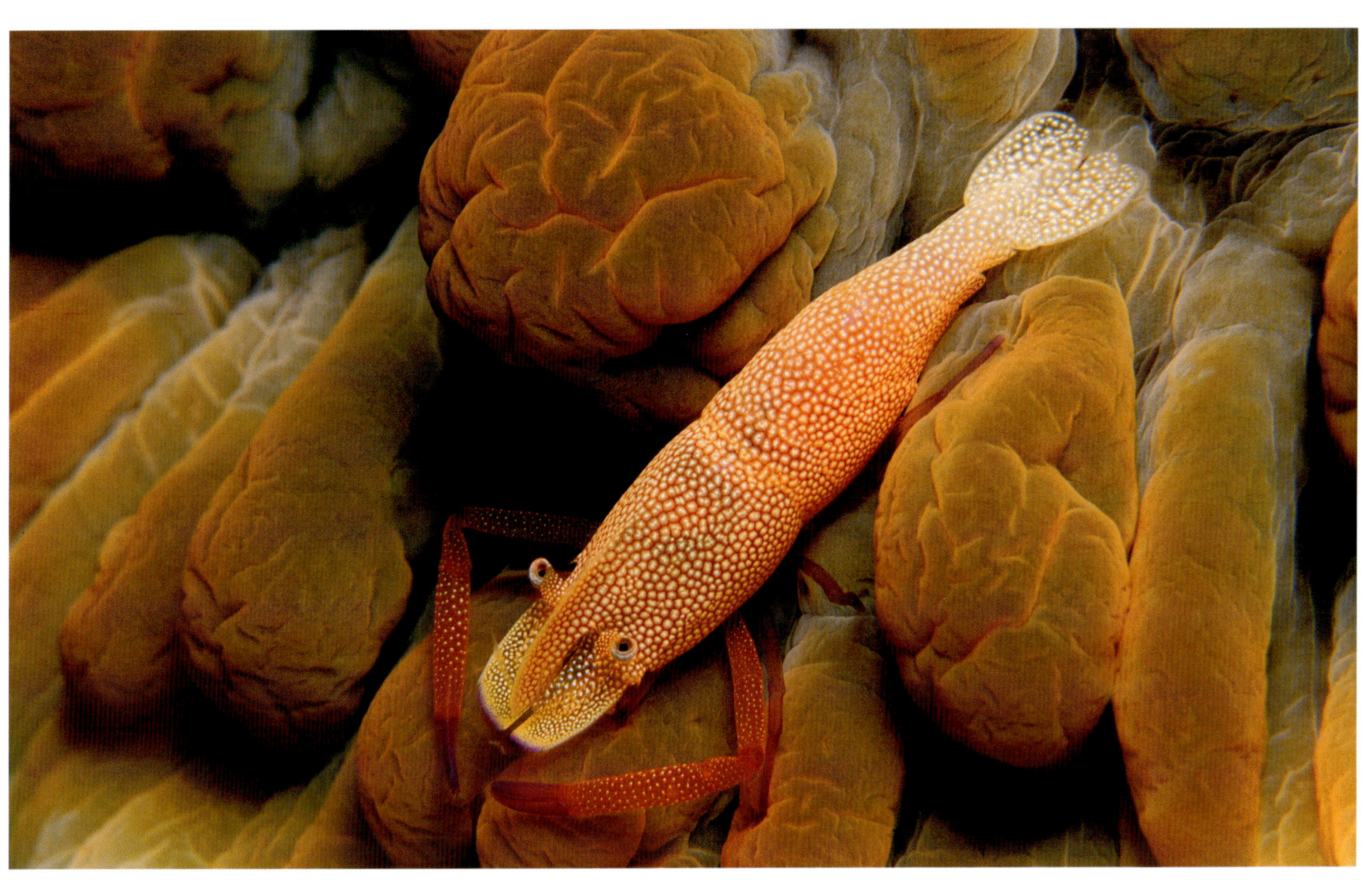

IMPERIAL SHRIMP ON DENDRODORID NUDIBRANCH

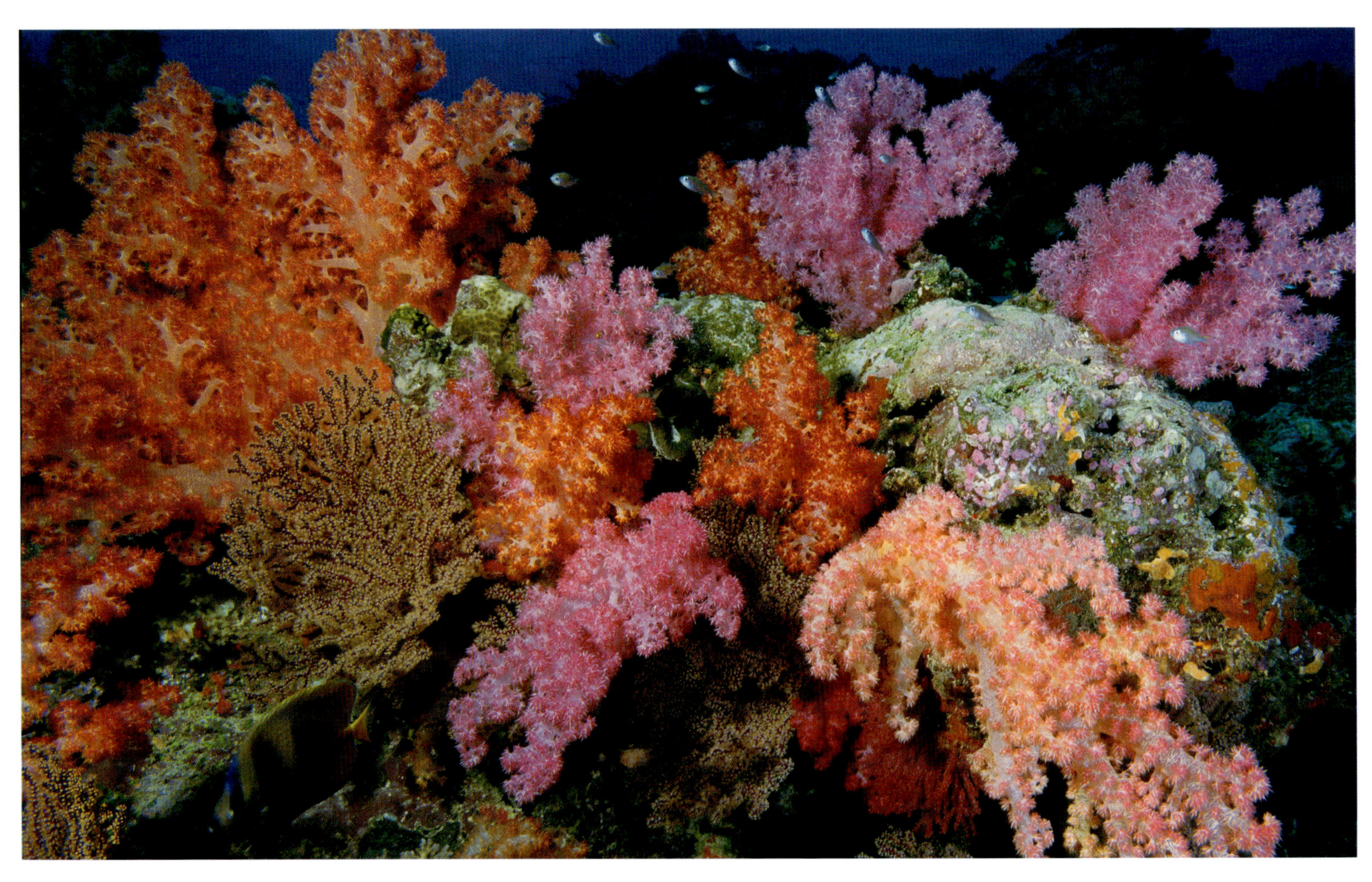

REEF WITH SOFT CORALS

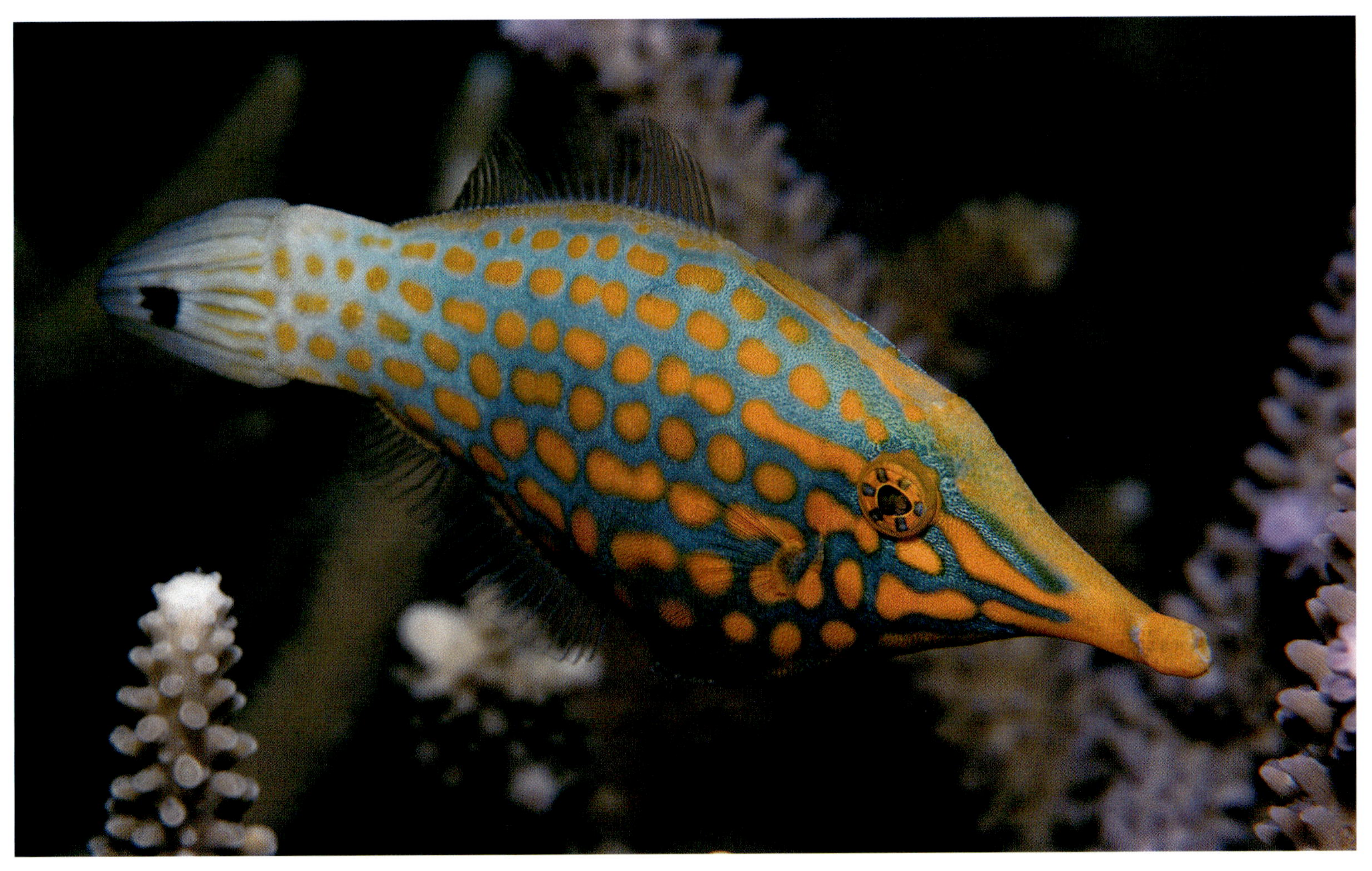

LONGNOSE FILEFISH

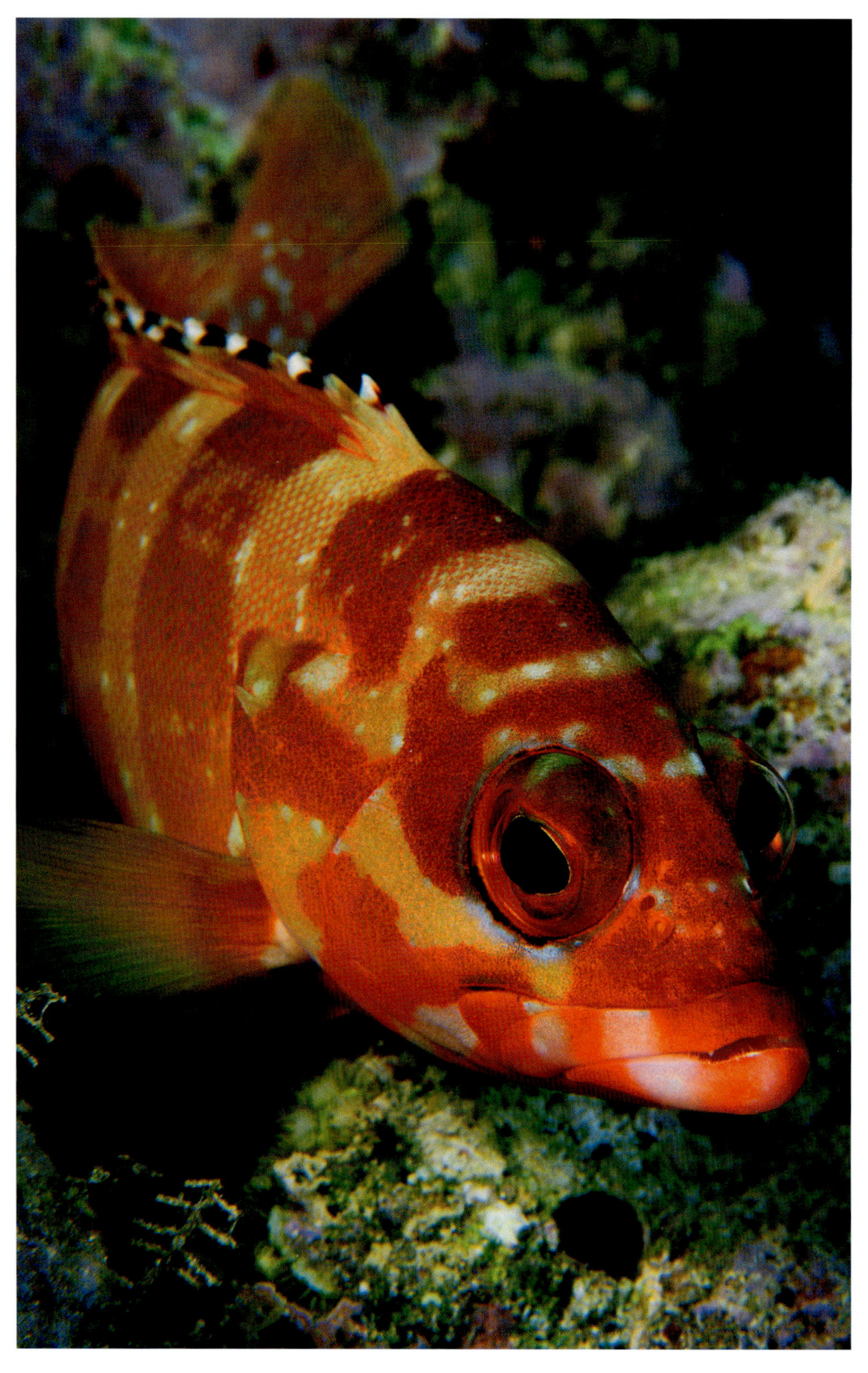

BANDED ROCK COD

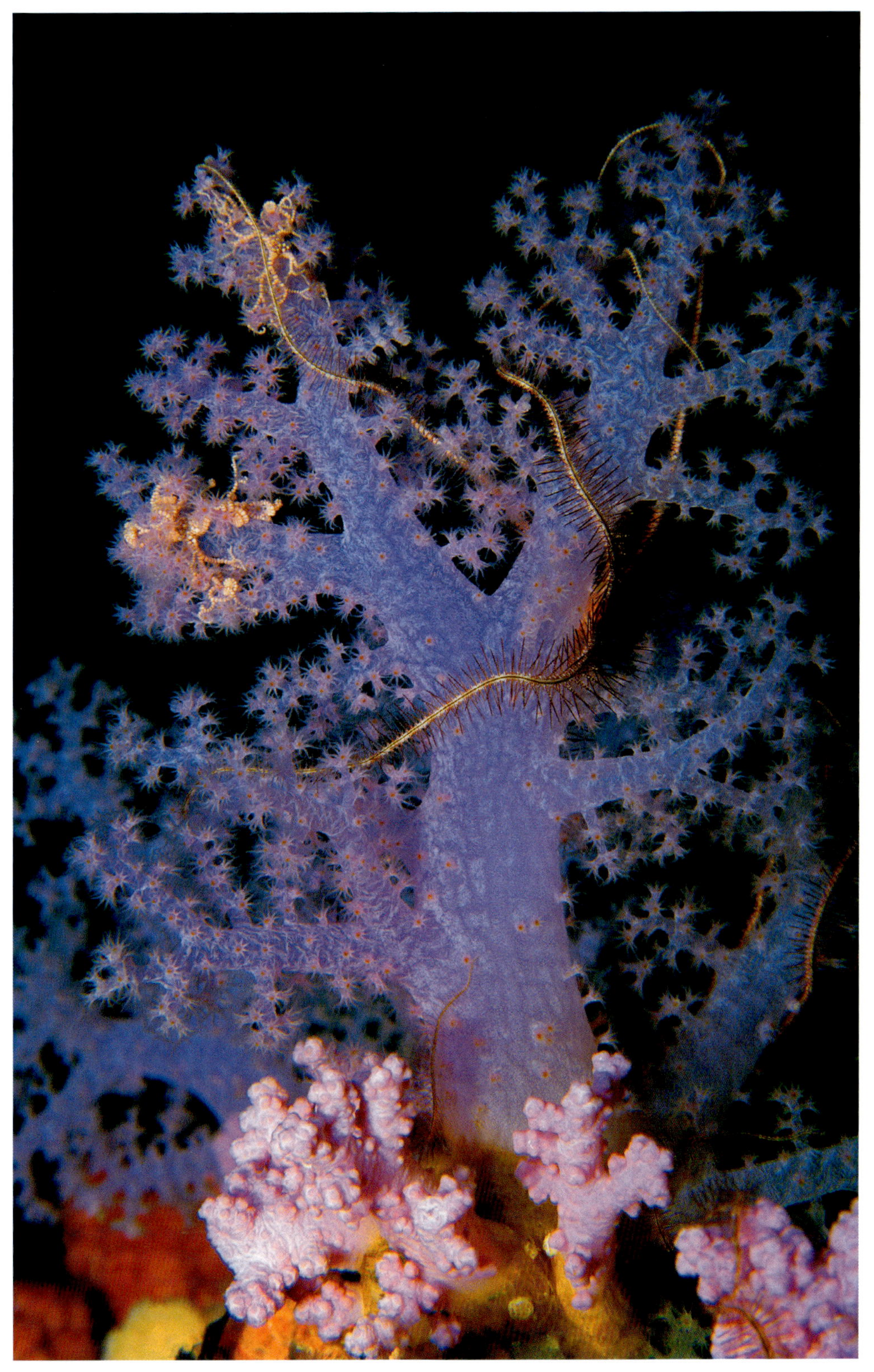

SOFT CORAL TREE

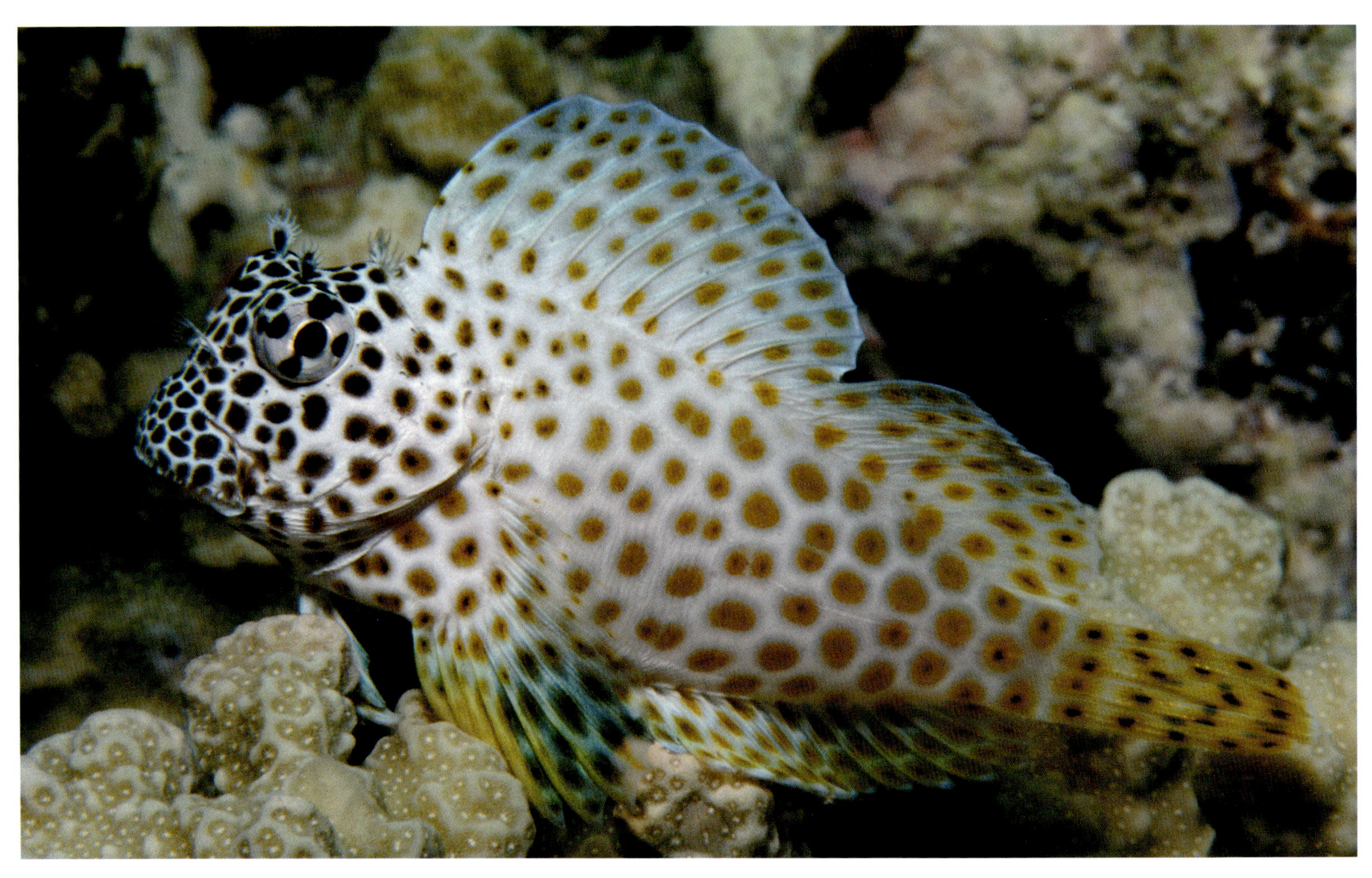

LEOPARD BLENNY

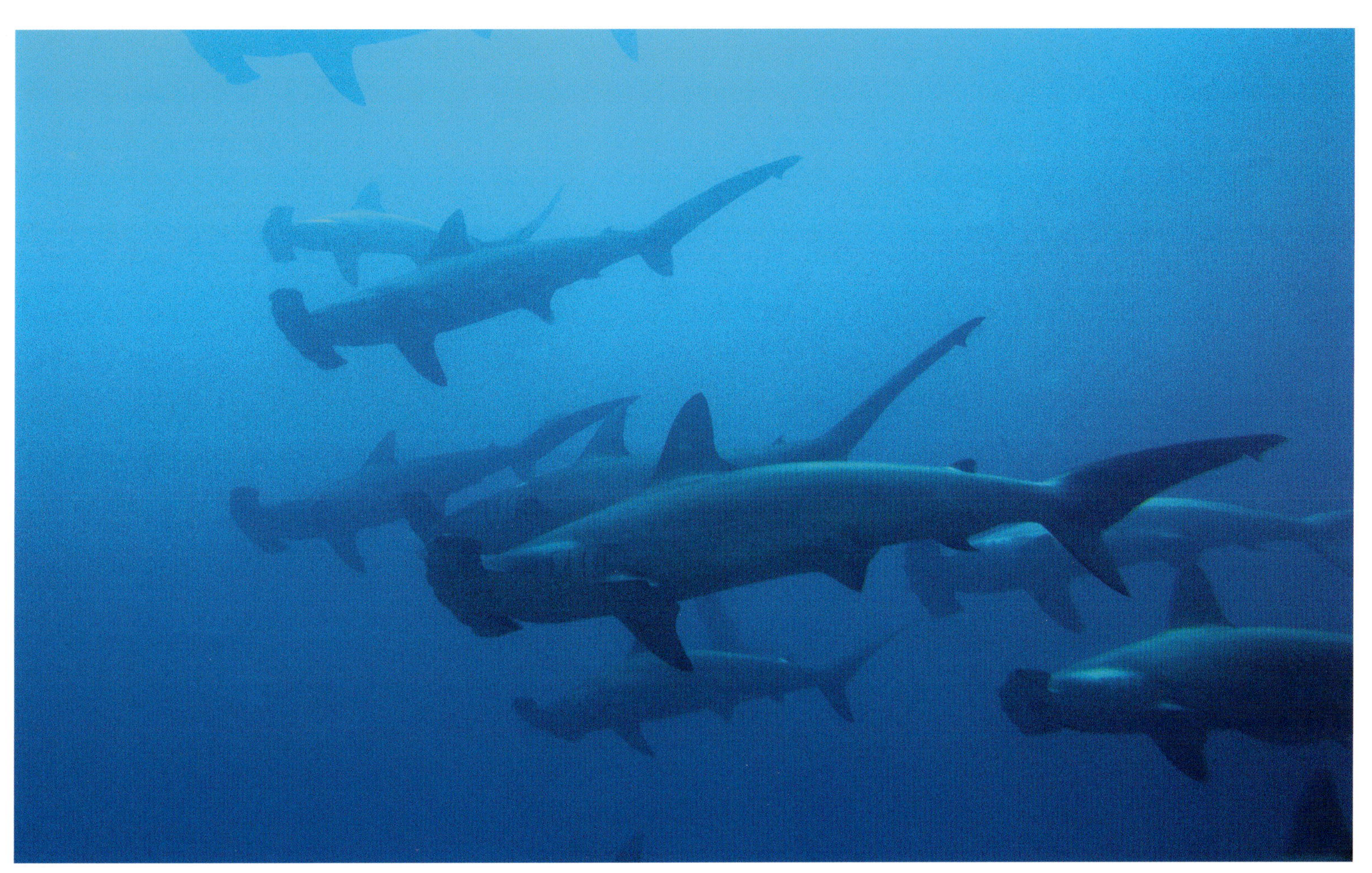

SCALLOPED HAMMERHEAD SHARKS

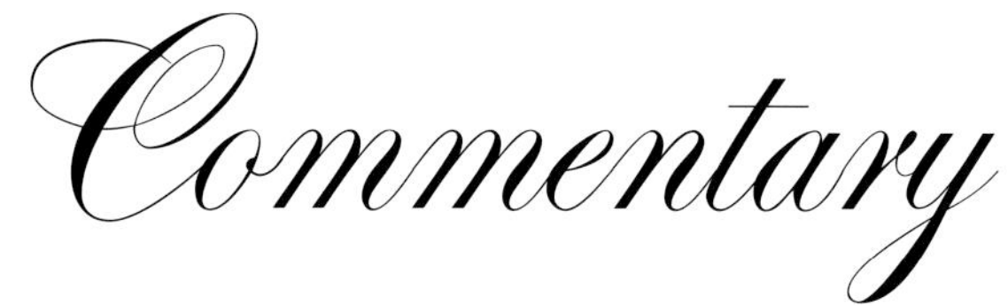

Commentary

TITLE PAGE: Clown Anemonefish, *Amphiprion percula,* Sulawesi Island, Indonesia

PAGE 2-3. Sunset, Palau Islands

PAGE 4-5. Caribbean Reef Squid, *Sepioteuthis sepiodea,* Bonaire, N.A.: These small squid are active nocturnal predators that feed in shallow waters of the reef. They, in turn, are a favorite food item for most larger reef predators such as grouper and sharks.

PAGE 6-7. Crown Jellyfish, *Cephea cephea,* Namena Island, Fiji: Juvenile jacks (fish) seek shelter amidst the nematocyst-armored crown jellyfish as it drifts through innerspace toward an undetermined destination.

PAGE 8. Squarespot Basslet, *Pseudanthias pleurotaenia,* Great White Wall, Fiji: This golden basslet can be found along sheer reef walls in deeper water, typically at depths below 25 m. This is the female of the species.

PAGE 9. Squarespot Basslet, *Pseudanthias pleurotaenia,* Great White Wall, Fiji: This incredible beauty is the male of the species. Members of the basslet family exhibit chromatic differences. The males have distinctly different colors than the females. They also maintain a harem of females within their territory. Should the male be removed, the dominant female in the harem will begin to change both color and sex. This amazing transformation may occur in as little as three weeks, according to some studies. The dominant male moves continuously, constantly corralling his females, in an effort to keep the harem together. The perpetual motion, coupled with its deepwater habitat, make it a difficult subject to photograph.

PAGE 10. Colemans Shrimp, *Periclimenes colemani,* Rinca Island, Indonesia: These delicate shrimp are only 2 cm. long. The female is the larger of the pair. They liv exclusively on the venomous Fire Urchin. This is a prime example of how life is stacked upon life on the coral reef. As they feed, the shrimp are escorted across the reef in an armored limo.

PAGE 11. Forster's Hawkfish, *Paracirrhites fosteri,* Namena Island, Fiji: The incredibly colorful hawkfish are carnivores that feed on small fish and invertebrates. To obtain their prey, the aptly named hawkfish "perch" motionless among the outermost branches of coral and scan the surrounding areas. Once a prey animal is detect ed, a small shrimp for example, the hawkfish swoops down on its victim with lightning speed. Forster's Hawkfish can reach a length of 20 cm.

PAGE 12. Polycerid Nudibranches, *Nembrotha kubaryana,* Father's Reef, Papua New Guinea: This is a mating pair of nudibranches. If you are reading to your children, you may want to stop now. All nudibranches are functional hermaphrodites (i.e., they possess male and female reproductive organs). They can mate with any other individual of their species. The everted genital organs are clearly shown in this image. Mating duration is variable and may range from seconds to over an hour, depending on the species. This pair remained together for less than a minute.

PAGE 13. Lined Nudibranch, *Nembrotha lineolata,* Sangiang Island, Indonesia: This specimen is in the process of laying eggs. Nudibranches typically lay their egg masses in a spiral or circular pattern. Whenever I have observed the egg-laying process, the nudibranches have deposited their egg mass by moving in a counterclockwise spiral. This species is approximately 5 cm. in length.

PAGE 14. Stonefish, *Synanceia verrucosa,* New Britain Island, Papua New Guinea: This is the face of a Stonefish. It is as venomous as it is ugly. A puncture wound from the dorsal spine of this sedentary animal will cause excruciating pain. Fatalities have been reported. The Stonefish in this photo was taken at a depth of 20 m. Note the brilliant colors. Those specimens found in shallower water typically have far less color and look exactly like a piece of coral rubble. THEY WON'T MOVE UNTIL YOU TOUCH THEM OR STEP ON THEM! In other words, be very careful where you put your hand or foot when you're diving or wading near Indo-Pacific reefs. They can reach a size of 40 - 50 cm.

PAGE 15. Longlure Frogfish, *Antennarius multiocellatus,* Bonaire, N.A.: I suppose you could say we're in the "ugly face" portion of the book, but to a female frogfish, this piscine predator may be a real prince. I'll tell you more about this amazing member of the anglerfish family later in the book.

PAGE 16. Stargazer, *Uranoscopus bicinctus,* Sumbawa Island, Indonesia: Is this just the coolest face you've ever seen? There are many species of Stargazers. This par icular species inhabits sandy, gravel substrates where it lies on the bottom, its body fully covered except for the mouth and eyes, and waits to ambush unsuspecting rey such as small fish. The best time to observe a Stargazer in action is late evening or after dark. Marine life predators have devised numerous strategies to capture rey. On the coral reef, nothing is more efficient than extremely camouflaged fish that remain motionless until their prey ventures too close. Then, in classic ambush tyle, the predator (in this case the Stargazer) lunges upward. At the same time, it rapidly opens its mouth, creating a vacuum, and literally inhales its victim.

AGE 17. Balloonfish, *Diodon holocanthus*, Bonaire, N.A.: Some time ago, while on assignment in Bonaire, I noticed the Balloonfish population had...well, it had allooned. Balloonfish (15 cm. in length) were tucked into numerous nooks and crannies in the reef. The cute, little critters were everywhere. One was bedded down nside an abandoned bivalve shell. Another was hiding under a submerged palm frond. Having numerous subjects to choose from, I selected a Balloonfish with attiude. It was lounging in an open recess between two sections of hard coral. A cleaning goby was roving around its eye. It must have felt good because the repeated ash of my strobe did nothing to dissuade the tiny Balloonfish from abandoning its "cleaning station."

AGE 18. Creole Fish, *Paranthias furcifer*, Bonaire, N.A.: Many of the Creole Fish in Bonaire harbor parasitic isopods. Isopods are crustaceans. The attached ymothoid isopod pictured is a large female. Smaller male isopods also reside in and around the mouth of the Creole Fish. Oddly enough, these circumtropical paraites tend to favor different fish species in different regions of the world.

AGE 19. Scalloped Hammerhead, *Sphyrna lewini*, Wolf Island, Galapagos: This magnificent shark is one of the reef's apex predators. It can reach lengths up to 4 ı. and preys on various fish species. Squid may also be an important part of its diet. Believe it or not, these sharks are terribly shy. Any scuba bubbles or sudden novements will instantly frighten them away. Scalloped Hammerheads are often observed during the day traveling in schools. Some of these impressive congregaions can number in the hundreds. Watching them swim by with the accentuated movement of their heads from side to side is a scene straight out of a science fiction novie. It is always a thrill to see these incredible animals. And make no mistake: sharks are attacked and killed by humans far, far more than humans are attacked by harks. The number of sharks taken by man each year is staggering. The most regretful aspect of the shark fishing industry is how wasteful and unnecessary it is.

AGE 20. Ghost Snake Eel, *Brachysomophis cirrhocellus*, Mabul Island, Malaysia: This is another of the ambush predators that resides in the sand adjacent to the eef. Anything that gets too close to this voracious predator will be consumed. The Ghost Snake Eel is about 60 cm. long and is infrequently encountered on shallow eefs (always in the sand) throughout the Indo-Pacific. The fleshy appendages lining the mouth obscure an impressive display of dental work. They are another of ature's great oddities.

AGE 21. Lizardfish, *Synodus variegatus*, Namena Island, Fiji: The ambush took place with a sudden burst of incredible power and lightning speed. The 30 cm. izardfish had procured its meal in a fraction of a second. Summoning forth all its learned skills as a predator, it had flawlessly performed the task with deadly precion. The incident appeared violent and brutal, as if the act were perpetrated out of anger or hatred. The victim in this instance was the False Cleaner, *Aspidontus taeiatus*. Indeed, an interesting twist of fate. How many times, I wondered, had this 10 cm. "con artist" played out its role on the reef? Mimicking the Cleaner Wrasse, ne False Cleaner (a blenny) entices a host fish into the area for cleaning services. But instead of cleaning the host fish, it bites off scales and small pieces of flesh, nereby obtaining its meal at the expense of another unsuspecting fish. On this day, however, the tables were turned on the hapless blenny; the deceiver had become ne deceived. Perhaps the Lizardfish was getting revenge or perhaps it was just business as usual on the reef. Predator capturing prey - a simple act of nature.

AGE 22. Sailfin Leaf Fish, *Taenianotus triacanthus*, Wakaya Island, Fiji: The Leaf Fish uses camouflage to ambush small fish. It reaches a length of about 12-15 cm. have known the specimen in this photo for several years. It stays under a reef ledge along the top edge of a sheer coral wall. When the tides or the time of day are ight (usually late afternoon, just before sunset), it moves from beneath the ledge and takes up position on top of a plate coral. As it rests on the plate coral, it sways ently back and forth in the currents, much like a paper-thin leaf. Dozens of centimeter-long purple basslets constantly swarm around this area, so the Leaf Fish has a onstant food supply. Despite being completely exposed, it simply looks like a part of the reef.

AGE 23. Lionfish, *Pterois volitans*, Derawan Island, Indonesia: Lionfish are reef predators that are quite common throughout the Indo-Pacific. While their venmous dorsal spines merit caution from divers, they do not pose a serious threat like the Stonefish. Lionfish are both beautiful and inquisitive. I have had them follow ne around the reef like puppy dogs for no apparent reason. I once spent 15 minutes watching one of them stare at its reflection in my camera port. And I have oticed that when they are lying motionless on the reef structure, they do a wonderful job of mimicking crinoids (feather stars). This close-up is of one of my photo ssistants who followed me around the reef for three hours one evening. Accustomed to divers, this ingenious Lionfish had learned to feed by utilizing the illuminaon from diver's lights. In fact, every time I would try to take a photograph of a macro subject (small fish and shrimp), my dive buddy would dart in and consume it! olding the light made things a bit tricky because the Lionfish would hover just below my hand as I swam along. I tried to be careful, but eventually one of its dorsal pines punctured the side of my hand. Moral of the story: Never let a Lionfish assist you with underwater photography.

AGE 24. Yellow Sentinel Goby, *Cryptocentrus cinctus*, Mabul Island, Malaysia: The family of Sentinel Gobies has somehow managed to find servants to do the eavy lifting. The colorful goby stands guard outside of its burrow while the Alpheid shrimp does the house cleaning. During daylight hours, the shrimp constantly removes pebbles and sand from the burrow. Whenever the shrimp is outside its burrow, the goby is outside the entrance standing watch. The shrimp always maintains contact with the goby while outside the burrow. One twitch of the goby's tail and the shrimp scurries back into its hole. Usually the goby follows close behind. This odd couple can be found in the sand/rubble areas of the reef. They represent one of the classic examples of symbiotic behavior in the reef community.

PAGE 25. Caribbean Reef Shark, *Carcharhinus perezi*, Nassau, Bahamas: The ultimate enforcers on the reef, these bruisers constantly patrol the drop-off. If an opportunity to feed arises, they won't miss it. These sharks are known to be aggressive and bold. Despite their reputation, they rarely display aggression toward divers. As with most sharks, if food is introduced into the water or spearfishing is taking place, it can spark a dramatic change in their behavior.

PAGE 26. Orange-Fin Anemonefish, *Amphiprion chrysopterus*, Namena Island, Fiji: This Orange-Fin Anemonefish has found sanctuary inside the oral groove of the anemone, *Heteractis aurora*. The adorable little Orange-Fin was a juvenile when I first found it. At the time, it fit in the anemone's oral groove with ease. With any provocation, it would dive into the opening and then poke its head out just enough to see what was going on. The following year when I visited the site, the anemonefish and its host were still there. The anemonefish had almost tripled in size and could no longer fit inside the oral groove. It was almost larger than the entire anemone.

PAGE 27. Flathead, *Thysanophrys sp.*, Sumbawa Island, Indonesia: Death is never far away on the reef. In this photo, taken at night, a Flathead (an elongate fish) with only its face exposed is waiting in the sand to ambush its prey. As I readied my camera to photograph the Flathead, a cardinalfish swam into the frame. I took a quick shot of the pair. It was the last photo ever taken of the cardinalfish. The attack was so quick and so overwhelming, yet it barely rippled the sand.

PAGE 28. Unicornfish Surgeonfish, *Naso brevirostris*, Namena Island, Fiji: This photo was taken at night while the surgeonfish was at rest on the reef. During the day this bizarre species swims along drop-offs, feeding on zooplankton. It can reach a length of 60 cm.

PAGE 29. Blotched Bigeye, *Heteropriacanthus cruentatus*, Mabul Island, Malaysia: The Bigeye is a secretive species that spends its days secluded in caverns or under ledges. At night, it comes out to feed on zooplankton.

PAGE 30. Chain Moray, *Echidna catenata*, Bonaire, N.A.: "Cleaning stations" are the health spas of the coral reef. These stations are specific locations on the reef where fish and invertebrates can go to get parasites removed and/or wounds cleaned. For example, this Chain Moray is having small parasites and sloughed mucous (breakfast of champions) removed by a Lysmata Shrimp. This is a highly ritualized behavior and may last for many minutes. Normally, shrimp is on the menu for a variety of fish or cephalopods. However, during the cleaning ritual, a certain bond is formed between the shrimp and its host. Fish that desire to be cleaned typically arrive at the cleaning station and will assume a relaxed or non-threatening position. Their body language may also include a shift in color (especially groupers). Once cleaning is initiated, the cleaner will enter the mouth of its host if necessary, apparently without fear of being consumed. Both parties benefit from this interaction and the host fish seems to thoroughly enjoy the experience. Sharks, groupers, mantas, morays, and most other reef fish are cleaned on a routine basis. In the Atlantic and the Caribbean, various species of shrimp and gobies are the primary cleaners. In the Indo-Pacific, various species of shrimp and wrasses perform the service. Numerous studies have shown that this relationship is vitally important to the overall health of the reef.

PAGE 31. Javan Moray, *Gymnothorax javanicus*, Wakaya Island, Fiji: This giant moray is 2.5 meters in length. It was a big `un. It is being cleaned by a very trusting Banded Coral Shrimp. There were occasions when this shrimp was so far down the eel's throat that it was barely visible. This location was the entrance to the massive eel's lair. At the entrance, there was an entire family of shrimp. The Javan Moray was their primary client. Believe me, there was enough for everyone.

PAGE 32. Juvenile Regal Surgeonfish, *Paracanthurus hepatus*, Rabaul, Papua New Guinea: They are about 4 cm. long. In this photo, they are using the coral for shelter. Every time I approached, they would slip deep into the coral in unison.

PAGE 33. Reef Scorpionfish, *Scorpaenopsis sp.*, Namena Island, Fiji: Typical of the reef's ambush predators, the Scorpionfish is well camouflaged and lies in wait for its prey. When a small fish or invertebrate ventures too close, the Scorpionfish attacks quickly. It is found throughout the Indo-Pacific at various depths and reaches length of 30 cm. Its dorsal spines are venomous and can inflict painful wounds.

PAGE 34-35. Mushroom Coral, *Fungia fungites*, Namena Island, Fiji: This beautiful disc-shaped, hard coral is not attached to the substrate. It looks like a colorful mushroom cap laying loose on the bottom. The mouth is shown in the center of the photo. The depth range is 10-20 m. Photo by GKB.

PAGE 36. Gorgonian Fan, *Acabaria sp.*, Witu Islands, Papua New Guinea: These delicate fans reside on deeper reef slopes and walls.

PAGE 37. Tridacna Clam Siphon, *Tridacna sp.*, North Astrolabe Reef, Fiji: This is a close-up of the siphon of a Tridacna Clam. Tridacna Clams are the largest bivalves in the world. The color seen in this image is due to the zooxanthellae embedded in the clam. These giants can grow to hundreds of pounds and attain lengths f over 1 m. That, my friend, is a lot of chowder.

AGE 38. Soft Coral Tentacles, *Sarcophyton sp.*, North Astrolabe Reef, Fiji: In this photo, miniature polyps of this soft coral species are actively feeding.

AGE 39. Ornate Ghost Pipefish, *Solenostomus paradoxus*, Komodo Island, Indonesia: This strange, little fish (10 cm.) is living proof that aliens live among us. Not ally...but can you imagine a more bizarre animal than this? This weird pipefish is relatively common on coastal reefs throughout Indonesia and New Guinea. owever, being a master in the art of camouflage, it's almost impossible to find. Once the Ghost Pipefish finds a suitable crinoid or soft coral, it can remain hidden mongst the crinoid arms or coral branches, in the same general location, for long periods of time. Observant divemasters who frequent these waters continuously ird-dog" the reef until they find these ornate ghosts. When the photographer arrives on site, the divemaster can escort them directly to the location. To a wildlife hotographer, a good guide is priceless.
ll the fish/invertebrates photographed in this book are photographed using strobe light (flash photography). In other words, divers do not see these vivid colors nderwater without some kind of artificial light source, thereby making the Ghost Pipefish all but invisible to the unaided eye. The spectacular, vibrant colors of this ecimen were unknown to me until the film was developed in the U.S. weeks later.

AGE 40. Peacock Flounder Eye, *Bothus lunatus*, Bonaire, N.A.: This wily predator is mostly covered in sand except for that amazing eye which acts like a eriscope, always in search of the next meal.

AGE 41. Crocodile Fish Eye, *Cymbacephalus beauforti*, Mabul Island, Malaysia: If there is a more unique eye in the animal kingdom, then I haven't seen it. The rocodile Fish can reach over 50 cm. in length. It is a well camouflaged predator right down to that amazing eye. It is found throughout the Indo-Pacific on shallow- medium-depth reefs.

AGE 42. Soft Coral Feeding, *Dendronephtya sp.*, Ruang Island, Indonesia: Soft corals are among the most beautiful invertebrates on the reef. They are represented y a variety of vivid colors and are found in current-driven reef environments. This image shows the feeding polyps. Note the eight tentacles on each polyp.

AGE 43. Fringefin Goby, *Eviota sp.* on Hard Coral, Rabaul, Papua New Guinea: As I was taking a close-up, detailed photo of the hard coral, this beautiful goby pped into view just as I was pressing the shutter release.

AGE 44. Crinoid Arms, *Oxycomanthus sp.*, Komodo Island, Indonesia: Crinoids are also known as feather stars. These beautiful echinoderms are best viewed at ight when many of them are out on top of the reef collecting plankton with their incredibly designed arms. The number of arms varies with the species. Members of is genus may have as many as 100 arms.

AGE 45. Umbellate Tree Coral, *Dendronephthya sp.*, Banta Island, Indonesia: This distinctive coral looks very much like a colorful stalk of broccoli. It is observed areas having strong currents.

AGE 46. Orange Ball Anemone, *Pseudocorynactis caribbeorum*, Bonaire, N.A.: This gorgeous species isn't a true anemone, but belongs to the coralimorphs. By day, remains hidden in crevices and under ledges in the reef. After dark, it unfolds, exposing translucent tentacles to feed. Bright orange balls are found at the tip of ach tentacle. Once the beam of a light (dive light or strobe light) hits the Orange Ball Anemone, it will begin to retract its tentacles. The tentacles actually seem to ither as the unusual invertebrate begins to close. The body wall folds around and over the tentacles forming a protective dome.

AGE 47. Sabellid Tube Worm, Family-Sabellidae, Komodo Island, Indonesia: Sabellid worms live in tubes on the reef. The only part of the worm that is exposed is e head which is an ornate spiral of feathery tentacles used for filter feeding and respiration. This photograph is an extreme close-up showing the outermost tip of e feeding/respiratory apparatus. Only on the reef can "worm parts" appear so artistic. Sabellids are also known as Fan Worms. I've been a marine life photographer/ quatic biologist for the past 25 years. So I ask myself, "Is worm parts the best you can come up with?"

AGE 48. Parrotfish Fin, *Scarus sp.*, Namena Island, Fiji: This is the exquisite, pectoral fin detail of a Parrotfish. It was photographed at night.

AGE 49. Coral Trout, *Cephalopholis miniata*, Witu Island, Papua New Guinea: The Coral Trout is undoubtedly one of the most outstandingly colored fish on the ef. The question is, why? It seems a predator such as the Coral Trout (actually a species of grouper) that relies on stealth and concealment would favor a cryptic olor scheme, not one that screams for attention.
his species is a hunter that lurks in the shadows of reef ledges and crevices. It is a predominantly crepuscular species, feeding at twilight and early dawn. During this me, the lower aspects of the coral reef are in darkness while the waters overhead are contrastingly bright. The grouper uses this unique lighting situation to silhou- tte its prey against the lighter blue water above. Meanwhile, the smaller prey fish cannot detect the presence of a killer waiting patiently in the dark waters only a

few meters below. Because light is significantly filtered as it penetrates water, the bright reds and sky blues we see on the surface quickly fade to muted, cryptic hues amidst the reef's recesses. The Coral Trout is, in fact, very well adapted to its environment. In other words, the colors red, brown, and black all tend to look the same at depth. Thus, the better question may be, why not?

PAGE 50 - 51. Aerial Scene, New Britain Island, Papua New Guinea: It was a perfect, cloudless day in paradise. Our chopper had lifted off and we were headed ou over the reefs surrounding New Britain Island for some aerial photography of our dive sites. Through the headphones I heard, "Greg, better get those shots now, the helo's not running real well." Luuceee, you got sun splaining to do. You know those times when you have to ask a question you don't really want an answer to? "What does that mean?" I asked with fearful curiosity. "It just means the engine needs a bit of maintenance and we might not be able to stay up as long. No worries, mate." I said, "Oh, I'm not worried." Worried wasn't exactly the proper word choice. There's something about the phrase, "we may not be able to stay up as long" that can humble a man, especially when a pilot flying a helicopter is the one saying it. So, off across the reefs we flew, with me hurriedly photographing the gorgeous scenery and frantically praying at the same time. No worries, mate.

PAGE 52 - 53. Flamingo Tongue, *Cyphoma gibbosum*, Bonaire, N.A.: This stunning specimen feeds on gorgonian soft corals. Typical of the ovulids, its mantle fans out over its shell. In other words, the spots you see are a part of the animal, not part of the shell. The Flamingo Tongue reaches a length of only 4 cm. It is relatively common throughout the Caribbean.

PAGE 54. Vase Sponge, *Callyspongia sp.*, Bonaire, N.A.: One of the trademarks of Bonairian reefs are the beautiful purple Vase Sponges and large, purple Tube Sponges.

PAGE 55. Keeltail Needlefish, *Playbelone argalus*, Bonaire, N.A.: Needlefish are common inhabitants of shallow reef areas. They stay just beneath the water's surface feeding on small baitfish. They reach a maximum length of 45-50 cm. This pair was photographed at night just under the water's surface.

PAGE 56. Blackbar Soldierfish, *Myripristis jacobus*, Bonaire, N.A.: This secretive species is often sheltered in crevices or under reef ledges by day. During this time it can often be found in small schools. At night, it moves out on to the open reef to feed on zooplankton. The large eyes are good indicators of its feeding and habitat preferences. Photo by GKB.

PAGE 57. Pedersons Shrimp, *Periclimenes pedersonii*, Bonaire, N.A.: Only 2 cm. in length, this delicate shrimp is one of the reef's most important invertebrates. It is one of the primary "cleaner" species on Caribbean reefs. In this photo, it is perched atop the strikingly colored tentacles of a giant sea anemone.

PAGE 58. Juvenile Queen Angelfish, *Holacanthus ciliaris*, Bonaire, N.A.: The Queen Angel is arguably the most beautiful fish species in the Atlantic/Caribbean basin. This gorgeous juvenile is only about 8 cm. long. As juveniles, they are typically shy and move amongst the shadows of reef crevices.

PAGE 59. Mantis Shrimp, *Odontodactylus scyallarus*, Bonaire, N.A.: In this book, I've tried to show you some of the most unusual and some of the most beautiful animals on the coral reef. None of them is more "out of this world" than the Mantis Shrimp. It lives in holes within the reef rubble. It usually moves about at night, but will, on occasion, leave its burrow during daylight hours. This amazing crustacean is also known as "the thumbsplitter" because of its powerful raptor-like claws. In this photo, these intimidating weapons are folded into the body much like those of a Praying Mantis. If a small fish or your finger (or other body part) gets too close, the mantis can extend its claws with lightning speed to subdue its prey or seriously damage the offending body part. From its burrow, those bizarre, alien eyes rotate 360 degrees on turret-like stalks, always on the lookout for predators or potential prey. Within the eyes, there are dark flecks that are constantly moving about This species ranges from 8-12 cm. in length. In the Indo-Pacific, there are some species that can reach lengths of 25 cm. The Mantis Shrimp is painfully shy and has usually disappeared into its burrow long before it has been observed. For this reason, photographers must approach the burrow cautiously to have any chance of getting a good photo.

PAGE 60. Longlure Frogfish, *Antennarius multiocellatus*, Bonaire, N.A.: This island is one of the few islands in the Caribbean where frogfish may actually be considered a common species. In Bonaire, I have photographed them in a variety of colors. These unusual anglerfish are voracious predators. On a dive years ago, I observed a dead frogfish next to a sponge. It had attempted to swallow another reef fish larger than itself and had apparently choked to death as a result. If these extremely we camouflaged fish were two meters long, no one would ever dive in Bonaire. Fortunately, they top out at a length of approximately 20 cm. While there seem to be plenty of them on the reefs, they are, nonetheless, extremely difficult to find. However, the local divemasters always seem to know where a few specimens are located. They're the best bet for finding frogfish. The importance of a guide familiar with the reef is a theme that is repeated throughout this book.

Note the pectoral fins of the frogfish on your left (male). These fins have been modified to allow the frogfish to slowly walk along the reef. The larger female is to the right. Like all anglerfish, frogfish have a modified dorsal spine they can twitch up and down. There is a fleshy lure at the tip of the spine that is used to attract prey. This "fishing lure" is concealed against the body when not in use. Photo by GKB.

PAGE 61. Bullseye Lobster, *Enoplomeopus holthuisi*, Bonaire, N.A.: This is an extremely colorful, nocturnal lobster that resides beneath coral ledges or in deep crevices. At night, it emerges from its lair, but never ventures too far from its den. It is very wary and elusive. Any light source will cause it to promptly retire to its hideaway.

PAGE 62 - 63. Hermit Crab, *Trizopagurus strigatus*, Mabul Island, Malaysia: The flattened body of this unusual hermit crab conveniently fits into the abandoned shells of cone snails.

PAGE 64. Western Clownfish, *Amphiprion ocellaris*, Mabul Island, Malaysia: Clownfish are popular because they're cute, colorful fish. Anemonefish (including the clownfish) all share a very close symbiotic bond with their host anemones. Removed from its host, the anemonefish generally does not survive. These energetic fish will spend their days luxuriating and frolicking amidst the stinging tentacles of the anemone without getting stung. It looks as if they're thoroughly enjoying themselves. How is this possible? It is theorized that the mucous coating on the integument (skin) of the anemonefish contains certain chemicals that prevent the anemone's nematocysts (stinging cells) from firing. The coating is biochemically similar to that of the anemone and may be a coating taken from the host anemone. Naturally, the anemone would have no reason to sting itself. Researchers have noticed that when the anemonefish is removed from the host for several days, it loses the ability to protect itself from the anemone's sting. It must then spend a period of time re-acclimating to the host.

PAGE 65. Sailfin Leaf Fish, *Taenianotus triacanthus*, Mabul Island, Malaysia: A pair of Leaf Fish sit atop Acropora coral waiting for unsuspecting prey (small fish) to venture too close.

PAGE 66. Ribbon Eel, *Rhinomuraena quaesita*, Mabul Island, Malaysia: The Ribbon Eel is one of the strangest eels on the reef. It lives in holes in the coral rubble. It is rarely observed completely out of its lair. Usually only the top third (as pictured) is exposed. This weird creature will turn its body side to side while spastically bobbing its head up and down. The reason for this behavior is not clearly understood. Of particular interest are the enlarged anterior nostrils which are a distinctive trademark of this species. As the name suggests, Ribbon Eels are comparatively thin but can attain lengths of more than one meter. Photo by GKB.

PAGE 67. Chevroned Barracuda, *Sphyraena sp.*, Sipadan Island, Malaysia: While diving off Sipadan I encountered a graceful school of Chevroned Barracuda on a few of our dives. As they swirled around me, the school took various shapes, including circles, artistic S-curves, and V-formations like a fighter squadron. They left as quickly as they had arrived. One day, after the barracuda ballet, a school of 20 Japanese divers approached. All were decorated in matching wetsuits, buoyancy compensators, fins, and sported the most popular new camera rigs. As they swirled around me, the school took various shapes including circles, artistic S-curves, and V-formations like a fighter squadron. They left as quickly as they had arrived.

PAGE 68. Aeolid Nudibranch, *Pteraeolidea ianthina*, Mabul Island, Malaysia: This incredible nudibranch may reach a length of more than 10 cm. It feeds on hydroids. Typical of Aeolids, once the hydroid has been consumed, this species has the ability to transfer the hydroid's nematocysts (stinging cells) to the gorgeous, blue cerata (filaments) that run the length of its body. It can then employ these stinging cells for its own defense. The cerata are also used for respiration.

PAGE 69. Flying Gurnard, *Dactyloptena orientalis*, Mabul Island, Malaysia: The Flying Gurnard is a distinct species recognized by its wing-like pectoral fins. When these amazing fins are spread wide, the Flying Gurnard glides effortlessly along the reef bottom. At other times, it may lie partially buried in the sand. Reaching a length of 30 cm., it feeds on small fish and invertebrates.

PAGE 70. Flamboyant Cuttlefish, *Metasepia pfefferi*, Mabul Island, Malaysia: The incredible Flamboyant Cuttlefish is one of the wonderful secrets of the sea. Its diminutive size (less than 10 cm.) and its extremely secretive nature make it very difficult to find. Once again, this is where a good, local dive guide comes to the rescue. Perhaps the most amazing thing about this species is its ability to change both shape and color. The entire time I spent photographing this specimen (about three minutes before it disappeared), the brown and white bands you see were moving across this animal like the stripes on a barbershop pole. The dimples on its skin would also expand and contract. It reminded me of a billboard in Vegas! The Flamboyant Cuttlefish is a very appropriate name.

PAGE 71. Nautilus, *Nautilus pompilius*, Mabul Island, Malaysia: This primitive cephalopod is considered a "living fossil." Some of my younger friends are beginning to call me the same thing. The Nautilus prefers very deep reefs where it feeds on lobster, shrimp, and crab molts. It is typically found at depths between 200-600 m. To photograph this specimen, I approached a local fisherman who had trapped several Nautiluses the night before. These captured invertebrates were headed to the local market. Their shells are routinely sold in curio shops. I made the fisherman an offer he couldn't refuse: I would purchase all five of his Nautiluses. They had been kept in buckets of fresh seawater and were very much alive. I gathered a few of my friends and we began our preparations to release and photograph them. Our goal was to take them down to about 15 m., release them, and photograph the Nautiluses as they headed toward deeper water (home). Try to imagine the scene: five adult (in theory) scuba divers at a depth of 15 m., side by side, each with his own cephalopod, tossing them into the water column, and frantically trying to take photographs as the Nautiluses make a jet-propelled dash for deep water. From my perspective, it was a Far-Side cartoon. I believe the primary flaw in our plan was thinking the Nautiluses would reward us for saving them by hanging around and posing for pictures. If you can't trust a cephalopod, then whom?

PAGE 72. Sargassum Anglerfish, *Histrio histrio*, Mabul Island, Malaysia: One morning I stepped outside my bungalow to assess diving conditions. There had been some wind earlier and the seas had come up a bit. Close to shore I spotted a large raft of floating sargassum weed. Never wanting to miss an opportunity, I donned my dive gear, grabbed my camera, and headed toward the weed mat. The sargassum was loaded with tiny shrimp, crabs, nudibranchs, and filefish. Each of these species is cryptically colored to blend in with the floating plant. As I circled around the giant weed mat, this gorgeous little Sargassum Anglerfish dropped out of it and immediately began a frantic swim back to the safety of the mat. I was able to compose one frame before it scurried back into the protective sargassum and disappeared. The fish and invertebrates that live in the sargassum weed spend their entire life floating on the open sea, always adrift and at the mercy of the wind and tides. On this day, the confined ecosystem had, if only for a moment, become part of the reef.

PAGE 73. Green Sea Turtles, *Chelonia mydas*, Sipaden Island, Malaysia: There are certain places on this travel-worn planet that are very special to me. Sipaden Island is one of those places. This tiny island (you can walk around it in 20 minutes) is one of the few places on Earth where sea turtles show no fear of man. This sea turtle/coral reef sanctuary has, for the most part, remained protected from commercial fishermen, reef dynamiting activity, and tropical fish and turtle egg collectors. While nearby reefs and attendant sea life have long since fallen prey to the ravages of man, Sipaden is a beacon of light and hope. It demonstrates what a few willful people with a mind for conserving wild things can accomplish. There are really only two rules necessary to ensure close encounters with these magnificent reptiles now and in the future. The first is to take only photographs, leave only memories. The second is, DO NOT TOUCH THE TURTLES.

PAGE 74-75. Komodo Dragon, *Varanus komodoensis*, Komodo Island, Indonesia: Why do I have a photo of a Komodo Dragon in a book about the coral reef? Fair question. When I was a child, I used to read about the giant dragons of Komodo in my encyclopedia (no Internet in those days). The island they lived on seemed so prehistoric, so mysterious, and so far away. To me it was another world, a place that would, forever, only be visualized through my fantasies.

Unbeknownst to me, it would take forty years, but one day my fantasy would become reality. Of course, the world I had conjured could never meet my expectations. Right? Wrong. Both above and below the water, Komodo was everything I had imagined. The experience was phantasmagorical. The island was mysterious and the diverse reefs were nothing short of magical. My childhood memories came flooding back. My fairy tale was alive. And like any good fairy tale come true, at the center of it all was the dragon.

Komodo Island and its surrounding reefs are nature's masterpiece. As I gathered the images for this book, I could not, in good conscience, exclude what is, for me, the heart of the masterpiece and the embodiment of my fantasy ...the primitive, monarchal Komodo Dragon.

PAGE 76. Sangiang Island, Indonesia: The volcanic island of Sangiang was one of our stops on the way to Komodo Island. The black volcanic sands and the reefs surrounding the island are alive with an impressive array of unusual marine creatures.

PAGE 77. Soft Coral, *Dendronephthya sp.*, Sangalakki Island, Indonesia: This is one of the numerous, colorful soft corals that flourish in the current driven waters surrounding the remote island of Sangalakki.

PAGE 78. Lyretail Angelfish, *Genicanthus melanospilos*, Kakaban Island, Indonesia: This elusive beauty resides in deeper water along reef drop-offs with luxuriant coral growth. It can reach a length of 16-18 cm. Unlike most angelfish, this species is a planktivore. The male is pictured here.

PAGE 79. Juvenile African Pompano, *Alectis ciliaris*, Komodo Island, Indonesia: The trailing dorsal fins of these steely predators identifies them as young adults. They will loose the filamentous portion of the dorsal fin as they mature. They travel in small schools and are rarely observed by divers. This school was photographed at 40 m.

PAGE 80. Sea Cucumber, *Colochirus robustus*, Komodo Island, Indonesia: This unusual, brightly colored Holothurian is found on reefs exposed to strong currents. In this photo, the tentacles are in feeding mode.

PAGE 81. Blue Ringed Octopus, *Hapalochlaena lunulata*, Komodo Island, Indonesia: Southern Komodo Island and the neighboring Rinca Island feature some of the most diverse coral reefs on Earth. These islands, among several others, are ideally situated in an area where the deep, cool, nutrient-rich waters of the Indian Ocean collide with the warm, tropical seas of the Pacific basin. The result is an explosion of marine life that is unrivaled in the animal kingdom. This southern rim of Indonesia is also home to active volcanoes and strong, unpredictable currents. In a very literal sense, it is an ocean of fire and a land of the dragon. So there I was, diving in this swirling cauldron of marine life, this underwater photography mecca, this... o.k., you get the idea; I was in a happening spot.

Near the end of the dive, I found a Blue Ringed Octopus! Although common in Australia, they are rarely observed in this region. These miniature cephalopods average only 6 cm. in diameter, yet they are among the most venomous animals on the reef. A bite from the Blue Ringed Octopus can be fatal if not treated immediately. It is reported that death can occur within 30 minutes of a bite. The blue rings tend to brighten when the octopus becomes agitated and the intensified color may serve as a warning to potential predators.

PAGE 82. Orangutan Crab, *Achaeus japonicus*, Sumbawa Island, Indonesia: This is a small (4 cm.) decorator crab that will often attach pieces of debris to the long hairs on its body, thereby making it very well concealed. It is often found on bubble coral (pictured here). The Orangutan Crab is easily overlooked because of its size and the ability to use pieces of its surroundings to construct a suit of camouflage.

PAGE 83. Squat Lobster, *Galathea sp.*, Sangiang Island, Indonesia: By now I hope you've realized that we don't need to go to distant galaxies to find alien life. We have our share of weird creatures living among us. They have simply adapted to life in the sea. I found this strange little Squat Lobster (2 cm.) late one night at a depth of 25 m. It had a tiny burrow in the reef where it seemed quite content. As I photographed the lobster, I could see in my periphery phosphorescent trails flying through the inky blackness above me. I took a few more shots of the Squat Lobster, then extinguished my light. The bioluminescent light show was spectacular. The blue streaks were caused by a species of free-swimming shrimp. Dozens of them were zipping all around me, creating eerie, blue light trails. They had been attracted by the zooplankton. The zooplankton had been attracted to my dive light. Now that my light was off, I was being treated to an innerspace living light extravaganza, the likes of which few will ever see. I was alone in the depths of a far away sea, enveloped by a cloak of darkness, but the night was alive, and I reveled in the magic of the moment.

PAGE 84. Zebra Crab, *Zebrida adamsii*, Rinca Island, Indonesia: Only 2.5 cm. in length, this species is able to form a symbiotic association with several urchin species. It is seen here amidst the spines of a venomous Fire Urchin.

PAGE 85. Glassy Sweepers, *Parapriacanthus sp.*, Derawan Island, Indonesia: Glassy sweepers are found in dense schools in coral caves or under large reef overhangs during the day. By night, they disperse onto the reef to feed. Each individual in this school is approximately 7 cm. long.

PAGE 86. Leaf Ghost Pipefish, *Solenostomus cyanopterus*, Sumbawa Island, Indonesia: These pipefish are also called Robust Ghost Pipefish. They are typically found in seagrass beds where they sway alongside a strand of the seagrass. This particular specimen was drifting across the sand. It looked and behaved exactly like a blade of the seagrass that was being carried across the bottom by a gentle current. Their ability to disguise themselves is phenomenal.

PAGE 87. Ornate Ghost Pipefish, *Solenostomus paradoxus*, Sumbawa Island, Indonesia: This beauty is photographed in 20 m. of water against the backdrop of a blue crinoid (feather star). It positions itself to look exactly like the arms of the crinoid. Without the flash of the strobe light, the Ghost Pipefish and the crinoid appear to be exactly the same color, a dark brown. Once again, it was only after my return home that I discovered this image sported the colors of the American flag.

PAGE 88. Pygmy Seahorse, *Hippocampus bargibanti*, Komodo Island, Indonesia: At an adult length of 2 cm.(not much larger than your fingernail), the Pygmy Seahorse is one of the hidden gems of the sea. It lives on the branches of gorgonian fans in deeper water (15-25 m.). It is difficult to find, even when you know exactly where to look. The dive guide pointed out the seahorse pictured in this book and I still couldn't see it until I looked through the magnified viewfinder of my camera. It blends perfectly with its surroundings. Its size, location on a swaying gorgonian fan, the deeper water, and its amazing ability to disappear when it's right in front of you make the Pygmy Seahorse an eye-straining, photographic challenge. It is also adept at moving away from the photographer to the opposite side of the gorgonian branch. Like a squirrel, when you're on one side, it shifts to the other. Despite its ability to frustrate marine life photographers, the delicate Pygmy Seahorse is one more reason why Indonesian reefs are revered by all who dive in these waters.

PAGE 89. Spotted Egg Cowry, *Calpurnus verrucosus*, Rinca Island, Indonesia: I encountered this magnificent animal crawling across the open reef during the day. Most cowry species of this size are both secretive and nocturnal. The spots are actually part of the animal that inhabits the shell. This species reportedly feeds on soft corals of the genus Sarcophyton. The Spotted Egg Cowry inhabits inshore reefs to a depth of 20 m.

PAGE 90. Chromodorid Nudibranch, *Hypselodoris apolegma*, Sulawesi Island, Indonesia: This stunning sea slug is but one of the numerous, incredibly colored specimens that are present on the reefs surrounding the island of Sulawesi. It reaches a length of 4-6 cm.

PAGE 91. Manta Ray, *Manta birostris*, Sangalakki Island, Indonesia: When the tidal currents are running, the mantas of Sangalakki hover in mid-water as the current funnels plankton into their open mouths. I don't believe I could ever tire of watching them. Their graceful maneuvers are artistry in motion.

PAGE 92 - 93. Sunset, New Britain Island, Papua New Guinea: Wow!

PAGE 94. Triplefin, *Helcogramma sp.*, Kimbe Bay, Papua New Guinea: This transparent, colorful fish is only 4 cm. long. It scoots along corals and sponges.

PAGE 95. Sabretooth Blenny, *Plagiotremus rhinorhynchos*, New Britain Island, Papua New Guinea: This innocent-looking blenny has a large pair of fangs in its lower jaw. It uses this dental work to bite chunks of flesh out of unsuspecting fish. Once the devilish blenny has procured its meal, it will often swim to its hole, back in tail first, and then peer out with that angelic smile.

PAGE 96. Cuttlefish, *Sepia latimanus*, Kimbe Bay, Papua New Guinea: The Cuttlefish is a fascinating cephalopod found on Indo-Pacific reefs. Adults of this species can reach a length of 50 cm. Like their relatives, the octopus and squid, they are masters of camouflage, able to execute rapid color shifts and change body textures to blend with their environment. When I first encountered this specimen, its tentacles were thrust deep into a head of staghorn coral. For 10-20 seconds this behavior would take place. The Cuttlefish would then slowly back away and retreat to a sheltered ledge some 6 m. away. There it remained for about a minute before beginning a slow, deliberate swim back to the same location where the ritual would be repeated. An hour passed. Whenever it moved toward the coral, I readied my camera and took a picture. As the strobe flashed, the Cuttlefish would quickly announce its disapproval by moving an impressive display of angry colors through the length of its body. What a show! By now quite curious, I risked breaking the rhythm of our encounter by closely inspecting the coral head. Peering deep into the coral recess, I observed a soft, opalescent egg mass. Each egg was about 5 cm. in diameter. Momma was tending her eggs. She would tirelessly continue this vigil until the eggs hatched.

PAGE 97. Lyretail Basslets, *Pseudanthias squammipinnis*, Fathers Reef, Papua New Guinea: This is a colorful harem of females. Lyretail Basslets inhabit shallow to medium depth reefs. Their numbers can reach into the thousands on these reefs.

PAGE 98. Coral Hermit Crab, *Paguritta harmsi*, New Britain Island, Papua New Guinea: Less than 2 cm. in length, this awesome little hermit crab takes shelter in the abandoned holes of tube worms. It feeds on plankton by using the long antennae as a straining device.

PAGE 99. Porcelain Crab, *Neopetrolisthes maculata*, Witu Islands, Papua New Guinea: These tiny crabs are found in sea anemones. There may be several of them on the larger anemones. They reside on the undersides of their host or deep in the anemone's folds, preferring to remain hidden from view.

PAGE 100. Eggshell Shrimp, *Periclimenes brevicarpalis*, Rabaul, Papua New Guinea: This is another of the reef's magnificent jewels. It is pictured here walking across its host anemone. It is about 4 cm. long. Time and again we are reminded of how important symbiotic relationships are on coral reefs.

PAGE 101. Tunicate, *Polycarpa aurata*, and Starfish, *Fromia sp.*, Rabaul, Papua New Guinea: The reefs of New Guinea are rich with a variety of colorful invertebrates.

PAGE 102. Blue-Face Angelfish, *Pomacanthus xanthometopon*, New Britain Island, Papua New Guinea: The stunning blue pattern on the face almost appears to be painted. This beauty is usually shy and secretive.

PAGE 103. Fan Goby, *Bryaninops sp.*, Father's Reef, Papua New Guinea: This miniature goby is 2.5 cm. long. It is resting on its home, a deepwater gorgonian fan.

PAGE 104. White Striped Anemonefish, *Amphiprion perideraion*, Rabaul, Papua New Guinea: This species is one of the more common species throughout the Indo-Pacific. Nevertheless, against the backdrop of this gorgeous purple anemone, this little gem becomes a very desirable photo subject. At this juncture, I'd like you to consider the importance of sea anemones on the coral reef. There are probably hundreds of fish and invertebrate species that rely on sea anemones for survival.

PAGE 105. Silvertip Reef Shark, *Carcharhinus albimarginatus*, Rabaul, Papua New Guinea: This is one of the most beautiful species of sharks. The white trim on the fins seems to glow in the depths. Silvertips are typically found on steep slopes on deeper reefs. I have watched them explode up and over the lip of a drop-off, appearing from out of nowhere, and found myself in the middle of a natural, full blown feeding frenzy. It's an incredible sight. This particular event lasted no more than 10 seconds. However, for that brief period, there were sharks flying around the top of the reef like stray bullets. Their speed and agility is overwhelming.

PAGE 106 - 107. Triplespot Blenny, *Crossosalarias macrospilus*, Mbengga Island, Fiji: This hyperactive blenny is seldom in one place for very long. Infrequently, it will pop its head up to inspect its surroundings and then hurriedly retreat to a hiding spot deep in the reef. It may reach a length of 8-10 cm.

PAGE 108. Red Anemonefish, *Amphiprion melanopus*, Wakaya Island, Fiji: The Red Anemonefish is distinguished by its bright orange color and the single, white stripe that runs from top to bottom along the operculum. Scurrying amidst the stinging tentacles of its host anemone, this 10 cm. beauty presents quite a photographic challenge. While photographing any anemonefish species, it is important to take advantage of their curious, aggressive nature. A diver who is willing to remain in one place while photographing these little jewels will discover that, again and again, they return to the same location within their host anemone. Once in this "sweet spot," they will often remain motionless for a second or two, which allows time for a photo. With patience and slow, non-threatening movements, photographers can closely approach anemonefish.

PAGE 109. Giant Sea Fan, *Subergorgia mollis*, North Astrolabe Reef, Fiji: These giant fans can reach lengths of over 3 m. They are found on reef drop-offs.

PAGE 110. Gray Reef Shark, *Carcharhinus amblyrhynchos*, Ngau Island, Fiji: These graceful animals are the "Lords of the Passage." In Fiji, much of the diving occurs in the reef passages of atolls. These cuts in the reef allow clear, ocean water to flow into the lagoons during high tide and warmer, nutrient laden lagoon- water to flow toward the open ocean on an ebb tide. During these tidal fluxes, the current races through the passages and the reef becomes an ecosystem in motion. It is alive with a variety of feeding and reproductive activities taking place. The passages harboring these sleek, silent predators may be as shallow as 10 m. However, they prefer reefs with immediate access to deeper water.

PAGE 111. Longnose Hawkfish, *Oxycirrhites typus*, Namena Island, Fiji: This beautiful species (10 cm.) is found on deeper, outer reef walls and drop-offs. It is almost always associated with black corals and gorgonian fans, both deepwater corals. Depth and the sheer angles of the reef slope create less than ideal circumstances for photography. Black corals are also very "bushy" and do a wonderful job of hiding the Longnose Hawkfish. Once again, successful photographs will require infinite patience, multiple visits to the site, and knowledge of your subject. This generally holds true for all wildlife photography.

PAGE 112. Banded Pipefish, *Corythoichthys sp.*, Ngau Island, Fiji: This delicate pipefish, a relative of the seahorse, was photographed as it scooted through a bed of soft coral. It is relatively small, reaching a length of 14 cm.

PAGE 113. Sailfin Goby, *Amblyeleotris randalli*, Namena Island, Fiji: The Sailfin Goby is another of those skittish fish that are difficult to approach without them retreating to the safety of their holes in the sand. This species is found on sand bottoms beneath reef ledges or in reef caverns, making them an especially challenging species to photograph. I spent an entire day working with this particular animal.

PAGE 114. Ocellated Nudibranch, *Phyllidia ocellatus*, Namena Island, Fiji: This is a common, yet distinctive species found throughout the Indo-Pacific. Photo by GKB.

PAGE 115. Manta Ray, *Manta birostris*, North Astrolabe Reef, Fiji: It doesn't matter how many times I've encountered these gentle giants, each new observation brings with it a sense of wonder, awe, and excitement. Talk with anyone who has been in the water with these animals and they'll all tell you the same thing...the encounter was unforgettable. Mantas are plankton feeders that seem not to swim, but to fly. Having wingspans that can exceed 4 m., mantas are frequent visitors to the reef. It is not unusual to see small groups of 4-5 rays feeding just beneath the surface. Their graceful, streamlined bodies and their athletic maneuvers give them the appearance of a squadron of Star Wars Fighter Craft that have taken time off to perform an in- water ballet. They truly are among the most elegant acrobats in the sea.

PAGE 116. Yellowtail Basslet, *Pseudanthias flavicauda*, Great White Wall, Fiji : Typically found in depths greater than 30 m., this is the female of the species.

PAGE 117. Yellowtail Basslet, *Pseudanthias flavicauda*, Great White Wall, Fiji: This gorgeous specimen is the male. Although I have dived this area many times, I have only encountered this species on one occasion. The potential for discovery on the reef is neverending.

PAGE 118. Baroness Butterflyfish, *Chaetodon baronessa*, Wakaya Island, Fiji: It's not unusual to see 15-20 species of butterflyfish on a single dive around Wakaya. I am especially fond of this species. They seem so delicate and well-mannered when they feed, taking only small polyps from the more fragile staghorn coral species. Butterflyfish usually flutter by in pairs, stop briefly to feed, and then move on to the next coral formation. They frequent areas where hard corals flourish.

PAGE 119. Imperial Shrimp, *Periclimenes imperator*, Namena Island, Fiji: This 3 cm. crustacean was photographed while crawling across the back of its host, a giant Dendrodorid nudibranch. The Imperial Shrimp can also be found on other hosts such as sea cucumbers or Spanish Dancer nudibranches.

PAGE 120. Reef with Soft Corals, *Dendronephthya sp.*, Ngau Island, Fiji: In the current driven passages of Ngau, this species of soft coral flourishes, providing a carpet of living color to the reef.

PAGE 121. Longnose Filefish, *Oxymonathus longirostrus*, Astrolabe Reef, Fiji: This tiny filefish can usually be found in groups of two to four. It gingerly swims around reefs with heavy growths of hard coral. It uses the elongated snout to feed on the delicate polyps of Acropora corals.

PAGE 122. Banded Rock Cod, *Epinephelus fasciatus*, Namena Island, Fiji: I love photographing groupers. They're the puppy dogs of the sea. They're curious, often friendly, and always seem to be up to something. I was in relatively shallow water decompressing after a deep dive when this grouper approached. At first it remained several meters away. However, within the next 45 minutes, after it became convinced I was no threat, it would lay against my arm, using me as a hideaway from potential prey.

PAGE 123. Soft Coral Tree, *Scleronephthya sp.*, Great White Wall, Fiji: Fields of these gorgeous lavender soft corals adorn the sheer, vertical drop-off known as the Great White Wall. These corals begin to dominate the wall at about 20 m. In the dimly lit depths, they create a heavenly, white glow. The White Wall is an enchanting dive experience.

PAGE 124. Leopard Blenny, *Exallias brevis*, Astrolabe Reef, Fiji: This energetic blenny moves feverishly within the reef's cracks and crevices, rarely exposing itself for more than a few seconds.

PAGE 125. Scalloped Hammerhead Shark, *Sphyrna lewini*, Wakaya Passage, Fiji: At 40 m. and sheltered from the current, I waited late that afternoon as the fading light foretold of another day's end. I knew that somewhere off the sheer reef wall they were on constant patrol, like silent sentinels. At first, there were only two, swimming past at the edge of visibility, ghostly apparitions appearing briefly through the eternal blue, then disappearing. Finally, the main event occurred. The school of Scalloped Hammerheads materialized out of nothingness (they always do). They seemed to be some form of extraterrestrial craft that, for a fleeting moment, passed through my consciousness, then vanished into my dreams. And I wondered...when will they come again?

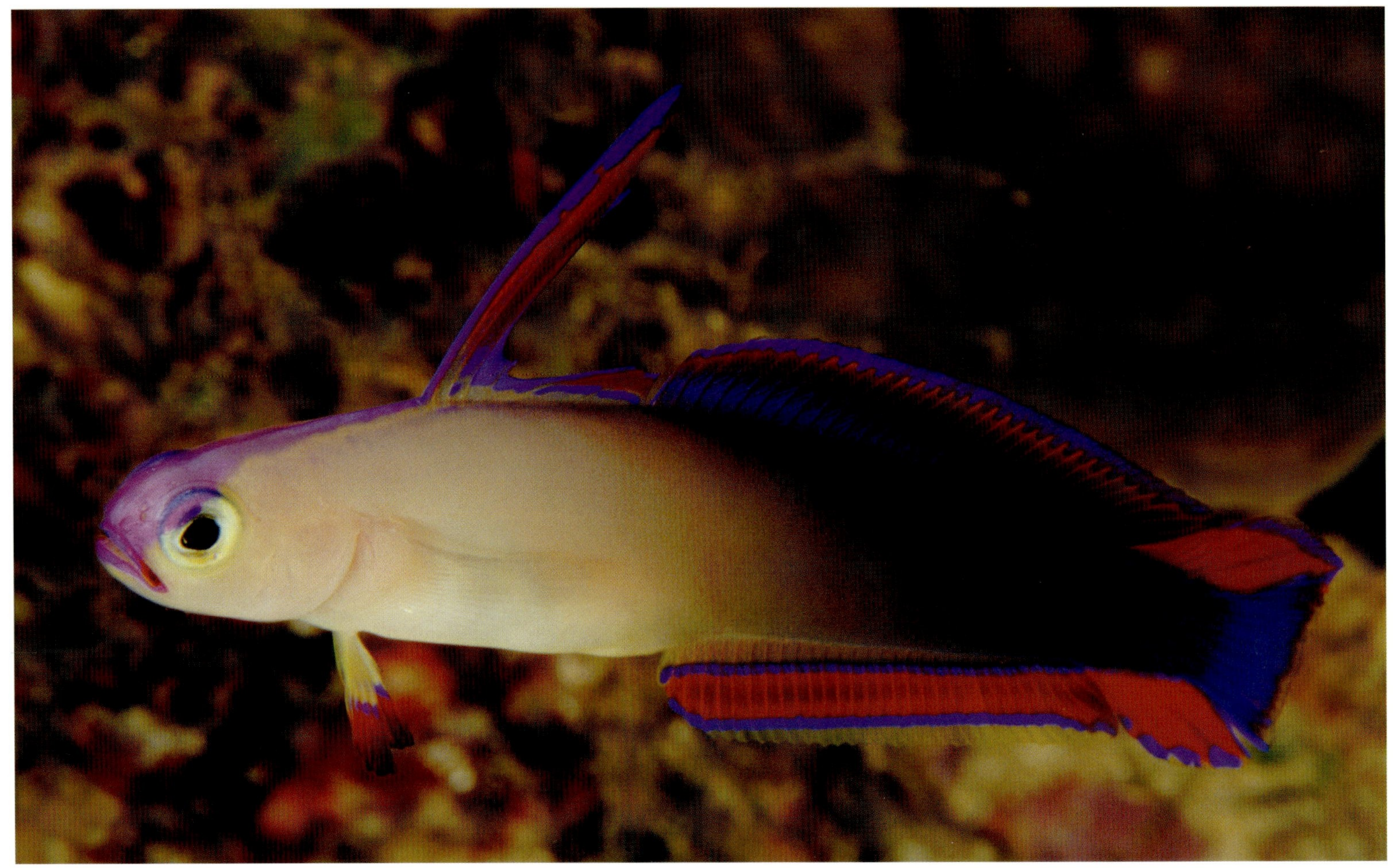

"...these are the times of dreamy quietude, when beholding the tranquil beauty and brilliancy of the ocean's skin, one forgets the tiger heart that pants beneath it; and would not willingly remember, that this velvet paw but conceals a remorseless fang."

-Herman Melville

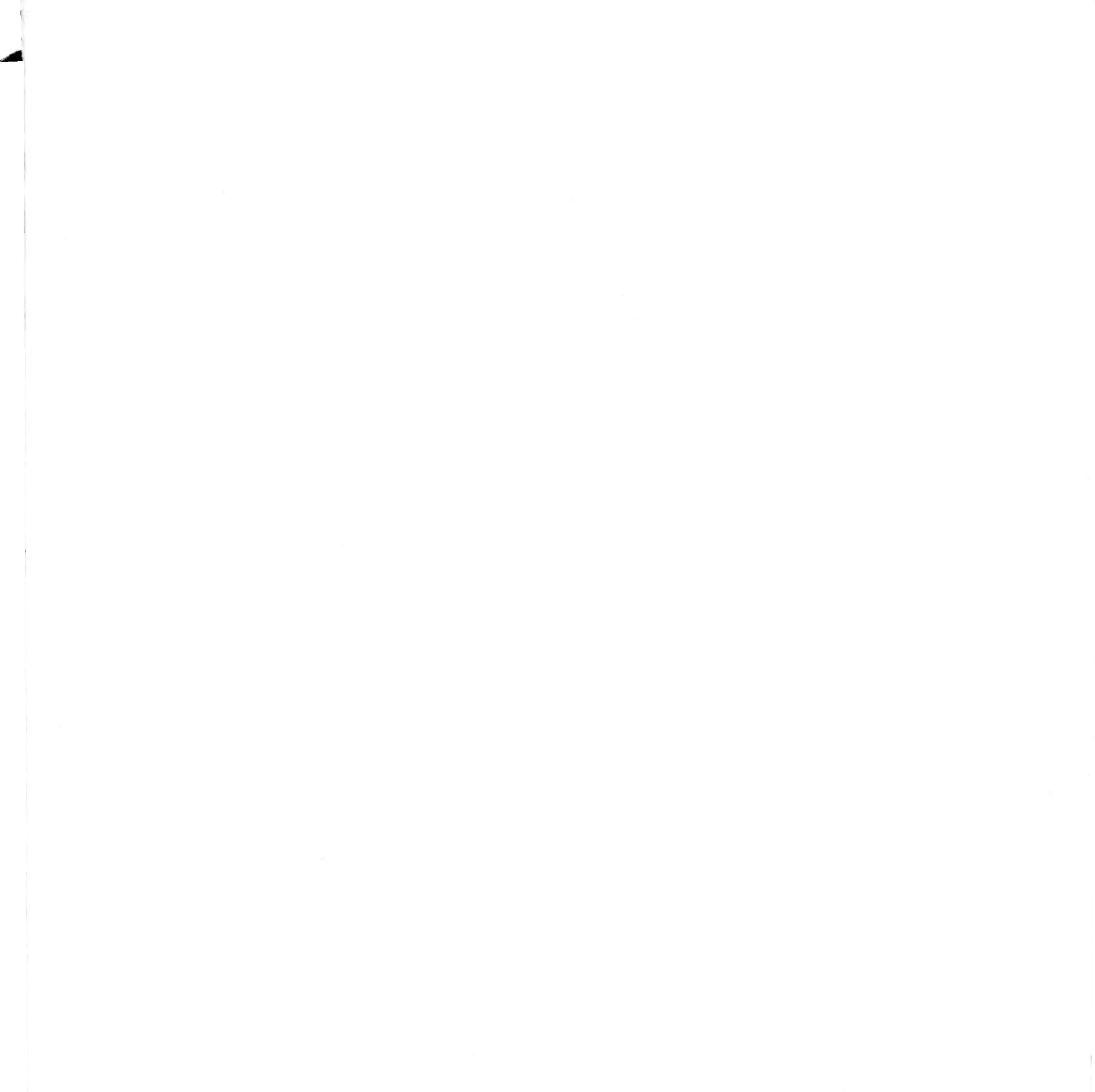